Indefinite

Indefinite

Doing Time in Jail

MICHAEL L. WALKER

OXFORD

UNIVERSITY PRESS

OXFORD
UNIVERSITY PRESS

Oxford University Press is a department of the University of Oxford. It furthers
the University's objective of excellence in research, scholarship, and education
by publishing worldwide. Oxford is a registered trade mark of Oxford University
Press in the UK and certain other countries.

Published in the United States of America by Oxford University Press
198 Madison Avenue, New York, NY 10016, United States of America.

© Oxford University Press 2022

CIP data is on file at the Library of Congress
ISBN 978-0-19-007286-5

DOI: 10.1093/oso/9780190072865.001.0001

1 3 5 7 9 8 6 4 2

Printed by LSC Communications, United States of America

For Rhonda, who loves me through tribulations
For #1, who survived my tribulations
For Heather, who made it possible

Contents

Acknowledgments

Ellen Reese, without your support this project would never have happened, and I don't know that I would have survived my time—not with my whole mind. You invested in me and asked nothing in return. I appreciate you for your indispensable guidance and help. Thank you for encouraging me. Thank you for seeing what I could not see and for supporting me every step of the way. I am forever in your debt.

Edna Bonacich, you have been a friend. I have not deserved your love or the tenderness you have shown me. During my darkest days, through my brightest moments, you have stood by me, as I transitioned from a feisty undergraduate student to this moment. Thank you. Thank you and Phil.

Damion Thomas, my dearest friend, my wise counsel, and the source of so much of what has pushed me and inspired me to be a better writer and scholar, thank you for drumming to your own beat and teaching me to find my own rhythm. And damn it if you ain't one of the most brilliant people I know!

To my "Mighty 2014" Racial Democracy Crime and Justice Network (RDCJN) crew: REPRESENT! In particular, thank you Patrick Lopez-Aguado for answering late night calls about concepts and connections between ideas. I'm so glad you are two hours behind me. Thank you, Evelyn Patterson for daytime discussions of ideas and for the right kind of encouragement when it was needed. And to, Reuben Miller, my brotha from anotha, I am indebted to you for our endless discussions about big and small ideas and for the times you pushed and inspired me to continue. Thank you for pushing me to write fiercelessly! Nicole Gonzalez van Cleve, thank you for always having my back. Of course, I never would have met y'all if not for Ruth Peterson, Laurie Krivo, and Jody Miller, the best damned mentors anyone could have had at RDCJN. Ruth, your comments helped me to reshape the book for the better.

To Waverly Duck and John Eason, if I got it, y'all got it! I love you brothas. To Joyce Bell, I miss you here in Minnesota! Thank you for never letting my bullshit ride without calling it out, and thank you for being so damned smart, funny, and kind. I'm lucky to call you friend. Your support has never wavered. Thank you so much Laurence Ralph for offering insightful thoughts on early drafts of some chapters, and for your friendship and guidance. I owe you, brotha! To Randol Contreras, your work inspires me. Thank you for being one of my toughest critics. *If I can convince Randol, then I've got something*, I continue to say to myself. Thank you for line-item suggestions! Also, thank you Heather Schoenfeld for detailed comments on early drafts of some chapters. Megan Comfort, I so greatly appreciate the time and care you put into offering me comments—praise and critique—to improve this book. Thank you for calling me "friend." Melissa Guzman, your fiery insight transformed a chapter from a mess to something much more respectable. Thank you!

To my colleagues here in the Department of Sociology at the University of Minnesota, I appreciate you all for letting me pop into your offices unannounced with what must have seemed like random sociological inquiries. Joshua Page, I appreciate your friendship so damned much. Thank you for lending your thoughts as I wrote. Your input was invaluable. Thank you, Michelle Phelps, for organizing a very supportive writing group with historians Malina Lindquist, Will Cooley, and Will Jones. Your suggestions helped me to improve this book.

I received a first-class education at the University of California-Riverside Department of Sociology. Thank you, Scott Brooks for your support and understanding. Thank you for introducing me to ethnography. To Jane Ward, thank you for the letters and books you sent me while I was locked away. I looked at the pictures of trees often, and I appreciate you having introduced me to feminist theory. To Jonathan Turner, your work has inspired me to do the best kind of sociology I know how to do. To Kevin McCaffree and Seth Abrutyn, my former graduate school peers and now outstanding scholars, I relied upon both of you for your deep wells of sociological knowledge, and our conversations—promised, as they were, to be only twenty minutes—helped me to think through problems and would-be pitfalls as we rounded our 90th minute in various conversations. I truly appreciate you both.

To "Ken," I'm so glad that we're in touch. Thank you for talking through some mysteries that could not have been solved by my field notes. To Letta Page, my editor extraordinaire, thank you for being exactly what I needed to improve this book—and at lightning speed! James Cook, thank you for believing in this book when it was a mere idea and for continuing to support me and this project when I first articulated the ideas poorly. Ha! It cannot be overstated that your belief in me translated to belief in myself.

On this note, I have a group of friends without whom, I could never have reached this moment. Wil Greer, you first taught me knowledge of self and to stand up for others because it's the right thing to do. Chizobam Okoro, thank you for always believing in me. Malinda Williams, you have had my whole back since way back like fo' flats on a Cadillac! Dr. Bernard Hardy, no one has ever been more deserving of their title, and thank you for being my layperson guinea pig for sociological arguments. I'm not sure you totally qualify as a layperson, being so damned smart, but I need you to know that your work ethic inspires me to be about my business even when I'm exhausted.

Last, but certainly not least, to my wife, Heather Miller, this whole damned thing would have been a pipe dream without you. Thank you for taking call, for solving medical emergencies, and then coming home to take over with our Littles so I could write. Those were 36-hour work shifts for you, and when I think back, I don't know how you did it. You must really love me. For the time to sleep in after an all-nighter, for the tenderness you showed me through 72-hour migraines fueled by book-related stress, for helping me to develop ideas and concepts when you were fatigued, and for holding this household together while I kept promising, "After this book," you have my undying gratitude. You are simply amazing, and I'm lucky to have you! A friend once told me that earning a PhD is an incredibly selfish venture. You were with me for all of that, but this book meant a new level of self-centeredness, and I am so glad you're here, finally, in the "After this book" phase. We made it! I love you. I appreciate you. This is the culmination of your efforts as much as mine.

Introduction

Palace de Excreta

When I think about jail,[1] my mind goes to Tuesday, February 7, 2008—my birthday, not that it mattered because who celebrates being 31? At only 9:00 a.m., I was slow roasting in my uninsulated campus housing unit. I'd walked my son, Micah,[2] to school and was mulling the day's agenda. In a few hours, I would go before a university judicial affairs committee to beg for a reprieve for having been arrested on university property several months before. The charges had nothing to do with the university and the case was in the early stages of adjudication, but if my hearing with that committee went unfavorably, I could be suspended from the graduate program or expelled from school altogether. I stared at the dust clinging to my TV and obsessed on wild contingencies always with the same end: some combination of losing my son, prison time, and a violent death.

In moments like these—when standing at the cusp of fortune and tragedy—my grandmother played music and cleaned the house. She handed that habit down to my mother, so when I was a child, if I heard the Gap Band or Kool & the Gang or Luther Vandross playing on a Saturday or Sunday morning, I knew my mother was cleaning the house and maybe clearing her mind to see more clearly whatever it was that she was dealing with. Music marks all potentialities. The meeting wasn't for a few hours, so I figured maybe if I took the bus down to the courthouse and set up a payment plan for old traffic tickets, the gesture would work like a deposit in the Cosmic Good Deed Bank that I could withdraw with interest later in the day. I put on my "clean up" playlist and piddled around my place to Michael Jackson, Earth, Wind & Fire, and Heavy D. I skipped around on the CD until I heard the opening chords to "Little Bluebird." I was a kid again in the kitchen with a spoon, throwing my back into every "Oh!" with my grandmother in the audience. I grabbed Maulana Karenga's book, *Maat*, and headed out the door.

I'd started and stopped the book more times than I could remember—certainly as often as I started and stopped anything else. Still, working through the day's calculus, it seemed sensible to take a treatise on ethics to the court-house. On the bus I stared at the book's cover, from which I'd gotten my tattoo. Rubbing the Egyptian hieroglyphics on my neck, I wondered whether it says what I mean for it to say or was I one of those idiots who thinks he's inked "dragon hearted," but it's actually the Japanese word for "pencil"? I reminded myself of an encounter with Tiamoyo Karenga after a meeting to put sub-acre farms in Los Angeles communities: "Nefer maat," she read from my neck with soft confidence. *I must have it right.*

The courthouse waiting area was populated with the usual suspects: a frustrated baby, people talking too loudly into their cell phones, people in work clothes huffing their annoyance. I hadn't read a single word from *Maat* when my name was called ahead of others. The clerk stabbed his fingers at his keyboard, toggling between screens without looking up while I explained, cheerfully for some reason, that I wanted to set up a payment plan for whatever traffic violations I might have. His eyes never left the screen, and I caught myself filling the air with extraneous information before realizing I wasn't there to make a friend or even to exchange in friendly small talk. I was there to facilitate the filling in of electronic forms. It was like being one of the legions of faceless bad guys whose sole purpose in movies is to get whooped on by the protagonist. In that instant, the clerk appeared to me as *the government clerk*—a kind of social object that I'd encountered in other courthouses, DMVs, and social services offices. Our silent mutual objecti-fication was broken when he unceremoniously dismissed me to the waiting area because he needed "to prepare some documents."

I sat on one of the colorful plastic chairs and thumbed through *Maat*. I was surprised to see that according to scribbles in the margins, I'd made it all the way to page 173 at some point. But I didn't remember any of it, so I started at the beginning. I was still committing my mind to reading the book in-stead of looking at the first pages when two sheriff's deputies approached. "Mr. Walker," one began, "stand and face the wall." Stunned, I complied. My wrists readied themselves for handcuffs before the deputy took them from his belt—long before I understood why I was being detained. (Later, I learned that the charges associated with my earlier arrest had been changed. A war-rant had been issued, and I had merely simplified its execution by presenting myself in the courthouse.)

"Is this your book?" the other deputy asked. I nodded with docility. One of the pair then guided me by a wrist down the hall through a door camouflaged by paneling and into a series of narrow capillaries stealthily connected to the building's arteries. We made what seemed like an unusual number of lefts and rights through so many doorways before arriving at a cramped office. I doubt I could have found my way out without help.

My escort sat me in a chair in the thoroughfare between doors on opposite ends of the office. The tiny room was an administrative get-away where deputies filled in forms, traded jokes, and apparently held arrestees. Something about the blinds and the window turned the room's sunlight a shade of amber. Gray filing cabinets seemed piled into towers, and there was a cartoonish amount of paperwork on nearly every surface. My escort sat at a desk and began fiddling with papers and chatting with another deputy. Until that moment, everything seemed to be happening in silence, but as I sat handcuffed and facing the clock on the wall, shock started wearing off. Reality thundered in. *This is really happening right now.*

Few activities—if we can call it that—are as troubling as watching a clock tick. What exquisite torture to watch the secondhand tick forward, and the more I stared, the more it seemed to tick slower, then in place, and then backward before ticking forward again.

Deputies came in and out of the office, walking around me, talking past me. I fidgeted in my chair—but not too much—while deputies playfully punched each other's arms and made evening plans. At first their carefree banter seemed to have nothing to do with me, but then I got it in my head that they were ignoring me on purpose—like they wanted me to feel unimportant. I felt a growing tension between wanting to be left alone—*Maybe they'll give me a ticket and let me go*—and a desire to be acknowledged as a fully sentient being and active participant in the ongoing situation. A deputy asked me if I needed to call anyone. *Shit! Micah!* I left a message on my mother's cell phone—just the facts: I've been arrested. I'll probably be in the Providence Downtown Jail. Please pick up Micah from school.

More than an hour passed before my escort announced he was ready to take me to jail. He didn't say that. He just put a hand on my left shoulder and told me to stand. I stood. He moved his hand down to my inner bicep and began guiding me through a labyrinth of corridors crawling with a colony of deputies that greeted each other like ants as they passed. We took an elevator down—*Where are we going?*—and arrived rather magically at the entrance of a bunker: the Providence Downtown Jail's intake area. Before that moment, it had never occurred to me that the jail was connected the courthouse like that. But that's the thing about jail: It gives you a netherworld feeling while being in the center of city and town life. You're strangely home and not; disappeared and present.

Shit

A deputy working intake opened the door, and my escort handed me off. Intake was the same cold, banausic place it had been weeks prior. A dinosaur of a voice gave the standard commands: "Gentlemen! Stay inside the red line. Face the wall. No talking." I did as I was told. When one of the deputies pacing the line gave the instruction, I removed and held my belt, socks, and shoes in one hand, using the other to hold up my pants. When it was my turn, I approached the property desk, placed my palms flat in front of me, and spread my feet to the desire of the deputy standing behind me.

The deputy behind the desk worked like an automaton, filling in parts of a form for me the way he had done for every captured man in intake. I made the dumb decision to read the form. There was a place to catalog my personal items, and there was a place to record my general disposition. I signed it and should have been done. But, call it frustration—and it was, partly, though it was much more about interrupting what felt like the violence of procedure to claim some small measure of dignity and be acknowledged as a person because I was, after all, in fucking jail on my birthday when all I'd wanted to do was pay some traffic fines—I pointed at a particular line on the form, looked flatly at the deputy, and declared: "You shouldn't have checked that box with 'no history of mental illness.'"

He studied me and then asked whether I thought I might be a danger to myself or others in that moment.

"I don't know what I might I do," I replied without breaking eye contact.

He remained impassive and quiet as he gathered my property and paperwork. He didn't say another word. Another deputy appeared at my side instantly and led me to a small staging area. There he calmly instructed me to strip naked. That wasn't how intake normally went, but he didn't offer an explanation, and I didn't ask. Instead of the standard disintegrating socks, broken eraser-colored sandals, white T-shirt, sullied boxers, and faded orange top and bottom pieces, I was handed a heavy, green, nylon gown. It was like a hospital gown but held together on one side with Velcro straps. He shuffled me past the usual pre-housing holding units before nudging me into a single-occupant cell. He closed the door behind me. No words. No explanation. I didn't ask any questions.

I stood by the door for a moment; then my senses brought the 10' x 10' cell into focus. The walls were painted the familiar shade: institutional agony—a McDonald's-french-fries-and champagne-beige-vomit color. The floor was soft epoxy—chilled by a malevolent breeze that crisped my ankles and wafted the fetor of festering rectums bygone. The gag-inducing stench was no mystery: a mad man—*Could one man produce this much shit?*—had made a masterpiece of tactile art. Everywhere I looked fresh, pungent shit was smeared, smudged, splattered, and clumped. An encased security camera in the upper left-hand corner of the room was covered in wads of feces. The security lighting fixture was blotched with flung excrement. In the bottom-right corner of the room was a metal grate around which the floors sloped. No bench, no bed, no toilet-sink combination, no table, no chair: the cell was an empty box. The floor was checkered with ordure and dried urine stains. *Because if you don't give fuck about your own crap, why worry about where you piss? Wait am I standing in piss?* I turned on the balls of my feet toward the cell door. *Gah!* The 4" x 8" safety glass was besmirched with fecal streaks. I stared at that sin with my lips curled. A person had made that cell look like that. Other persons allowed and ignored it. And apparently civilized beings believed it was rational to put me in there. *I don't know what I might do. I don't know what I might do. Why in the fuck did I say that?*

The goings on in the hall were muffled by the walls, and I could barely make out anything through the smeared safety glass. *They've forgotten me.* I stood before the little window and hoped someone would come get me.

By now Mom has gotten Micah. At least, she's heard my message and got on the road or called Nicole. Thoughts darted like shooting lasers in different directions. I needed my mother to come through for me—for Micah. *I'm fucking up. Like, my whole life right now, like, I'm fucking it all the way up. And I gotta stand in this literal shit. I gotta stand here in all this shit and piss and god only knows what else. I gotta stand in it all.*

Had I been in the cell for an hour—longer? There were no obvious markers of the passing of time, so I decided to sing songs. A verse or two didn't count: it had to be the entire song, including the adlibs, for an *accurate* measure of time. If I would've had music, I could've sung along to thousands of songs, but in that moment, I could only call to memory Guy's "Let's Chill," Bilal's "Sometimes," and the Notorious B.I.G.'s "Unbelievable." So, I stood just inside the Palace de Excreta, singing and rapping to myself—those songs.

I guessed that each song was about three and a half minutes long, but I lost track of how many times I sang each one. Often, I started over when I stuttered or enjoyed a particular verse or when I wanted to get the adlibs just right. Also, I'd been standing long enough for my legs to be tired, and I reasoned that if my legs were tired, I must have been standing for six to eight hours. But I argued against myself that using the tiredness in my legs missed the whole point of singing in the first place—that it was insane to think I could accurately track time by leg-tiredness, especially with a more viable tool at my disposal if I would have just counted how many times I sang.

That camera must not work. Why else would they allow this room to look like this? They must not know what it looks like or what it smells like in here. Shit. I'll be dead in here weeks before anyone remembers to find me. The fuck time is it? It's a wrap for school. I gotta sit. I can't stand forever.

There was no obviously safe place to sit. I settled on a spot to the left of the cell door, hopscotching there and wondering whether my weary quadriceps would go limp or ease my body to the ground. My legs split the difference, and I performed a controlled fall into place with my legs at a skew to avoid resting in crap. The nylon gown was at least a barrier between my back and the wall.

Stillness. Then, the terrible cycle: fear heated and rose brightly before sinking and darkening as I cooled it. But then more feelings rose—brighter, more intensely hot ones—and I couldn't cool them all at once: just raw emotions, tied loosely to images but no clear thoughts. I couldn't manage them. I bellowed, loudly and shamelessly like an animal caught in a trap. The sound was startling—like hearing the sorrowful cries of someone else, but it was my chest heaving and my bottom lip sucking in and out between gasps. I cried like I lost a child, and in a way, I had. I lost a portion of my intrinsic innocence: that moral simplicity that's uncomplicated by the knowledge of experiences like that safety cell.

When my lamentations passed, there was yet the cold draft on my feet, knees, and scrotum, the reality of fecal finger paintings, and me—alone. And I hated myself for crying useless tears.

Keys at the cell door: I sprang up. A deputy offered a Styrofoam carton of food and skim milk through a slot in the door that I somehow hadn't noticed. I accepted the food, for some haunting reason, with a pleasant attitude, using the normal niceties. *The fuck do I have to be so happy about?* Frustrated, I returned to my spot to tough down a ham sandwich on white bread, cookies, and the jail's version of coleslaw. My hands were unwashed hands and I was surrounded by excrement. *It's gonna be some super cholera or E.coli that gets me.*

Exhausted, I figured that I was getting the jail's version of mental health treatment for persons perceived as a danger to themselves or others: "Take him to the Palace!" I blamed myself. I could have been processed like anyone else, but I was a frustrated smart-ass who grabbed a stupid opportunity to disrupt the deputy's automatonic behavior. But did deputies really believe that time in the Palace would be helpful? It seemed I was being told, "We know how to handle guys like you."[3] I had no idea how long I'd been in there, but I guessed that I would be there for at least 72 hours, so I accepted that I could not stay awake the whole time.

Sleeping against the wall wasn't going to work; I might have dozed, leaned too far to one side and landed in shit. No. I stood, opened the nylon dress, spread it on the floor, and climbed my naked body atop. It was a raft in contaminated waters. My bare back bore the brunt of the wintry breeze, as I curled into a fetal position trying to keep my legs from touching the floor. My tendons fought the effort, so I gripped my legs around the shins, interlocking my fingers to prevent even a toe from touching the toxic floor. I closed my eyes.

How long have I been here? Did I sleep at all? Wait: the trip on the bus, the arrest, intake. When is the last time I peed? I'm not gonna be able to hold it until someone comes to get me—if someone comes to get me.

My bladder was near failure before I decided to do something about it. No one was watching, but I refused to deign to the level of the cell. I stood, covered myself, and then navigated the gauntlet of human waste so that I could pee into the grate in the far corner of the room.

I returned to my spot on the wall—no sleep for now. Almost immediately a weighted sadness settled on my chest, and my guts started cramping. I felt like I was imploding and exploding at once. The more I sobbed, the more I hated myself for it. My humiliation, guilt, regrets, and wretchedness seemed manifested in the *everywhere* shit. I didn't think about it. I acted. I opened the Styrofoam food container and broke the plastic spoon I'd been given, trying to get a sharp enough edge to open my wrists. The spoon wasn't sturdy enough to snap into shards, and I couldn't sharpen the plastic against the soft walls or floor. I bit a thumb nail off to the quick and used it to dig into my skin. I stabbed at my wrists, knowing that I needed to cut lengthwise if I was to bleed out properly. My hands were sweating, as I rotated between the fingernail and the spoon, working at my wrists until I could see a vein behind the white meat on one arm. I was so tired that I had to encourage my-self to keep going. *There's gotta be an easier way. You gotta be insane to break your own neck. Are you insane, Michael?* I applied torque to my neck. *Fuck! I ain't crazy, but I don't need to be to open these veins. Just gotta be determined, but this would hurt less if I were insane.* Having drawn blood on one wrist, I closed my eyes and hoped life would drip from my body.

Did I fall asleep? How long has it been? I hadn't bled enough for even a small pool of blood to form, so I gnawed at my wrist, but it hurt, and I wasn't sure whether I had the resolve to bite and bleed the way I needed to. I wasn't insane—yet.

A deputy delivered more food, and later a cup of water. I couldn't re-member the last time I'd had water. I ate, drank the skim milk and the water, and I stored my trash in the corner to the right of my spot and the left of the cell's door. Suddenly, a subtle grumble grew into a wrenching in my bowels. It felt like a strong man was scrunching my intestines. *This must be how this room got like this: the food!* There wasn't an obvious place to relieve myself, and I could not envisage myself pressing poop through the metal bars of the floor grate. The Styrofoam container would have to be my commode. Afterward, I stored the container and its ignoble contents in the farthest corner away from me.

I switched between standing at the door, sitting in my spot to pick at my wrists, and laying down. After food was delivered a third time, I stacked the empty milk cartons into a makeshift pillow. This meant I could scoot my shoulders to the edge of the nylon dress-bedroll apparatus because my head was resting on the cartons instead of touching the floor. That way, I didn't have to work so hard to keep my legs tucked. The drawback, of course, was that I had to remain perfectly still, or the stack of cartons would tumble, and I'd have to catch my head before it touched the ground. I was playing a ver-sion of the childhood game, "hot lava"—except touching the floor really was dangerous.

Deputies brought more food—more water. "Do you need to flush?" a deputy yelled at the cell door. I was utterly confused, so he gestured with his eyebrows and pointed past me to the corner grate. "Do you need to flush?"

Oh! The grate. It's covering a pipe—a septic pipe! I thought for a moment about the human waste that must have been idling in that pipe. "Yeah," I responded, nodding simultaneously. The deputy reached to his right be-yond my view, and a rush of suction and water carried away a portion of my plight.

Later another deputy opened the metal slot to the Palace. She wanted whatever trash I had. Shame volted down my spine, as I handed over some mostly empty food containers and milk cartons—I kept my "pillows"—before passing what felt like material disgrace and explaining mortifyingly: "This one has waste in it." She nodded and accepted it.

Had I been in the Palace for a day—two days?

A young Asian American woman visited me. She kneeled to speak to me through the food slot, and I kneeled in my spot by the door, hoping she could see the sanity in my face. She showed me her badge and said she was from the county's Department of Mental Health. She stammered through a one-size-fits-all survey, glancing at me only occasionally. Several times, she began a question, then halted and moved on when she realized that it was irrelevant to my situation. I was facilitating the filling in of a form again. I asked her whether she was there to help me or to read questions at me.

"I want to help you," she replied unconvincingly.

I started pushing her on the meaning of every question she asked. I sarcastically repeated her questions about whether I felt like hurting myself. "Do you mean before or after I was put in this shithole because that matters." I suppose I pushed her too far—or maybe she was looking for an out.

On the next survey item, she stopped herself: "You know what? It doesn't matter." She closed the hatch and was gone.

I stayed kneeled at the door until I lost feeling in my toes and my knees ached. "It doesn't matter." The words were strangely freeing. I gave up working on my wrists. The effort required feelings, and having resolved that "it" didn't matter, my emotions were evaporating.

My legs still ached from kneeling at the door when the strong man's hands returned to wring my bowels. I used two spoons to lift the grate that covered the ragged hole in the septic pipe: no more Styrofoam containers. There my waste festered until I could convince a deputy to flush the pipe for me.

Unaccounted hours later, another woman came from the Department of Mental Health. Older, Black—she had "auntie" energy, like a woman who greets you with a smile and a warm plate piled high with more food than you could possibly eat. She wasn't carrying a survey. She wasn't there to evaluate me: hers was a rescue mission. We conversed lightly. She told me that if I wanted to get out of the Palace, I would need to tell the doctor who would be visiting me next that I was not suicidal or dangerous anymore. She assured me that if I told him I was better, he would get me out. It was a bit like being told that I needed only to click my naked heels three times. After all, I'd been put in that god-awful place for my own good, right? And for the good of the jail? But all I needed to do was say I was fine, and I could be out of that cell?

Perhaps a day later, perhaps 10 hours later, an east Indian American psychiatrist visited me—just like my auntie said he would. He was an oddly merry man with an infectious, upbeat attitude that gave me something like biblical faith in him. He asked me how I was feeling and whether I wanted to get out. *Call and response.* I said that I was better—that I wanted to live. "OK. We'll get you out of there," he smiled.

Revelations

When the deputy came for me, it was perfunctory, like he was getting a pair of white socks from a dresser drawer. Straightaway, he marched me from the safety cell to a shower around the corner. I must have smelled like 10,000 dung beetles. I hadn't brushed my teeth or put soap and water on any part of my body for days. As I rinsed ("shower" would be an overstatement), I felt abstract—exaggerated and deformed in that way when you emerge from an overly deep nap filled with terrible dreams and you're confused and unsure about the contours of the waking world. Everything hurt.

While getting dressed, I asked the deputy why no one had cleaned that cell.

"We try to hose it down—clean it from time to time," he said.

I left the issue alone. I was pleased to be dressed like a respectable criminalized person, to be in my county oranges and ready for more conventional forms of punishment. The uniform hid my humiliations as much as it hid the jail's failures. No other residents would know that I'd been in a suicide cell, and deputies would have to want to know. It was as if my time in the Palace never happened. In fact, because deputies sent me to the Palace before I could complete intake procedures, I hadn't been formally processed into the jail yet—no booking number or identification wristband. I'd been tucked away in liminal place-time, not formally anywhere, so my jail time had not started.

My escort ushered me to the front of the processing line. On the way, I worried about Micah and my mother. And then I spotted a control panel with monitors. *Holy shit!* There, clear as spring water, was a live feed into the cell from which I had just been freed. My tribulations flitted through my mind: the singing and talking to myself, the gnawing at my wrist, my nakedness on the flayed safety dress. All my debasements had been on full display for deputies and curious residents passing by. The Palace had imbued me with the sense that I was utterly alone and beyond the reach of the social world. That soft-surface shit storm of a cell felt like a total institution unto itself in the way sociologist Erving Goffman[4] described: a walled place where the barriers between the spheres of social life are more or less destroyed, and all social activities occur in the one place under the rubric of some rationalized plan. I don't presume to know the goals associated with the Palace de Excreta, but here's what my time in there did: I was profoundly shamed, degraded, broken, and confused.

Seeing that live feed made me lightheaded. I wondered whether deputies had been laughing at me or maybe they pitied me. *No. No. No one was watching you, Michael. They couldn't have been. No one ever intervened—ever.* I kept telling myself that no one could have seen me in there because then deputies would have to explain what I was experiencing. If I had successfully committed suicide, I reasoned, deputies wouldn't have had a good explanation for what happened to me. Maybe in their story of how I died, they would blame the cell's condition on me, too. But none of that mattered because I survived, and I figured no one was watching me when I was in there. I hope no one was watching me.

I completed the intake process without further incident. Deputies fingerprinted, photographed, and assigned me a booking number. After a few hours in a standard pre-housing holding cell, I was taken to a permanent housing unit without any special instructions to follow-up with a mental healthcare worker. Apparently, the "treatment" had worked, and I was all better.

American Jails

American jails constitute one of the largest people processing machines in the United States. In 2019[5] state and federal prisons admitted 530,900 people. Jails, however, admitted over 10 million people each and every year between 2005 and 2018 (a notable 13.6 million in 2008).[6] And what this really means is that while the average daily population counts in prisons are higher than they are in jails, far more lives are touched by jails than prisons. Part of why that's true is because not everyone who goes to jail will go to prison, but everyone in prison has done some jail time. The flow of American criminal justice is arrest, then jail, and if a conviction comes with a sentence longer than a year, in most cases you "do" that time in prison.

Given the reach of American jails, I'm struck by how little we know about them. I don't know that it's anyone's fault. Prior to being arrested, I certainly couldn't have told you anything about jails. But even my colleagues who study punishment and criminal justice seem to have trouble dealing with jails in their own right. I tell them that I've conducted an ethnography in a county jail system, and they start to talk to me about prisons. I keep saying "jail," and the longer we chat, the more they say "prison." Imagine studying high schools and having everyone lump them in with colleges and universities.

In at least two ways, prison chauvinism makes sense. Prison seems to hold a unique place in our collective imagination. This is certainly true in popular culture.[7] But whether it has been a matter of research interest or access to research sites, there are far more studies of prisons than there are of jails. The entire field of punishment can accurately be described as the multifocal study of prisons and social life. A simple search of sociological generalist and specialty journals concerned with punishment bears this out.

Notwithstanding a relatively small number of articles,[8] the most important work on jails was published over 35 years ago. Of these, Ronald Goldfarb's book is the most harrowing, James Spradley's is the most sophisticated, and John Irwin's is the most popular among social scientists. And while all three make an argument about jail as a place to hide away groups generally held in low social esteem,[9] their thematic commonalities have not developed into something like "jail studies" as a unique form of punishment or even the study of jail as a kind of organization.

A second explanation for why prison studies are more common than jail studies might have to do with the average length of stay in jail: 26 days. There may be an assumption that nothing of consequence is happening in jails— that people are not there long enough for anything interesting to occur. Perhaps 26 days in jail seems quite doable (or even too-brief a period to justify a book). Keep in mind that the experiences I detailed in the opening of this book occurred within three days, and still I was not officially "booked" into jail until after I got out of the Palace. And then there's this: Suicide[10] is the longstanding leading cause of death in jails—followed by heart disease. Between 2006 and 2016,[11] there were 16,962 deaths in jails: 40 percent of those occurred within the first seven days of being incarcerated; and about 31 percent of all deaths were suicides at a median of just nine days in jail. Most jail suicides did not happen in what the Bureau of Justice Statistics calls "mental-health units." Indeed, only one percent of suicides occurred in some version of the Palace de Excreta. Most were in general population housing units (47 percent)—where I was sent after my treatment in the Palace. And while we may not know the stories of those who died in jails, we do know that in the decade leading up to and including 2016, no less than 70 percent (with a peak of 76 percent in 2016) of the people who committed suicide in jail were the innocent-until-proven-guilty. There's definitely something going on in American jails, and 26 days is more than enough time for it to happen.

Quite frankly, if you have never been to jail, a day inside can feel like a week. I'd like to suggest there be a *grab and hold* policy whereby judges, defense attorneys, prosecutors, legislators, law enforcement personnel, and correctional officers are randomly grabbed off the street, interrupting whatever plans they had, and held in an American jail away from their home county for an indefinite period of time: no less than 18 hours and no more than a month. Why that time span? I figure if you know that it's possible to get out after 18 hours, you might get your hopes up that you'll leave sooner than later. I can tell you that the knife really twists in the wound when your actual time in jail exceeds your expected time. But more than that, I am betting that we will get a much truer sense of who is concerned with justice, legitimate means of punishment, and basic standards of humanity if those who maintain and justify the Palace de Excreta are potentially subject to it.

The fact is the average length of stay in jails conceals more than it reveals. One of my earliest "discoveries" about jail was that a person could be there for years while fighting a case. Going back at least 40 years, the largest subpopulation in American jails has been the unconvicted (65 percent in 2017).[12] But their punishment is no less severe than those serving jail sentences. In fact, it is more distressing to "do" years of indefinite jail time without having been convicted. Procedural continuances and delays and overwhelmed courts: the right to a speedy trial quickly becomes little more than an ideal.[13] And so there develops a core of jailed residents who anchor the social structure of interpersonal relations in the housing units. They stabilize social interaction and give jail life a culture. *Indefinite* is a study of that culture—a way of examining from the inside out a place that processes about 1 in 30 Americans every year.

This, then, is the goal with this book—as reasonable and paradoxically bold as it may be: I intend to speak to my colleagues in the academy while detailing experiences that are wholly recognizable to anyone who has been to jail. Having lived in both worlds, this goal is only appropriate.

How I Came To This Study

During the fall of 2006, just a couple of weeks into my first semester of graduate study, I was arrested and I spent a night in Golden County's Cardinal Detention Center. I treated the experience as a one-off. It was embarrassing, but I confided in Scott Brooks, a professor in my graduate program at the time who told me, "Well, you know what you gotta do now, don'tcha? Gotta write it up." I didn't see the value in it, but I did as he suggested and filed away my description of the events surrounding that night in jail and the adjudication of the case. I completed my first year of graduate training without further run-ins with the criminal justice system.

The following fall, I spent more time in Golden County jails: the Providence Downtown Jail and Barracks Jail. I treated those arrests and jail stints as a series of unfortunate experiences, but I wrote about them nonetheless—nothing too deep—just what happened and how I felt without trying to analyze them beyond my normal self-reflective ways. My plan was to continue graduate school, specializing in general social theory and social psychology. I had no interest in studying the criminal justice system—even less in examining my own experiences. Besides, at the time, I didn't see how social theory or social psychology could apply to a penal environment.[14]

Finally came the winter of 2008 and the events with which I opened this book. My time in Providence was brief, but my troubles were far from over. I returned home to a notice that my tax refund would go to past debt, to a notice of eviction from the university's housing administration, and to a notice of expulsion from the university. I suppose not showing up to that appointment with judicial affairs didn't help. That's that. And there was little time to process *that* because I was scheduled for a series of court hearings in which I no longer had the emotional fortitude to put up any kind of fight. I agreed to a plea deal for a 180-day sentence—120 with "good time," and I had about two weeks to get my affairs in order: to move my stuff out of my campus apartment and to register Micah in a school near my mother, with whom he would be staying.

Preparing for jail time, I was of two minds. On the one hand, I thought I'd likely get out early because I knew the jails were overcrowded and the sheriff ran a program that released penal residents with nonviolent charges to make room for those with violent charges. On the other hand, I half believed that I was going to die in jail—that *something* would happen so that I never got out. Still, I wrote a list of books that I hoped someone would purchase and send to me in jail. The night before I was to surrender myself, I spoke with Professor Ellen Reese from my former graduate program. It was one of the first times we had ever had a conversation, but she wanted to encourage me to "pay attention" to what I saw in jail and to take notes—maybe, she reasoned, jail time could be an opportunity. I didn't see that way—not at all. I am the first in my family to earn a college degree, and it meant nothing because the very next day I would be in jail. My life was over; it wasn't a research opportunity.

About two weeks after my birthday arrest, I surrendered myself, was taken into Providence, and was transferred to Golden County's Sunland Detention Center. There I completed 120 days before being released on a hot June day. My mother drove me home. I spent the next two years working terminal positions in nonacademic jobs before I was able to return to the same graduate program. Admission wasn't a simple process. I had to cover a debt to the university, and I was made to write a research paper on the effects of parental incarceration on children. I wonder who read that and if they felt sufficiently satisfied that I was properly shamed as a single father. When I returned to graduate study, I did so with ethnographic field notes covering roughly 134 days in jail—give or take a few hours. I'd heeded Ellen's advice—partially, anyhow.

I had difficult-to-get data, but I had little interest in doing anything with it. Ellen, who was overburdened with students, graciously agreed to chair my dissertation committee, and I gave her the blues on more than one occasion as I vacillated between two ideas: one that used the ethnographic data that eventually became this book and one that chased down patterns in the romantic relationships of Black immigrant women. Ellen and I had some interesting discussions about which way to go. One that sticks out in my mind: She was flabbergasted with my indecision. I was worried about self-exploitation, how my family would view me, whether I could do the experiences any justice, and whether the Academy would take me seriously. More specifically, I'm a tall Black man, and I have a sense of how I live in the minds of others. Sociologist Katheryn Russell-Brown[15] provided a useful concept here: "criminalblackman." It's a single word because, for many, "criminal," "Black," and "man" intersect to form a single terrifying image of what crime itself is. Of course, the myth of the "criminalblackman" is not some happenstance but a carefully contrived image dating back to the Reconstruction.[16] It's hard enough to escape that myth without having been charged with a crime; it is all the more difficult to shake it once convicted. Thus, I worried about embodying Devah Pager's work in *Marked*.[17] Would academia see my Blackness and my criminal record and determine me too risky for a career no matter how good a sociologist I might become? If I could get an academic job, did I want to be known as the "jail guy"? And could I do a just analysis, or would I produce some lowbrow book of titillating stories about race, violence, and redemption? I wasn't sure, but Ellen said that I needed to reach a sufficient level of comfort with the ethnographic data, and if I couldn't get there, it was best to move on in a different direction.

Around that time, a friend told me that having been incarcerated "is the seventeenth thing" he thinks about me. That suits me just fine. Ultimately, I agreed with Scott Brooks, who once told me that I cannot control how others think of me or my work. People have a way of deciding who you are no matter how you present yourself. The upshot is that I specialized in race and crime without abandoning my interests in general theory and social psychology. As for self-exploitation, I'm in this book but it's not about me, and you won't find a satisfying Hollywood story arc with a White Jesus character and the Black human project who is ultimately set upright. Having said that, my inner voices of worry remain restless, but I forged ahead in writing this book because I think this research is important, and, if for some, my race, record, and gender impact how they receive my scholarship, that was going to happen anyway, so *it is what it is*.

How I Did It

I'm not now, nor was I then, a thrill-seeking researcher. I was arrested, jailed, evicted from my campus housing, expelled from a university, and I suffered the consequences of all those experiences in flesh and spirit. This ethnography evolved organically from my habit of writing, my natural curiosity, support from Ellen Reese, and the realization that there would be no magical early release for me. In all honesty, I never thought I'd get back into graduate school, and if I did survive jail, I wasn't convinced I'd be sane or have usable data.

But once I committed myself to doing a study and not just writing how I felt and what I saw, I confronted a number of challenges. First, as a jail resident, I couldn't just walk around talking to whoever I wanted. Wherever I was, I made it a point to interact with others. That included taking advantage of medical, dental, and mental healthcare in jail, going to "church," going to court while in custody, participating in recreation time, and generally mixing with others whenever possible. And I didn't just speak with other residents. I purposefully struck up conversations with deputies and staff members with varying degrees of success.

Second, deputies formally classified penal residents by risk and informally by race. My data reflect my racial classification and social life in general population housing units. The result is that I had minimal interactions with residents not classified in general population and, because race relations were so consequential, I didn't have unfettered access to interact with residents in racial groups different from mine—though there were some exceptions. One way I met that challenge was through what residents called the "county tour." To quell fights, head off conflicts, and (according to resident lore) earn money, Golden County custodial deputies transferred residents between housing units and bussed them to different jails altogether. All that shuffling around is what we called the "county tour," and my tour afforded me chances to interact with residents in different jails from different racial groups with different measures of jail experience. I took advantage of those opportunities to the best of my ability.

As for recording field notes, I purchased golf pencils and pads of paper from the jail commissary, and I mostly wrote while on my bunk or in a cell. Being free of the onslaught of social media applications, television, radio, phone calls, and text messages, residents tended to have the same conversations repeatedly, and I am sure that I was able to remember more than I would have if those distractions were there. Whenever possible, I quoted what was said and when I couldn't, I described the spirit of what was said. Additionally, I regularly sent letters describing social life in jail to Ellen Reese and professor emeritus Edna Bonacich. Both graciously returned those letters to me once I was home.

Finally, professors Ellen Reese and Jane Ward sent me books. Ellen went the extra mile of writing me frequently, sometimes putting money in my commissary account, visiting me, and generally helping me to stay sane and focused. At some point, she sent me Erving Goffman's *Asylums*.[18] That book did two things for me: It told me that I could do meaningful research in a jail, and it gave me new leads—new questions and ideas to chase down.

An Organic Ethnography

As I said, this research evolved organically, which means more than the obvious—that I hadn't planned on doing a study in jail. This *organic ethnography* included five practices. First, I focused on experience[19] and structure. By the time I turned an analytical eye—my sociological imagination,[20] if you will—to the life I already belonged to, I understood some relations, emotions, and dispositions very well. I knew them in my own body; others, not so well. Either way, my goal was to be able to explain social life in jail to someone who has never been there. A large part of this meant taking social life in jail as an independently worthy place to study. The social rules, values, behaviors, and ways of organizing were not some set of human pathologies but were actual solutions to problems germane to jail time: culture in action. And I intended on studying that culture without subjecting it to chauvinistic standards of different subcultures. Whenever I made comparisons, I did so to highlight what is common across social arenas that might normally seem very different from jail.

Also, I paid attention to what it feels like, smells like, what is often heard and seen, and what food tastes like in jail. I mapped out who was who, in what roles, the relationships between those roles, and what made those relationships work or not work. I thought a lot about the relationship between residents and "jail" as a nebulous edifice, and I tried to avoid expressing social behaviors and ideas in this configuration: *Jail makes people do this or that.* Such statements are familiar in social science, but they don't actually tell us much. Are we to anthropomorphize "jail" as an actor behaving against individuals? I have taken a different path, and though not always faithful to this principle, I have tried to tell you who specifically did what. In some cases, it makes more sense to say that "jail time" has different effects on residents. Even if that feels vague, it is nonetheless accurate because residents did respond to a conception of time as a "thing."

Second, I made emotions a principal pathway to understanding the experience of jail time. I cared a lot about how residents expressed their emotions, and I didn't ignore or hide how I felt about being in jail and interacting with others.[21] There is something very strange, I think, about sociologists pretending to be unaffected by their environments. I don't wear my emotions on my sleeve in this text, but I don't write as though I didn't feel anything. I very much want you to know—and so I worked hard to present—the various emotional stances that I and residents had in different jail experiences.

Third, I used conversations as interviews, fact-finding expeditions, and a way to track down counterfactuals. It may have been that I had a guess about how something worked, so I'd clumsily broach the topic to get others talking about it. Other times, I tried to slowly push the conversation in the direction

I wanted. I did that, for instance, when I wanted to see if there were multiple ways of keeping track of the passage of time. In other instances, I just plainly asked what I wanted to know—like when I wanted to learn penal sign language. But keep in mind, I wasn't actually conducting formal interviews. I was in the natural bounds of typical social behavior, and in many cases, it would have been weird for me to step outside those bounds for the sake of curiosity. For instance, I never heard the word "truck" used the way residents did in jail but I worried that asking the meaning would put symbolic distance between me and those around me,[22] so I never flat out asked anyone what it meant. Like most slang, the meaning of "truck" was somewhat situational, and I picked up the subtle differences in usage until I had a sense of what it meant.

Fourth, and this relates to highlighting the role of emotions for investigating social life, I kept *paired field notes*. In the one set are my personal feelings—a place for me to exorcise my own demons and to be "Michael the person" instead of "Michael the sociologist." I wrote about my son. I wrote about my mom and how much I sometimes hated some residents and how I admired others.[23] I dedicated the other set of field notes to more traditional sociological analysis, and the language in those notes reflects that: "social structure," "stratification," "social status," "status hierarchy," "masculine narratives"—these are the kinds of terms found in those field notes. To keep both sets of field notes, I decided whether an interaction was more or less "sociological"—that is, did it help me to understand social life in jail, was it part of a pattern of events, and did it inform the way I understood other events through confirmation or disconfirmation? If the answers were "yes," I recorded the event in the sociological field notes. When an interaction or observation struck me viscerally, and I needed to deal with how I was feeling, I wrote in my personal set of field notes. Very often, I experienced something that fit both, so I just documented it in both sets of field notes. I had time to do that in jail.

Finally, my writing is three-dimensional. Throughout this text, I switch between one of three voices: Michael the subject, Michael the narrator, and Michael the sociologist. To organize these three voices, I have paid close attention to what novelist and literary critic, John Gardner, referred to as "psychic distance,"[24] or the closeness the reader feels to the events being described. Sometimes, I give you Michael the sociologist and the distance is purposefully wide to provide some conceptual framing, theoretical scaffolding, or analysis—my comments on mutual objectification with the courthouse clerk, for instance. Other times, there is virtually no distance between me, you, and what happened as when I bring you into my thoughts. And there are yet other times when the psychic distance is more middling so that I can narrate a bit, like when I tell you about how deputies shuttled me through courthouse hallways to jail. It's not easy to balance these three voices in an academic text. Gardner has an illuminating discussion about narrative inviting the reader into a dream world, how immersion in the dream can be quite satisfying, and the dissatisfying experience of being "woken" from that vivid dream. As an academic book, interrupting the dream state of deep description is sometimes necessary to provide analysis. Switching between these three voices—sometimes *waking you up*—is what I mean by three-dimensional writing, and I think it is one of strengths of organic ethnography.

What does organic ethnography offer that we would otherwise not have? The point of ethnography is to learn about the social world of others, and there are only two ways to do it. We can be told about different social worlds through some form of media, or we can experience those worlds for ourselves. I am not advocating for every would-be ethnographer to join the social world of others—either organically or by imposition. But I am saying that some things are only understood through experience, and the analysis and writing of that experience must be true to how every sense was stimulated.

On this point, sociologist Erving Goffman[25] said that it is only through subjecting yourself—your body, your personality, your social situation—to the contingencies of the social world that you hope to know that you will, in fact, be able to know it. He reminds us that to the people in a given social world, the rules therein make sense. But researchers must cast away their cultural selves if they are to experience the desires and fears and aspirations of others. Doing so is a large part of what is involved in organic ethnography, and it is why *The Jack Roller* and *The Derelicts of Company K* are among the most insightful ethnographies ever produced. But organic ethnography must go one step further. The analysis and presentation thereof must be grounded in the emotional content of the social world in question. Goffman's *Asylums*, for instance, is one of the most theoretically rich studies of organizational living ever produced, but we learn little of the emotional selves of the people Goffman encountered or of Goffman himself. Experience, though, *is* emotional. I advocate for more of it in sociology—more of the emotional stance[26] of the author; more of the emotional content of the life events we study.

Plan For the Book

This book is organized to cover social life in jail by highlighting moments[27] that best illustrate the moods, activities, people involved, motives, and constraints that capture the state of being at a time. Most importantly, I've included those experiences that anyone who has been to jail will recognize. This is not the same as saying every jail is the same. Every hospital is not the same, but anyone who has stayed overnight in a hospital will recognize certain experiences. So it is with this book. *Indefinite* should be read with the goal of understanding the emotional, physical, and cognitive experiences of jail as they are—piled atop one another and not encased in the smooth sociological trickery of a single process.

You will not find a neat narrative from arrest to release under the rubric "careers" or any other processual concept. To my mind, "process" requires an identifiable sequence of steps toward some goal. In social science, we like to call things a process because we observed something at time one and something different at time two, but change does not indicate process.[28] Jail time made that abundantly clear to me. Thus, this book is not a chronology of events. Instead, each chapter, and each vignette between the chapters, has the goal of submerging you in the emotional muck of social life in jail.

But while each chapter zooms into peculiarities of jail life, I remain attentive to what is familiar in social life more broadly. My perspective is that jail is a type of organization, and because I am dealing with social behavior in an organizational setting, no one should be shocked to find that humans are doing the same kinds of things humans usually do—albeit under more extreme circumstances. Too many studies of penal life fetishize the setting, and this partly why I use the term "resident" instead of "prisoner" or "inmate" or some other term married to prisons. I suspect some of my colleagues won't agree, but the fact is, people live in jail like they do in military academies and monasteries. Each population collects mail in an organizational home and the whole of social life occurs there. Using terminology that acknowledges those commonalities, I hope, points researchers toward seeing how a study of jails applies to hospitals and how it can help us to see what is special and not so special about military academies and even certain communities. And also, I want to deal with jail residents on grounds unsullied by the connotations that come with terms like "prisoner" and "inmate."[29]

Whenever it seems appropriate, I toggle between digging into the complexities that make jail life what it is and analogizing jail to other social arenas.

For instance, the person battling cancer, the family battling poverty, and the jail resident battling the vagaries of punishment have similar relationships with time and uncertainty. In fact, our experiences with COVID-19 in the United States cast the problem of uncertainty and time in sharper relief than normal. Extremes of uncertainty make long-term planning difficult, which increases the importance of the immediate if, for no other reason than we have more control over the present than we do an unknowable future. This is the basic reality for the unconvicted jail resident languishing with no sense of completion; it is the reality for the person battling cancer who is not told, "You are cured" but instead, "There's no evidence of disease" or "You're currently in remission"; and it is reality for the family mired in poverty that robs Peter to pay Paul, hoping they never meet. In each case, life becomes more immediate; there's a need to constantly renew one's energy for an internal fight to keep going. After all, 68 percent of formerly incarcerated persons are reincarcerated within the first three years of release; 79 percent within six years; and 83 percent within nine years.[30] You could go back. The cancer could return. You could be evicted or have your lights cut off. The potential in each situation leads to the personification of vulnerability, uncertainty, and time itself as beasts that must be fought. There is great value in ethnography that clarifies common denominators across social arenas.

The Vignettes and Chapters

Preceding each chapter is a vignette meant to introduce some relevant issue discussed in the following chapter. More than that, each vignette is an emotional moment that struck me during the doing of this organic ethnography, and I want you to have a sense of those moments, too.

The more analytical work is in the chapters, which are organized into two parts. Part 1 is primarily about the social structure of the Golden County jail system—the interrelation of actors in particular roles and statuses and the procedures that link them. In Chapter 1, I begin by using a factory production line as a metaphor for how intake procedures reconstitute people as "criminal objects." Chapter 2 introduces the "rep" and the principal management system deputies used in general population housing units. I discuss how deputies exploited the reps to manage the day-to-day caretaking responsibilities that would otherwise fall to deputies. Chapter 3 extends the discussion in the previous chapter, expounding on how deputies instituted race as a way of organizing social life in jail. I highlight the underlying logics of using race and where those logics are abandoned. In Chapter 4, I turn to deputy–resident relations. I use residents' dichotomous characterization of "cool deps" and "asshole deps" to discuss the nature of deputy–resident relations. Chapter 5 concludes Part 1 with a tour of going to court while in custody. Here I highlight how in-custody court appearances encapsulate the uncertainties and vulnerabilities to truly mark the character of doing indefinite time. Additionally, I theorize why court days are so dangerous relative to other events.

The chapters in Part 2 are decidedly more feelings-oriented. Chapter 6 is a deep dive into jail culture in action, including the vagaries of jail living for which residents could neither predict nor lessen the negative effect. In Chapter 7, I take up the issue of time—how it's understood and experienced very differently in jail than in free society, and I show what it looks like when a resident's emotional fortitude fails. Chapter 8 takes a novel approach to studies of carceral living. I investigate the relationship between sleep hygiene and mental and physical health. Chapter 9 follows the end of Chapter 8 by picking up the theme of care. I explore what expressions of care look like, and I present residents in their emotional and behavioral complexities.

Strictly speaking, the final chapter is not a summary of the book's arguments or an appeal to policy change—though I do explain how I came to understand my time in jail. Rather, I conclude with how this book began: in jail. In the end, residents needed to find ways to make sense of jail time, and I show how residents used the philosophies of *it is what it is* and *it is as it should be* to endure jail time. On this point, my argument is that enduring is really all any resident could hope to do.

Despair

"I already cry myself to sleep every night."

—Sisqo

1

Objectification

A deputy once told me, "If you're in here, you did something." He might have said it like this: "You're in here because you're a criminal." Or, more concisely: "You're guilty." I still think about the matter-of-fact way that deputy conferred guilt upon me. It was different from other kinds of interactions I'd had with law enforcement. Whenever I've been pulled over in traffic, I could bet on at least one more police cruiser appearing on the "scene." I'd sit with my hands at ten-and-two wearing an annoyed face to mask my fear. Just as often, I was asked/told to sit on the curb with my legs crossed. The extra officers would stand near me with an alert look. Police lights beckoned lookieloos. I may have been speeding. I might have performed a "California roll" through a stop sign, or I might have had an "obstructed view" by a scent tree hanging from my rearview mirror as one officer explained her reason for pulling me over. I've always hated the implicit accusation of nonspecific guilt in the spectacle of police interactions. I've felt similarly about checking "the box" to acknowledge having a criminal history, but it all still felt like an accusation—nothing like the finality in that deputy's statement.

The truth is, that deputy related a fact of life for penal residents in Golden County jails. Jail is where accusations are made true—or at least treated as such, and it begins with intake, where the ostensible goal is to admit persons into jail. But it is no less apparent that deputies working intake are involved in another, more consequential enterprise: making criminals.[1] Now, you may protest that it is their own behavior that earns each penal resident the ignominious status of "the criminal," but of course that's not true—not wholly anyway. For, we know that not everyone who has been charged or found guilty of a crime is deemed a criminal. No one refers to Martha Stewart as such. Part of why that's true is because differences in blameworthiness, honor, esteem, dignity, and respect map onto intersections of race, class, and gender. This is why the more socially marginal a person is, the more vulnerable that person is to accusations of guilt.

But in jail, deputies dispense with accusations and ascribe guilt in the making of "the criminal." And who, or rather what, is "the criminal"? We know the answer intuitively, but to be clear, "the criminal" is a kind of social object, and all social objects are essentialized in terms of their *uses* or their *motives*. "The slut," a distinct fiction of men's imaginations, is not exactly a woman of any kind but a collection of body parts for a man's use.[2] In essence, the criminal is a bundle of motives to do harm, to lie, and to steal. A cousin of mine is a correctional officer in a northern California prison, and he explained to me that during training, correctional officers were taught that "every inmate either has AIDS or is trying to kill you" because that's what "criminals" do.

Such a belief comes with serious consequences. It should be remembered that penal organizations are mandated to provide basic measures of care[3] as much as they are designed to punish. In practice however, it is far too often the case—sometimes with deadly results—that when faced with the choice to provide mental or physical healthcare or to lean into punishment, custodial staff choose the latter. And why? Well, the criminal is not to be trusted, invested in, or cared for because the criminal is unworthy of the dignities and concerns afforded fully sentient humans. The Palace de Excreta taught me that. Many others lost their lives in the learning of that lesson. Terrill Thomas was killed by Milwaukee custodial deputies in 2016 when they denied him water for seven days.[4] Rikers Correctional Facility staff subjected Kalief Browder[5] to tribulations that led him to a series of suicide attempts while in custody before the one that ended his short life after he was released without being found guilty of a crime. In 2018, Army veteran Gregory Lloyd Edwards suffered a deadly interaction at the hands of Florida's Brevard County custodial deputies.[6] Andrew Holland died from a pulmonary embolism after San Luis Obispo County Jail deputies strapped him in a restraint chair for 46 hours.[7]

None of this is terribly shocking except, perhaps, in our numbness to it all, but as students of the history of degradation, we know that the objectification of personhood is its own justification for torture and human atrocity.[8] When people are arrested and taken to jail, however, they enter as their whole selves, donning the accoutrements that signal something about who they might be in society. They enter with their first names and a complex of identities attached to different roles and groups to which they belong. But if Golden County custodial deputies were tempted to imagine their fathers, brothers, sons, uncles, and friends in the faces of those entering intake, they hid it well. Indeed, it would be harder to mistreat humans believed to be very much like ourselves.[9] Thus, through intake procedures, deputies systematically destroy and replace personhood with a single social object—one that is symbolically as different from dignified society as is possible: the criminal.

And let me completely clear, because while I continue to use the terms "social object" and "objectification," the underlying issue is one of value. Indeed, objectification is a theory of value in the sense that a theory is an explanation of things. The theory is social objects are of low value—very nearly no value at all. And so very weak intellectual energy is dedicated to explaining why we mistreat and degrade objects. In fact, the onus is on those likely to be devalued to explain why they should not. Once objectification is complete, then it is easy to shrug and offer a childlike "because" as sufficient justification for the brutality and degradation persons as objects will suffer. I do mean "will suffer," for objectification is not a passive social project. There are payoffs to low valuation. Reduce a person to uses, and those uses justify themselves. Reduce a person to motives, and your response to those motives are intrinsically legitimated and, most importantly, abuse can occur without the moral quandaries we would experience if we were dealing with actual people. After all, "If you're in here, you did something," which is grounds for what we will do to you next.

The Line

When the intake door shuts behind you, thousands of miles stretch you away from the free world. You enter on the surrealism of a Spike Lee double dolly shot only to be jerked to consciousness by the quick tempo of gruff jail procedures and shocked again into a dreamlike float. Your new reality will set in, but it will take a few tries. Just inside the door, you get snippets of the environment. Cold breezes whip up a stale mildew smell. Echoing off the walls is walkie-talkie static, indecipherable chatter, jingling keys, and the rollercoaster sound of heavy metal doors sliding shut with a mighty clang. Overhead fixtures light dull surfaces. Deputies are here and there. Some escort lines of listless men in orange tops and bottoms. Others blur into beige tops with shiny black boots and belts bookending forest green pants. Some deputies sport high and tight haircuts. Some stand tall—hands on their belt, chin high, eyes steely (they must teach that stance at the academy, too). Every deputy wears black nitrile gloves to avoid contamination by handling you, the raw materials on this production line. Somewhere in the distance, behind the cell doors lining the corridor, voices fruitlessly yell: "Hey dep'! Dep'!"

And above their pleas, a deputy booms commands in a militaristic cadence. His tone suggests he had been repeating the same directions longer
than his patience, pausing for effect between words: "Gentlemen, stand—inside—the—red—line—and put your nose—to—the—wall." You saw the line
when you first entered intake, but you look down and see it for what it is
for the first time. It runs throughout the intake area and the jail hallways.
More significantly, the depersonalization process has already begun. For, it
is not you in line, but we. Intake occurs in bunches, so *we* step inside the red
line, shoulder-to-shoulder with *our* faces close enough to the grayish-green
painted wall for stressed breath to condense in front of us.

Maybe we stood there for a couple of seconds—maybe a couple of minutes,
but we remained in suspended anticipation until a deputy performed a frisk
and sat a brown paper bag by each of us. When given the instruction, we put
our shoes, socks, and belts (if wearing one) in the brown paper bag. "Spread
your legs," a deputy said in a series of choppy commands. In succession, we
showed the deputy the bottom of each foot; we held our pants with one hand
and showed the deputy the other. There was a lot going on at once: the quick
pace, the cold, the moving in and out of a dream state, the red line, the noise,
the shouted commands, and the strange left–right–right–left dance we were
doing to facilitate the search. It was easy to become confused. Inevitably,
someone raised the wrong hand or moved the wrong foot, and deputies
swooped upon him, castigating him for the confusion. Perhaps we were just
unable to follow instructions, deputies bitterly wondered aloud.

It was mean and bullying behavior, but how else should we learn to expect
degradation if not by experiencing it? "Hey asshole!" a deputy yelled at the
back of a head. "Do you know your left from your right?"

The rattled man began explaining that he hadn't heard the deputy clearly.
Another deputy chimed in that the man should just follow instructions—
"Without all the explanation," he added.

With the frisk done, a deputy tapped each of us in succession to turn and
face a chest-high desk behind which a deputy sat in a tall chair to match the
exalted position over us. Put your grocery bag of clothes on the ground; place
your hands flat on the desk; and spread your feet "two feet" apart. Those
who undershot the distance had their legs kicked apart from behind with
the added indignity of their beltless pants falling to their thighs or ankles.
This was the property desk where the deputy inventoried personal property,
counted and transferred to personal commissary accounts any money we
had with us. The deputy screened for sexual and mental health concerns, and

I suppose the proper process would have had each of us check the appropriate boxes to indicate known risks, but in practice, the property desk deputy filled in most of the form without discussion. The screening had more to do with fulfilling an organizational mandate than determining whether some intervention was needed. The deputy checked boxes and scribbled on lines and we were given insufficient time to review the document before being told to sign our confirmation that everything was accurate.

The uniform station was a short walk from the property desk. As instructed, we walked inside the red line with fingers interlaced. Standing and walking like that forces the head to bow a bit, giving the impression of being emotionally or physically broken, so some tilted their chins in the air, but that pushes the shoulders forward and down a little. It becomes a battle between the *penal posture* deputies wanted and natural comfort. With time and relentless reminders to walk in the penal posture, it became easier to stay like that. Eventually, residents fixed their bodies without being told, and some found themselves walking like that even when deputies weren't around to tell them to do it.

The uniform station was a nook where crates of white socks, jumbled sizes of orange tops and bottoms, white boxers, and eraser-colored sandals lined a wall on the floor. In free society, we use fashion to convey our personal selves to others. In penal society, the uniform station is where each of us traded the complexity of selfhood represented in fashion for the grouping and stigmatizing effects of the county jail uniform. Dignity impelled some to search through the crates with a bit of anxious laughter. You want to get the right sizes if nothing else. Someone inevitably held up some soiled boxers for others to see, but it was best not to let the mind linger on the origin of any given stain or discoloration. There was hardly time for that, anyhow. The deputy escort moved everyone along, so we grabbed whatever we could and returned to the red line in orange tops and bottoms in different stages of color fade. Some of us were in grayed boxers that were two sizes too large—or too small. If lucky, you found a white T-shirt that was more or less clean, but nearly everyone had on sandals in a state of disrepair.

However ill-fitting they were, each of us left the nook in a criminal's uniform, and it's worth sitting with the work that the uniform does, for it is not merely clothes. Indeed, clothes are not merely clothes—rather, clothes comprise a large portion of your "identity kit,"[10] signifying your relative prestige, your subculture, and even your blameworthiness.[11] I am reminded of a fraternity brother who bragged about his fine wool suit, and when he turned,

I saw that he did not know to remove the temporary stitching from the vent on his suit jacket. His suit was nice but he didn't know how to wear it, and I went from admiring his taste to realizing that he had only just acquired it. The jail uniform is far more consequential. It hides your charges and insists that you are guilty of a crime. It is the unambiguous shorthand for the *kind* of person you are, and few symbols engender stronger negative reactions; few convey clearer messages of indignity, immorality, danger, and untrustworthiness. The damned thing wears you, and in uniform, the circumstances of each man's arrest are hidden. Your charges may have been violent or nonviolent; you might have been arrested while at work, school, on the scene of the alleged crime, or while making love with your partner; you could have been in a suit, basketball shorts, or swim trunks; perhaps you are a newbie or a veteran of jail time. All such specifics are crushed under the pressure of organizational procedure, and there will be no nuance of distinction among soon-to-be residents on the production line—only uniformity and social objecthood.

Next was the march to the property lock up area where we hand over our grocery bag of personal clothes. Already there is a new line of people pressing their noses to the wall where we once stood, and we have become the listless bodies in orange tops and bottoms that we had seen upon entry.

Having dropped off our bag of clothes, we marched to the fingerprinting station. Modern fingerprinting doesn't involve stamping inked hands and fingers on paper. Golden County jails used a large contraption resembling a copy machine. It had a cylindrical optical scanner across which a deputy guided our palms, fingers, and the ridges on each hand. It took teamwork to get the machine to register a usable print. You had to stand to one side of the scanner while a deputy stood either on the side of you or slightly in front, arm-in-arm to control how to position your hands. Deputies gave strict instructions to hold still and let your hands go limp. If any part of your hand was too rigid, the scan might not take. The more attempts made, however, the more the optical scanner developed a film (a germaphobe's nightmare), so deputies frequently sprayed the scanner with water, repositioned whatever they were scanning, and tried again to register a usable print. It was an awkward situation—for us and them, I'm sure: the feeling of a gloved deputy softly guiding your hand to get a fingerprint because you have been charged with a crime and you're in jail mixed with the rushed pace and acerbic commands given in the background that you cannot help but to hear.

Because the fingerprinting scanner was so temperamental, the station was a bottleneck. Deputies sometimes made a competition of getting acceptable prints with the fewest number of passes over the scanner. That may have helped with the tedium of their work, but it did little for us. We had been hurried along at a disorienting pace to reach the fingerprinting station where waiting forced upon us an awareness that there were no visible clocks or natural light. Worse, while there was a bench next to the fingerprinting station, it sat only four or five at a time. The rest of us had to stand, and we could be standing for 20 minutes, an hour, or some other unaccounted period. Sometimes there were too many of us congesting the hallway, so deputies stored some of us in pre-housing holding cells or skipped fingerprinting until the line died down some.

That shuffling increased lapses in care. Sometimes, someone didn't get a meal during "chow time." On one occasion, a man spent hours begging for a meal from every deputy who passed, being sure to explain that it was not his fault that he hadn't been fed. Deputies offered only three meals a day, and if you were arrested just after a meal, you had to wait for the next official mealtime. "I don't know why you weren't fed," one deputy responded.

Another said the same thing and added, "But I don't have any control over that." He said he would see what he could do. No meal came, and another deputy explained to the hungry man that handing out food was the responsibility of some other deputy. That was my favorite response from deputies—pointing to the *mythical other* who was always responsible for the very thing residents were asking about. I never did meet that mystical creature.

I came to understand these kinds of responses from deputies as *polite indifference*: feigned interest to mask a deputy's determination to get through a work shift without addressing every concern or need we had. In permanent housing units, deputies mixed in a little help between moments of polite indifference, condescension, and disregard. This was much less the case during intake, where men at different stages of objectification had more than a few questions about the jail environment and next steps. Sometimes dedicating a few seconds to respond to a question afforded deputies a brief reprieve from the inundation of queries—even when the response wasn't actually a solution. A well-placed, "I'll see what I can do" can buy some time away from an anxious resident.

In any case, deputies eventually fingerprinted everyone, leaving a final station. Until this point, no one is formally "booked" into the jail, and the production line has not yielded its completed product. There are three stages to the final station, and depending upon how crowded the area was, deputies either started by verifying the soon-to-be resident's name, birthday, and social security number so that a booking number could be generated and assigned, or they sometimes started with the photographs. Standing in a well-lit space, each of us removed our orange top, white T-shirt, and pants—if necessary—so that a deputy could photograph any tattoos. I was always struck by the potential danger in the moment of having one's body photographed because it was a public area. Tattoos might signify gang affiliation racial ideology (or mistaken as such), or they might be used to identify someone who was trying to keep their identity unknown. Presumably, nothing ever happened as a result of the open photography session, or deputies never traced a conflict back to intake where someone's group affiliations were first revealed. Both could be true. After documenting tattoos, deputies positioned each of us on a marked spot on the floor, gave the instruction to "look up" at the camera perched high upon the wall, and they snapped a mugshot. Finally, the mugshot and personal information were laminated to a "wristband," and voila! From persons known by name to objects known by number: the production line is complete.

Many residents would come to despise their wristband as a kind of animal tag that doubled as an access card. It was supposed to be wrapped around the wrist too tightly to be removed, but lots of residents found ways to slide theirs off and on. Without it, though, deputies denied residents the chance to exchange worn clothes for cleaned ones. Visitation, church, your mail, recreation, and commissary orders could be denied if a resident didn't have on his wristband. I had a less emotional response to my wristband than did most others around me. Instead, I found it an important indication of how active the jail machinery was and how long someone could be in jail. Booking numbers began with the year of admission followed by the numerical place in a running count of admissions. As I learned, someone could be in jail for a shockingly long time.

On one occasion, a deputy escorted four of us past a set of single-man cells. The cells were a form of administrative segregation for residents with medical conditions. They looked like little hotel rooms with a shower, toilet, and bed all in the same space. The deputy escort stopped us near a cell emblazoned with a resident's booking number: 199916XXX.[12] In other words, in 1999, he was the 16,000-and-something person admitted to the Golden County jail system. It was February 2008. He had been in jail for nine years pending adjudication.

Pre-Housing Holding Cells

Deputies didn't explain this, but before newly minted residents could be assigned to a permanent housing unit, there needed to be a classification interview. Until that happened, residents were made to tarry in what I call *pre-housing holding cells*. Deputies and residents alike referred to all temporary places in jail as "holding cells," but I experienced and observed dramatic differences in the place-based[13] norms of interaction depending upon why residents were gathered in a particular holding cell. Later, I show just how different were the rules for interacting in *court* and *mental health holding cells*. For now, I want to highlight what made pre-housing holding cells so unique.

Initially, the most striking feature of pre-housing holding was that newbie residents didn't know why they were there. Deputies were loath to explain jail procedures. Answer one question, and there would surely be others. Hence, disregard was more common than polite indifference. It wasn't that we didn't know we were there to wait. We knew that, but as newbies, we wanted—indeed, we needed—to know what we were waiting for. I distinctly remember thinking that I was just waiting on the next *thing*—whatever that was, and I assumed it would be bad.

Also coming into focus while in pre-housing holding was the need to know the time—to locate one's self in *when*. Not knowing the time and not having any of the usual methods to create a sense of movement through time, it was easy to become slightly obsessed with constructing a timeline of events.[14] My nagging need for temporal ordering was no less distressing than others who pestered deputies for the time, but I preferred to keep to myself as much as was possible. Besides, deputies usually offered a smart-ass remark to questions about the time, so I saw no point in subjecting myself to that. Still, if I could have known the time, I could have neutralized some of the anxieties I had about my son and what my mother was doing. Sitting in pre-housing holding, I felt exposed to a universe of contingencies. Now, I have been "without money for food," as a Golden County Department of Social Services aid request form asked, and I have not known how I would pay my rent, but I experienced a more acute form of vulnerability to time and uncertainty in pre-housing holding than in my most insecure moments in free society. It just seemed as though *anything* was likely to happen in jail.

Relatedly, there was a stark change in tempo from the production line to pre-housing holding. During active-duty days, my mother used to describe extreme shifts in the tempo of action as "hurry up and wait" experiences. Deputies moved the production line along as if they were late and trying to catch up. Their commands were abrasive and delivered in quick stabbing sentences. There was never any time to pause. From signing the property release form to choosing the uniform to getting the wristband—the production line was a brisk experience. Then, deputies dumped us in pre-housing holding, and the stark shift to almost no activity at all augmented the feeling of being disconnected from time in any meaningful way.

For me, the inactivity accentuated the pre-housing holding cell's features. The cells were uniformly cold, filthy, and filled with the beast mode fragrant sillage of an uncleaned toilet and musty metallic anxiety sweat. Some of the cells were under 100 square feet; others were about 400 square feet. Some had hospital-styled bright, white lights, and other cells glowed under a pale fawn color. Some had wood or concrete benches running the length of the walls, and others provided no place to sit but the ground. Usually there was at least one phone, but some had two, and sometimes there was a corkboard with bail bonds company cards affixed to it. In some cells, there was a stained stainless-steel toilet-sink combination while others came with a porcelain toilet with or without a seat and no running water to drink. If there was toilet paper (and there often wasn't any), it was tucked into a cruddy little cubby—if not set atop drying urine splashes near the toilet. If lucky, you would be in a cell with a toilet that was partially hidden behind a four-foot-high cinderblock wall, but the toilet may have been in plain view, and sometimes it was rather close to the cell door. Many pre-housing holding cells had large windows to the intake hallway, but there might instead be a small steel-meshed window in the cell door or even just classic prison bars. Though every kind of holding cell fit these descriptions to one degree or another, by the time I was in a court or mental health holding cell, I knew how to ready my body for that experience. My mind spent less time spiraling down analyses of the contours of those cells the way I did in pre-housing holding where everything was still new.

But it wasn't just the environment that occupied my mind during prolonged periods of silent inactivity in pre-housing holding. My thoughts broke from my control and turned against me. In that pre-housing holding cell, you remember that you were free just hours before and that you had plans for your immediate future that did not include jail. There had been insufficient time to give serious thought to how things had unfolded, but speaking personally, pre-housing holding imposed my thoughts upon me. I worried incessantly about my son, my mother, and responsibilities going unmet. I ruminated on details of embarrassing events going back as much as 15 years prior. Those memories had nothing to do with my jail calamities, but they nonetheless surfaced against my will.

I wasn't agonizing alone, though. Some residents frantically called bail bonds companies, hoping whoever answered would get word to a friend or family member. In my own experience, it could be hours before your booking number was searchable in public databases, and until that was true, the bail bonds company could not make a determination as to whether they could help you. After all, if bail was denied, they had no reason to talk with you. Still other residents locked a dead stare on a spot on the wall, some the floor, some on nothingness. Periodically, deputies added to or subtracted from our numbers in the cell. We had been sitting in stoic silence, but upon seeing the deputy, someone jumped at the chance to ask the time, why we were in pre-housing holding, and what was to happen next. Then I knew I wasn't alone in my worries because I knew that only a deep unease about the uncertainty of the future propelled those questions.

Deputies generally ignored timeline-related questions because, in fact, they didn't really know how long it would be before any of us would be transferred to a permanent housing unit. It really could be hours or days. When, for instance, experience gave me the confidence to ask a Latino resident how long he had been in pre-housing, he responded, "Eh. I been here for what—" holding up three fingers, "this is my third day." *Three days in here!* In any case, most residents hid their anxieties—or at least attempted to, and when cracks revealed the soft, vulnerabilities that I shared with them, I felt somewhat comforted in knowing that it wasn't just me fretting over the time, the toilet, and the next thing to happen.

Still, not every resident had stoicism on their side. A young Latino resident joined our Providence pre-housing holding cell and immediately took a seat on the bench. He bounced his legs on the balls of his feet. His brow was furrowed. He clasped his hands and rocked a little before standing to stretch. An older White[15] resident offered advice: "It's Friday, man. You' gon' be here for the weekend." He added that it was best to settle in and that the arraignment would be on Monday. The Latino resident paused to briefly make eye contact, but he didn't seem any less concerned. "Do you know the charges," the White resident continued.

"Fuck. Not really." Pacing, the young resident asked, "Monday—really? What do they do then?"

The older White resident explained that an arraignment is where defendants learn their charges. The young resident seemed to be attempting advanced calculus in his head. Then he started talking—stuttering and repeating himself, jumping around from issue to issue. The flood gates were open. As he talked himself into sharing more details about his arrest, others offered advice. Some of us laughed at hearing that he had run from police. "You might be fucked, fool," a Latino resident sighed with a chuckle.

"Eh, just throw yourself on the mercy of the court, fool. Ha! Ha! Ha!" another Latino resident said through laughs. He explained that he knew someone whose family members submitted supportive letters to the court and that "it worked for him." Something about the way he said that was comical, and we all got a laugh, but the conversation fizzled.

We had been cordial—friendly even—but we weren't friends or even associates. We were just people in the same place and under the same general circumstances. There was more silence than conversation in pre-housing holding, but whenever there was a discussion of any kind, it generally sprung from someone making an observation—the older resident explaining the next steps to a young resident who was clearly nervous. As another example, in a Cardinal Detention Center pre-housing holding cell, I watched a resident stare through the cell door window and mutter, "Fucking cops." Then he turned toward the rest of us to continue his complaint: "They always fuckin' wit' you. Fuckin' wit' ya car. Rough you up. Violate your rights." Others started sharing stories about cops behaving like gangs, about near get-aways, and about a few "stand-up" officers who treated people with respect. But like every other discussion in pre-housing holding, we returned to protracted silence as quickly as we had abandoned it.

Being in a pre-housing holding cell was a bit like being in a medical waiting area. You don't know why others are there—not exactly. You sense it's bad form to ask, and you don't particularly care to share why you're there. You may guess that some have more experience in that waiting area than you do. You may share background characteristics with others—age, race, ethnicity, gender, class, and so forth—but your current situation is what brings you all together. Still, you're all strangers without a motive to do anything other than keep to yourselves. Hence, I never saw or heard of any bickering, antagonism, or fighting in pre-housing holding cells, and the simplest explanation for that is this: no one had a reason to fight.

Indeed, residents in pre-housing holding shared space, wisdom regarding their cases, and food—all without regard to experience, race, ethnicity, or age. This was somewhat remarkable because interracial sharing and conversation were virtually prohibited in most permanent housing units. That race in pre-housing holding wasn't the barrier to basic human decency that it was in permanent housing units revealed how illogical the administrative use of race truly was. More on that soon, but during mealtimes in pre-housing holding, newbies turned down their skim milk and certain food items with a toddler's disgust: "Anybody want my milk?"

The milk went to the first resident to holler, "Shoot it!" meaning to pass it over. In some instances, newbies gave away their bologna and mayonnaise sandwiches, their apple, and—god forbid—their cookies!

Newbies versus Experienced

Who were those residents hollering "Shoot it!" who had the intestinal fortitude to digest jail coleslaw? We might reasonably assume they were simply hungrier than others, but their ability to eat without complaint was one of several confidences in cultural competency that newbie residents did not have. When you have been through a particular jail system, that experience provides a confidence about how to negotiate relations with deputies and with other residents. Eating is more manageable, and there is less hand-wringing over what might otherwise seem like unpredictable moments. That doesn't mean the experienced resident was any less concerned about his circumstances. I certainly wasn't less worried just because I'd been to jail before. But culture is what people do in respect to the kinds of situations that tend to confront them,[16] and experienced residents knew more of the how-tos that Golden County penal residents had developed.

Eating jail coleslaw—an ice-cream-scooped, runny, vinegary, milky substance sweetened with carrots and set in its own juices in a division of a Styrofoam container—was a rather low-level indicator of a resident's relative cultural competency. Other differences included, for instance, the confidence with which residents interacted with others. Newbies tended to avoid eye contact with deputies and other residents. They spoke with trepidation in their voices in contrast to experienced residents who spoke clearly to whomever they chose without obvious signs of shying. Newbies and experienced residents also tended to differ by their ability to sleep. It was much easier to sleep when you knew the next steps and that violence in pre-housing holding was rare. In Providence, for example, not only did a group of experienced Latino residents sleep, they snored. In the same cell, a couple of White residents sleep-nodded in a seated position, remaining alert enough to keep from slumping onto a stranger's shoulder. Sleep was much harder for newbies who were exhausted by the experience of intake as well as by the energy expended to abortively calculate the indefinite contingencies of *what now*.

There were two other somewhat unreliable ways to determine a resident's level of experience: his use of slang and his muscle build. "Shoot it" isn't exactly jail slang, but it isn't as common in free society either. Referring to your orange tops and bottoms as "oranges" implied jail experience, but a newbie could have picked that up from others. Other terms, like "spread," were more germane to penal living and were a giveaway as to a resident's experience. On the whole, however, slang was more suggestive than conclusive. It was the same with one's muscular build. There are no weights available for California prison or jail residents, but push-ups, squats, crunches, and pull-ups are common exercises. Do enough of them, and your body takes on a "V" shape from the shoulders to the waist much like a gymnast. Of course, not every penal resident worked out, but the "V" shape indicates penal time. Prison residents were frequently transferred to county jail to face new charges or to be a witness in someone's trial, and they tended to have that V-shaped gymnast physique. I met one such experienced resident in Providence. Hulking and affable, he was exclusively concerned with chatting on the phone with his girlfriend and pestering deputies to ensure that his commissary money was properly transferred from prison.

There was, however, a nearly surefire way to differentiate newbies from experienced residents: toilet etiquette. Newbies often held their bowels and urine to the point of near failure. When they did relieve themselves in pre-housing holding, they did so in the conventional way, ending with a flush. Meanwhile, experienced residents used the toilet in a culturally competent way: flush continually while peeing and "float one; soak one," meaning flush at every natural break in stool to cut down on the stink. The experienced resident knew to sit down and flush while relieving gas—to let the industrial plumbing suction carry away the brunt of the smell.

Now why is this distinction important at all? Aside from competencies in etiquette, experienced residents understood jail procedures and how social life in the permanent housing units was organized. They also knew the norms around interracial- and intraracial-sharing in permanent housing, yet they made no attempt at aligning the rules in pre-housing holding with permanent housing. Whereas race was given no special significance in pre-housing holding, race relations would become the most salient factor by which social life in permanent housing units was organized. As will be discussed in the next chapter, deputies managed general population housing units by marshalling race relations with the rationale that widespread interracial conflict was inevitable if residents weren't classified and somewhat separated by race. If that were true, we would rightly expect to see interracial conflict in pre-housing holding—especially because there were always experienced and newbie residents in those cells. But the opposite was true. Pre-housing holding was among the safer places in jail with experienced and newbie residents alike happily sharing personal stories, food, and space without any more conflict than would be found in a hospital waiting area. Indeed, there was nothing inevitable or intractable about race relations in Golden County jails—nothing at all.

Classification

That fact didn't stop deputies from elevating the significance of race relations in Golden County jails. Residents didn't sit in pre-housing holding for just any bed in any permanent housing unit to become available. Deputies absolutely considered race and attitudes toward race as key factors in determining how they classified residents.

Penal classification serves a number of functions[17] that generally fall into one of two categories: safety or treatment concerns. The main goal is to use attributes like marital status, race, criminal history, charges, and so forth to predict the likelihood of a resident being involved in misconduct. There is reason to be skeptical of risk assessment as a tool,[18] but what matters is that a resident's classification determined his housing and the kinds of experiences he was likely to have while in jail.

Classification worked like this. One by one—and not exactly in succession but over time—deputies pulled residents from pre-housing holding cells to conduct the classification interview. "Lopez," a deputy called into the cell without any emotion. Two residents with that last name stood. "Lopez, A.," the deputy clarified, and the wrong Lopez sat down. Lopez, A. stepped just outside the cell door. Through the window, we could see the deputy's back, his hand gestures, and the clipboard he was holding. He gesticulated with that strained fake friendliness that authorities have when they want to extract information—his hands moving in waves to show his palms as if to say: "It's OK to share with me." Moments later, the deputy returned Lopez, A. to the cell, and we continued as we were. Like every other resident who returned from the classification interview, he didn't share the contents of his conversation with the deputy.

There was good reason to keep one's classification interview private. Until that moment, the main difference between residents was in experience and nothing more. But during the classification interview, the deputy asked his questions with a whisper. What's your sexual orientation? Are you in a gang? Has anyone threatened you? The deputy marked a form following each answer. "Do you get along with all races?" The savvy resident kept a tab on what was being asked: sex, gangs, threats, and racial conflict. *It must be fucked up wherever I'm going next.* I always answered "Yes" to the race question, and I suspect that deputies would interpret the person who answered "No" to that question as an increased security risk. Golden County jails did not have housing units for persons who hated members of one race or another, so that person was likely to be sent to an administrative segregation unit. In practice, though, deputies didn't tell residents their classification at the end of the interview. You discovered that you had been sent to administrative segregation, protective custody, the trustee pod, or general population when you got there.

A resident's classification was no small matter. There were differences in freedom, danger, and privilege between the classifications. ADSEG was the most restrictive classification. It was jail within jail. "Administrative segregation" is a formalized way of saying solitary confinement. I never was assigned to an ADSEG unit, but deputies frequently marched me past ADSEG cells in the Sunland Detention Center. Those cells were scorched by bright lights that reflected off white paint in a tiny cell outfitted with a metal slab for sleeping and a toilet-sink combination. Get into a fight or get caught with "pruno" (penal made alcohol using fermented fruit) or "water bags" to do curls— among other kinds of misconduct—and deputies may send you to ADSEG.

During one my trips to mental health, Deputy Brown instructed our small group to face the wall while another deputy shuffled a resident behind us. Peeking over my shoulder, I saw that the resident had a red band hanging from his waist chains. I'd developed a bit of a rapport with Deputy Brown, so I later asked him what the red band meant. "Administrative segregation. Twenty-three-and-a-half-hour lock down. No phones. No visits," he responded.

I asked whether residents ended up there because of fights. My question had a history. Months before my being in Sunland, I'd seen a young resident in a Providence court holding cell who also had a red band hanging from his waist chains. He was short and slightly built. I'm guessing he would be carded at an R-rated movie. There were no signs of puberty in his shoulders or face. He was experienced, though. That much was clear. He walked about the holding cell freely but not in a worrisome manner. I noticed that he was blinking an eye like it was bothering him, and upon a closer look, I could see there was a fresh, reddish-purple bruise streaking from the corner of that eye. I asked him about it, and he explained that a few hours earlier, he had seen a resident with whom he had beef from their time in "YA"—the California Division of Juvenile Justice or, as it once was and continues to be known, the "Youth Authority." He said that when he saw the guy who had sucker punched him however long ago, he wanted "to get'em back," so he rushed at him on sight. As the pair fell to the floor, he hit his eye on the edge of a court holding cell's concrete bench. *I know that shit hurt!* I pointed at the red band on his waist chains, and he shrugged, "Fightin." Not long after he explained his story, deputies started rounding everyone up to return to the housing units. It seemed like the red bands were suddenly everywhere, like when you buy a new car and then feel like everyone else on the road is suddenly driving the same make, model, color, and year as you. It was a revelation as to what I had been missing because my attention had been elsewhere.

I just wanted to confirm my suspicion that fights could lead to ADSEG. "Basically," Deputy Brown started, "it means that if I put him in the cell with you, he would jack your shit up."

I took that as a challenge, and I sarcastically asked whether he really thought that was true. He offered to put the ADSEG resident in the cell with me, and I accepted but then quickly declined, asking whether he was trying to get me into trouble. Deputy Brown laughed, ended our exchange, and I had my confirmation about ADSEG.

Whereas deputies sometimes classified residents to ADSEG for the safety of others, protective custody (PC) housing units were reserved for residents in need of protection from other residents. Some PC residents or "PCs" as they were also known, had a reputation for informally snitching or formally testifying against a "crimey"—the person with whom they were alleged to have committed a crime. Others had renounced their gang affiliation or were affiliated with a gang that put them in increased danger while in jail. Others still, had sex-based charges. And finally, some residents "PC'ed up" (requested a PC classification), because they thought jail time might somehow be easier in PC units. Ultimately though, deputies determined each resident's classification, and if deputies believed it to be appropriate, a resident might be classified and housed in a PC unit irrespective of his preference. For instance, during visiting hours, a Latino resident named Insincere told me that he was concerned about how one of his charges, "child endangerment," might be interpreted once given state prison time. He worried that he "might have to PC-up."

Insincere's concern was no less valid in jail. PCs were a despised group among the total population of penal residents. They were associated with repugnant behavior, so others discussed PCs in only the most derisive terms: "nothing but snitches and baby rapers," as one resident put it. In general population, I met residents charged with murder and domestic violence, but none garnered the disdain heaped on PCs. It was widely understood that PCs had to "debrief"[19] to gain PC status. That is, they were required to share whatever information they had on resident misconduct, gang activity, and anything else of interest to deputies. Consequently, there was a standing "green light" against PCs. Residents in the trustee unit, general population, or ADSEG could attack a PC on sight without worrying about how other residents would view the action.

Perhaps in part for their own protection, PCs formed a gang that embraced the snitch label. I first learned of this from a Sunland resident named Havocc. He returned from an in-custody court appearance and regaled us with news of a PC gang calling themselves "the 2-5." We discussed it briefly, but I didn't think much about it until weeks later, when my celly, Scott, returned from court and reported that he had heard of the "two point five" gang. We joked that they were halfway to being 5-O à la *Hawaii 5-O*, the old police show and slang term for police. Chino, who had done state time, added that the PC gang "even" had songs about how proud they were to snitch. Apparently, the gang was more widely known than we realized because in the coming weeks, I noted Latino residents sometimes discussing "pecetas," but it was a sociologist, Robert Weide, who explained to me that "peceta" is a Mexican 25-cent coin, and that to call someone that was to mock them as a member of the "2-5" gang on the "sensitive needs yard" (SNY) in California prisons—"sensitive needs" being another name for protective custody.

My single fleeting interaction with PCs came as I waited in a court holding cell for an in-custody court appearance. I stared out the cell door window to the residents across the hallway. They wore blue bands on their waist chains, but I didn't know what that meant. Just then, a voice from behind me grumbled, "Fucking PCs!" It was a Latino resident looking over my shoulder at the same residents I was, and in that moment, I connected the blue bands with being in protective custody. There wasn't anything outwardly special about the blue-banded residents. Given how PCs were discussed, I half expected them to be some sort of grotesque creatures. In the cell across the way, one of the Latino PCs stopped in front of the window. He looked at me with a sly smile, tapped another resident, and then yelled at the window: "You think you're better than me? You ain't better than me. You ain't shit."

Then I was *sure* he was a PC. The encounter made no sense otherwise. In most circumstances, a Latino resident shouting, "You ain't shit" to a Black resident had the potential to spark a major interracial conflict. That he was willing to yell at me at all evidenced the more relevant framing of the situation. Race wasn't salient in that encounter; classification was. I didn't respond.

The largest classification in every Golden County jail was general population (GENPOP). The classification was a kind of catch-all designation for residents who didn't really fit anywhere else. A resident might well be a white supremacist, as many were, they were nonetheless assigned to GENPOP housing units. In fact, an analysis of the heterogeneity of attitudes, dispositions, charges, and experience in GENPOP housing units comprises much of the rest of this book.

Finally, the most privileged class of residents were trustees. Trustees were the jail's workforce, and to be a trustee, you had to meet two conditions: you had to have a scheduled release date and you had to hold a job in jail. Deputies housed trustees together, as they did for the other classifications, but unlike the other classifications, trustees were easily spotted because they wore green tops and bottoms. They worked in the kitchens and laundry areas. Sometimes they worked somewhat odd jobs. Late one evening, I saw a deputy supervising a trustee who was painting a door jamb. And while that was work, it was also time away from the cell. Trustees enjoyed other job-related privileges. Work in the kitchen and you would eat better. Work laundry and you would have your pick of uniforms.

In my experience, if you didn't speak up during the classification interview, your chances of being sent to a trustee pod were low. Trustee housing units were renowned for having better creature comforts than could be found in other kinds of housing units, so when I surrendered myself for my longest sentence, I briefly interrupted the deputy conducting the classification interview to explain that I had a release date and that I'd like to be a trustee if possible. "Oh," the deputy said, scanning down the survey form.

"Mmm-hmm."

The deputy scribbled something and explained that my request was noted but that there was "no guarantee though. It's if there's space."

I'm glad I interjected because deputies started me off in the Providence trustee pod, and it was the easiest time I ever did.

The Boss

During dayroom time, Beast was always surrounded by guys asking him questions or nipping at his heels about one thing or another. Sometimes he stayed in his cell during dayroom time, and there was always a guy walking by his cell to ask if everything is OK, chatting briefly with him, or standing in the dayroom and signing messages to him. When does that man sleep? When do I sleep?

2

The Rep System

I stared a while at the bail bonds company cards affixed to the corkboard next to the phones before I thought to call one. *Who put these in here? Deputies?* I had what felt like a good spot on the bench in pre-housing holding: toward the back in the corner so I could see everyone without needing to turn my head. I'd have to get up and walk a few steps if I wanted to make a call. No one else was using either phone, so I thought maybe they were off or that I wasn't supposed to use them. Being in jail is a lot like feeling your way in the dark. I stared at the cards.

They were ostentatious in a janky, used-car sales kind of way. On each card, the word "collect" was stamped or printed in eye-catching relief against the rest of the writing. I was walking toward the phones before I realized that I'd made the decision to do so. I inspected the cards, looking for a sign that I was supposed to call one company over the others. I chose Genie Bail Bonds. Their card was white with purple writing. The name was cheesy, but the minimalist card design suggested a level of professionalism that was absent on the other cards. *Shit. I only know one person with a home number.* I stood facing the corkboard with my eyes locked at Genie's business card and then briefly lost focus when my mind tumbled down germaphobic anxiety. I wondered how many ears had touched those phones.

I placed a collect call to one of the numbers for Genie's local office. My memory of the call is spotty, and I regret not documenting the exchange, but here's the thing: Three times I've had a gun pulled on me. The first time my brother and I were playing basketball on a Nerf hoop in our duplex when a neighbor called the police. I was 19. My brother was 12. Apparently, hearing us yell "shoot" was mistaken for actual gun shots. It was a hot, dry, windless day, so we had the backdoor open. When the ball bounced out the door and onto the driveway, my brother chased it, and something made him stand erect with his hands in the air. Then I heard an officer yelling for me to come out. There were a line of officers backing each other up at stations alongside the house with their weapons trained upon my brother and me. Someone was giving commands, and we were made to lay chest-naked on the searing asphalt until they sorted out that there was no reason for them to be there. The second time, my cousins and I were surrounded by a group of young men just blocks away from our home. We stood there while the group tried to work up the courage to do more than threaten us. Fear stuttered my brain, and I kept saying, "Don't trip." The gunman pointed past me and yelled something. My cousins and I were permitted to walk away. The last time, I was pulled over for speeding and ordered out of the car at gun point. The California Highway Patrol officer had a nickel-plated gun, and I couldn't make out his increasingly tense commands over the gleam on his weapon.

Each of these events was so traumatic, so halting, that fear-adrenaline pumped into my ears, deafening whatever the men behind the guns were saying to me. I was, quite literally, stunned, and *that* is what it felt like to be a newbie speaking with a Genie Bail Bonds' representative from a pre-housing holding cell—paralyzingly disorienting.

What I am sure of, however, is that despite having a booking number and wristband, I was not yet "in the system," so the Genie representatives couldn't tell me my charges or my bail amount—two things residents want to know from a bail bonds company. Still, there was some level of comfort in speaking with someone beyond the jail's walls. One of the representatives took down my name, booking number, and my mother's contact information. I don't know whether he checked "the system" for my bail like he said he would "in a while," because a deputy called my last name.

"Walker," the deputy said dryly.

I stood and we made eye contact before he called two more names. We headed into the hallway, stood inside the red line, and faced the wall as we were told. I half wondered whether we were about to be released.

The deputy instructed us to assume the penal posture—hands clasped behind our backs, and we followed him through a maze of hallways while staying, always, inside the red line. We came upon a nook and were instructed to get a "property box"—a white, 12" x 12" banker's box that came with an "indigent kit" or "fish kit," as it was sometimes called: a bar of soap, a toothbrush and toothpaste, a razor, a small stick of deodorant, a bit of shampoo. Also in the box was a document ironically titled "Inmate Orientations." It was a fanciful document in the sense that it laid out a list of rights and responsibilities by which deputies and residents were supposed to abide. In case anyone wondered, the document begins: "You are being confined in the [Golden County] Jail System." *Thanks.*

We made a second stop for a bedroll. There were mounds of four-inch, smaller-than-twin-sized sponge mattresses. Each was covered in a dirty gray latex-like material, and none smelled new, lightly used, or clean. We also grabbed two flat white sheets and a grayish-green wool blanket sized for a tall middle-schooler. I'd seen blankets like that on the Kadena Air Base in Okinawa.[1]

The march through the hallways felt long. I couldn't make out how deputies knew when to take a turn. There didn't appear to be clear indications of where we were, and I wondered if that was on purpose—or maybe I wasn't seeing things clearly because I was scared. We took a an elevator that moved so slowly, it was hard to tell whether we were going up or down. I noticed our deputy escort's eyes weren't darting here and there, and his shoulders were rested. He seemed bored. The elevator door opened a level or two above where we started, and our escort instructed us to get inside the red line. After a brief stroll down a hallway past a control station operated by another deputy, our escort told us to face the wall. He checked and triple-checked a folded piece of paper before taking one of our three to the barred entrance of a housing unit. He unlocked the door, exchanged a couple of chuckles with some of the residents therein, and then there were just two of us.

A little way down the hallway, it was my turn: Providence Downtown Jail, 16D. The deputy stepped just inside the housing unit, he pointed at an empty slot on a three-high bunk stack, he chatted lightly with a couple of residents, and he left. His job was done. It had been many hours since the arrest and natural light, and there were no windows in the housing unit.

Orientation

There had been a pause in the action when I entered the dayroom; eyes from around the room scanned me up and down before looking me off. How did I walk? Did my gestures suggest gang affiliation or that I could handle myself in a fight? Was I a newbie? Was I afraid? No doubt, I was scared, but I wasn't exactly afraid. Whereas one can push through and overtake one's fears, to be afraid is to be stopped by potential consequences. I'm no tough guy but I told myself that whatever was about to happen, it is what it is.

I noticed that the Black guys were huddled in a corner, and a couple of them gave me the nod as I headed to the empty bunk. Most of the Latinos were on the other side of three rows of metal, picnic styled benches in the center of the housing unit, and there was only one White guy. He was leaning in the direction of the Black residents. I unrolled my bed on the bunk and set my property box atop. "I'm Carter. I'm the rep." I saw him when he stood and headed toward me. I'd readied myself for conflict, but he was just introducing himself. He motioned for me to follow him, and he gave me what I came to call *the orientation*.

We took a path around the tables on the predominately Black side of the housing unit, and he pointed and told me which toilet, sink, and shower were "ours." I followed his circuitous path back to one side of the tables. He tapped his fingertips on a table: "Our tables are right here. That's the Messican section," he pointed. "Don't cross between their tables." He was sure to make eye contact with me; then he opened his hands and cocked his head to the side as if to ask whether I understood the orientation he had just given. I nodded, and he went back to the Black section, resuming what he was doing before I interrupted. I sat on my bunk. I hadn't understood the orientation at all.

If it's unclear to you what a "rep" is, what a "rep" does, or what he meant by "our" tables, you're right where I was at the time. I was no less confused, but through mistakes, mimicry, and directly asking questions, I learned who reps were and what role they played between GENPOP residents and deputies. Now, the very idea of a rep is not a simple one, and every point of entry into explaining the role raises other questions, so across the next two chapters, you'll need to trust that I will deliver all the need-to-knows and as many of your want-to-knows as I can in an organized manner.

Let's begin with Carter. He was Black, as in he was a member of the African diaspora, but he was also "black," which was one of the three racialized groups in Golden County jails. Part of the reason that he introduced himself and gave me the orientation was because I, too, was "black"—though I didn't know that until a little later. Actually, none of this is intelligible without returning to the issue of classification, so I was wrong. We'll begin there.

During the classification interview, a deputy asked whether you got along with all races, but no deputy revealed that they would assign you to one of three racial classifications: "blacks," "southsiders," or "woods." That there were three racial groups instead of some other number had little to do with reproducing free-society racial groupings and even less to do with security—despite the claims of deputies and some residents. Rather, the number of racial classifications and who was sorted where was a matter of *organizational convenience: the implementation of organizational practices and policies as a consequence of resource limitations rather than principle.* Each racial classification was an aggregation of a variety of ethnicities, nationalities, and other social identities crudely united by skin tone, surname, and dialect. Deputies simply looked at residents and made a determination about which racial classification to assign them. If you looked Black or Asian to deputies, you were black. Thus, a Nigerian American could be celled with a Vietnamese American, and both were black in every way practical to jail life.

Southsiders, or *sureños*, included four subgroups, most of whom were Latino. There were non-gang-affiliated Latino Americans and gang-affiliated "homies." In southern California it is somewhat common knowledge among street-informed persons that when in jail, southern Californian Latino gangs are united under the rubric of the Mexican Mafia, so even if two southsiders were from warring gangs in free society, they got along in jail. (In a Providence court holding cell, I watched two southsiders meet, and one asked, "Are you a homie?" The other said he was, and the pair immediately relaxed, exchanged names, shook hands, and continued their conversation.) The final subgroups of southsiders were the smallest of the four: "Indios"— members of nearby Indian nations—and "paisas," which means countrymen but is a pseudo-slur for recent Latino immigrants similar to "fresh off the boat," connoting poor and rural.

The "woods," short for "peckerwoods,"[2] were the least diverse racial classification, and it strikes me that another way to think of racial classification in Golden County Jails is by dividing residents into either a "White" or "nonwhite" category in the sense that philosopher Charles W. Mills described in *The Racial Contract*. While racial groups of color were cobbled together masses of various social categories, whiteness was left untouched—and by a government organization, no less. If you were White, you were a wood with only an ideological subdivision. There were woods who expressed no particular belief about race relations, and there were "white power comrades" or just "comrades" for short, who greeted each other with the Sieg Heil salute and proudly identified as white supremacists.

If these racial classifications seem nonsensical to you, I shared that sentiment, but we should remember that race does not refer to anything immutable.[3] In and out of penal organizations,[4] racial classification has always been a fluid enterprise. No U.S. census[5] has completely replicated the ethnic and racial categories of the previous one, and who is included in which racial category has always been more or less tied to the sociopolitical and economic interests of White people.[6]

But racial classification in Golden County jails had little to do with the meanings normally tied to race or ethnicity; neither was racial classification an overt way of reproducing the subjugation of people of color the way it is in free society. As I noted earlier, it was organizationally convenient for "blacks" to include Black and Asian American men, which is not the same as saying there is no measure of racial domination in doing so. Still, in 2008, Golden County jails admitted over 1.5 million people on felony and misdemeanor charges. Of those, 41.2 percent were categorized as Latino, 35.2 percent as White, 17.4 percent as Black, and 6.2 percent as "other," including Asians and American Indians.[7] During my time as a penal resident, I never saw more than three Asian American residents at any time. Each had a Black "celly" (cellmate). Imagine, however, if there had been large populations of Hmong and Middle Eastern men cycling in and out of Golden County jails. Deputies might have established a fourth and fifth racial classification. As it stood, the numbers of those groups weren't large enough to justify such an expansion.

As a newbie, you didn't learn any of that critical information until you were assigned to a permanent housing unit; you had no inkling that race was any more significant than it is in free society. Recall that in pre-housing holding, even experienced residents shared space, food, and conversation unencumbered by race. But when you got to a permanent housing unit, you quickly realized that deputies were maintaining racial segregation in inte-grated places, as oxymoronic as that reads. It's helpful to have an image of the layouts in permanent housing units.

In the broadest sense, there were two kinds of permanent housing units: what I refer to as either *open* or *closed* units. Imagine entering a rec-tangular living-room sized box through a sliding prison bar gate. To your immediate left is a wall and on that wall, about eight steps ahead is a single payphone-styled telephone and a television perched above it at your arm's length. To your right is a series of three-high metal bunk beds hugging the walls in a horseshoe. Inside the horseshoe are three rows of picnic-styled alu-minum tables arranged parallel to the wall with the phone and television. In front of you, past the television and phone, in the far corner from where you entered, is a small hygiene section where there are two toilets, two sinks, two showers, and a single hot water spigot that deputies cut on and off at their discretion. This is the description of the housing unit in which I met Carter: Providence's 16D.

I use the term "open" to describe these kinds of housing units because aside from the norms of social behavior, the unit's amenities were *open* to residents housed in them. You could, for instance, hop off your bunk and sit at a table or walk back and forth a bit. Providence 16D was medium-sized, and open units (sometimes called "tanks" or "dorms") varied in size and available amenities. The smallest open units were about the size of a master bedroom large enough to justify double doors. In those units, the three-high bunks were to one side of the unit with the hygiene facilities on the opposing wall. My first jail experience was in Golden County's Cardinal Detention Center, where I was held in such a small open unit that had only two rows of tables for mealtime. It felt smaller than it was: dark and cold. Like many, if not most, housing units, it had no access to natural light but it did have a large window to a brightly lit section of the hallway where deputies sometimes passed, escorting residents here and there.

Some of the smaller open units were adjoined by a "Jack-and-Jill" shower and sink area closed off to residents by locked prison bars for most of the day. Deputies alternated between unit "A" and "B," giving us two and sometimes three brief periods of shower time. You needed to be quick to give others a chance to at least "hit the hot spots" of basic hygiene.

Showering was a bit easier in larger open units like the one to which I was assigned in Golden County's Barracks Jail. You entered through a metal door with a small window. The unit was a like a gymnasium converted into a shelter. There was a grid of three-high bunks in the center of the space—enough for at least 60 residents. Mealtime tables were arranged in rows to one side of the room with three showers, sinks, and toilets grouped in a space, and three phones lining a different wall.

Closed units were a bit different: They were comprised of two-person cells—the smallest and grungiest of which I saw lined a hallway across from a series of medium-sized open units. The cells had dirty yellow paint peeling from every surface. The bunks were exceptionally lip-curling in their filth, as were the toilet-sinks that forced residents to face the hallway if seated, and because the cells had metal bars rather than doors, there was no privacy for residents assigned to them.

The more modern closed units were called "pods" because they contained a "command pod" from which a single deputy could unlock every cell, speak into every cell via the intercom system, cut on or off the phones and lights, and make announcements via the dayroom's speaker system. In practice, there were usually two deputies (and sometimes three) operating the pod. One deputy, "the runner," performed regular security checks, delivered mail, retrieved outgoing mail and "kites." A kite is a written message or request, whether on a palm-sized formal "blue slip" medical request form or scribbled on any handy piece of paper. Meanwhile, the "pod primary" was at the controls in the command pod.

Some pods were standalone units, but most were a collection of units arranged panoptically like baseball diamonds with two tiers of cells facing the command pod—home plate, as it were. For instance, my longest stretch of time was in Golden County's Sunland Detention Center, where I was held in Z-4. That is, Z-Pod, dayroom 4, and there were three other dayrooms attached to the same command pod. Technically speaking, the "dayroom" is the shared space beyond the cells where residents showered, ate, made calls, and fraternized, but deputies and residents alike referred to the units comprising pods as "dayrooms."

From the hallway, deputies opened the slider to the sally port and then the slider to the dayroom to which you were assigned. There could be more than 160 residents spread across the dayrooms in a pod. In each dayroom was a single hot water spigot, at least two phones but as many as three, at least three but as many as four showers, and rectangular picnic tables that may or may not be movable.

Whether deputies put you in a closed or open unit was a matter of chance, and I saw no advantage to either type. Being in a closed unit (see Figure 2.1 and Figure 2.2) meant spending a lot of time in a cell, but that gave you some privacy and, if you got along with your celly, you two could play games, talk, and share food. If you two didn't get along, then time in the cell was tortuous. Either way, you never forgot that there was another person in a tiny cinderblock box with you. No one had to talk. At about 11' x 7', your celly's smells communicated with yours.

Open units, on the other hand, were paradoxes of solitude and crowdedness. You were never alone, and for privacy, you had to turn your back to the shared space and face the wall—if you were lucky enough to have a bunk abutting a wall. Yet, I recall feeling especially alone in open units. The bustle of residents around me fell into background noise, and in the quiet—an awful lot of quiet—I truly felt the weight of my time. Neither type of housing unit provided a "backstage" of the sort where people normally ready themselves for the "frontstage" of larger social interaction.[8] You couldn't hide when you used the toilet or drank water or had a nightmare or woke up feeling particularly drained of emotional energy. In the end, you might have a preference for open or closed units, but the decision was out of your hands, and from my viewpoint, there was no lesser of two evils.

Figure 2.1 Cell
Illustration of our cell from the viewpoint of the head of the bunks by the table.
You can see the cell intercom button to the right of the toilet to the left of the
cell door under one of the vents. It was higher than it appears in the picture. On
the floor in front of the cell door, we placed a towel to wipe our feet and take off
our slippers before entering. That was standard practice for residents who kept
a clean a cell. Sometimes we stored our slippers there—sometimes next to the
table on the ground. Done by Scott.

Returning to the issue of race, custodial deputies didn't maintain racially
homogeneous housing units, but what they did was assign residents to beds
in a race conscious manner. In open units, if a southsider was on the top bunk,
deputies assigned a southsider to the middle and bottom bunk, too. That way,
there would never be, for instance, a three-high bunk set with a black resident on the middle bunk and a wood resident on the top and bottom bunks.
It was the same in closed units. Deputies ensured that your celly was classified in the same racial group as you, but to what end? There were no physical
barriers keeping residents apart in open units. Given the motivation to do so,
a resident could leave his bunk, walk a few steps to a member of a different
racial classification, and start a fight.

Figure 2.2 Cell
Illustration of our cell from the viewpoint of the cell door. On the bottom bunk, my bunk, was an active game of checkers, a couple of letters, my field notes, and my orange top and bottom. Under my bunk was my property box. Scott's bunk was full of all the letters his girlfriend used to write him daily. To the left of the bunks, you can see the fixed-in-place table and chair. My books were organized on the table as was our toilet paper stock and a couple of food items. Under the table was a repurposed commissary bag for trash. Above the table was the opaque window that gave us no natural light. Done by Scott.

In closed units, deputies handled mealtimes and "dayroom time" (time out of the cells) on a tier basis, and on each tier were residents from all three racial classifications. Thus, the racial segregation of resident beds was a foolish practice at best. It created unnecessary problems at worst.

I want it to be clear that when future GENPOP residents languished in pre-housing holding cells, they did so because deputies were waiting for race-specific bed assignments to become vacant. Indeed, frustration and experience once led me to the blunt interruption of the classification interview to ask whether I was just waiting on another Black guy to make bail or something. "Pretty much," the deputy said. "Or space might open in other ways."

By "other ways" he meant transfers between housing units or jails. Keep that in mind as you recall the Latino resident—that is, the "southsider"—who told me he had been in pre-housing holding for three days.

Divide et Impera

To summarize, deputies classified incoming residents into one of three racial groups and assigned residents to beds in line with those racial classifications while the shared spaces in each dayroom were racially integrated. There were two consequences precipitating from these administrative practices. First, wherever deputies introduced (and later supported) race as a way of structuring social life, residents then racialized space, walking paths, phones, showers, tables, and basic interaction. By *racialization* I mean *the association of persons, places, things, and activities with racial categories.*

We commonly speak of Black neighborhoods, White sports, Asian fashion, and so forth. Those associations are not strictly about who we think is most likely to live somewhere, do a given activity, or exhibit a particular kind of fashion. There is a normative flavor to statements like, "Black people don't ski." It's a way of delimiting race and sport, but it's also a way of saying, "Black people *shouldn't* ski." To establish racial categories is to establish normative boundaries by race. It's a packaged deal. Hence, each racial group's claim for themselves was simultaneously a claim against the other groups, as will be clear in the next chapter.

Now, the logic—and I use that term descriptively, not denotatively—underlying racial classification rested upon an "institutional myth"[9]—a broad cultural and normative belief among penal administrators that racial classification[10] is vital to the security of any legitimate penal organizations. Supposedly, interracial conflict is intractable, so racial classification forestalls inevitable interracial fights. However, there was an abundance of evidence[11] to the contrary, beginning with the absence of interracial conflict in pre-housing holding cells. In fact, I learned that racial classification increased[12] (rather than decreased) the likelihood and potential severity of violence among penal residents. Still, deputies forged ahead not—in my estimation—because racial classification actually did what they claimed, but because deputies could marshal race relations for the more efficient management of GENPOP housing units.

This is the second major consequence of racial classification. By creating racial groups and supporting the racialization of jail facilities and resources, deputies instituted what I call a *mediating management model*—an *administrative system in which managers rely upon mediators to reduce the workload of managing groups of subordinates*. In this model, mediators are members of subordinate groups whose responsibilities may include: filtering information between management and subordinates; mediating competing interests between management and subordinates; and policing—sometimes with violence—subordinate behaviors to ensure organizational activities occur in an orderly and incident-free fashion.

There are plenty of examples of mediating management models outside of jail.[13] The Jewish kapo, the class president, the "house nigga," and the chair of an academic department are all mediators in this model. For instance, the chair of the sociology department at Highfalutin University is also a member of that department's faculty. In her capacity as chair, she may operate as an extension of the dean of the college or as a strong faculty advocate to the dean. Either way, a large part of the chair's job is to make the management of faculty easier for the dean, and the position is terminal. That is, the academic chair (like the Kapo, the house nigga, and the class president) does not promote to management in the way that a Target customer service representative can promote to a lead, then to a supervisor, and so on. The mediator is not a career building role but a more or less temporary and highly transactional bundle of responsibilities and relative privileges.

In this case, the mediating management model consisted of deputies (management), "reps" (mediators), and GENPOP residents racialized into three groups (subordinates). Each racial group in each GENPOP housing unit had a "rep." The term was likely short for "race representative," but I never heard anyone say it that way. Like the rest of us in those housing units, reps were GENPOP residents. They may have been sentenced and given a release date, or they might have been doing indefinite time like Carter in Providence 16D. The latter was quite common. Reps had a variety of privileges and responsibilities, but most importantly, it was a role maintained at the pleasure of deputies.

Why? Well, a deputy working our pod once explained the plight of his work like this: "You might think we aren't doing anything in the pod, but at any given time, you're dealing with 170 to 180 inmates, and everyone is on their button [cell intercom]. Plus, the phone is ringing off the hook, you're checking things on the computer, and there is always someone coming and going. It can be stressful . . . You got six guys on the button, and you don't know who is trying to con you, so everyone just gets a 'No.'"

At the time, I thought very little of what amounted to a deputy complaining to me about his job, but in the final analysis, his explanation of running the pod serves as justification for how deputies used the reps to manage us.

"Who's Your Rep?"

So, what exactly did reps do? The upshot is that reps were GENPOP residents who policed social behavior in the housing units, performed a lot of care-taking tasks on behalf of their respective racial groups, and filtered information from deputies to us and from us to deputies. In exchange for doing tasks that made managing housing units easier, deputies ensured the reps were privileged relative to the average GENPOP resident.

However enviable the rep position might at first sound, it was hardly that, and this is likely the case for the mediator role in most mediating management models. Few faculty members aspire to chair their departments; most tend to acquiesce to the position. Similarly, most penal residents did not hope to be the rep for their racial group. Part of the issue was the need to negotiate the tension of interests between management and subordinates. The degree of tension varies by organization, but it's always there because management—deputies in this case—had their goals and mandates that sometimes conflicted with what GENPOP residents wanted. The rep needed to balance those competing interests *and* manage his own competing self-interests that, no doubt, sometimes pushed him to lean in favor of deputies versus GENPOP residents, and he needed to do so without creating more problems than he solved.

One of the more surprising, but obviously necessary, facts about reps was that there were a number of ways a resident might become the rep, but none involved input from deputies. A deputy-appointed rep would be an obvious extension of management and likely lack the legitimacy to perform the role.

I asked D-Double, the Black rep in Sunland's Z-4, about how someone becomes the rep. "If you're the last one here," he began, "and then new guys show up not knowing shit—they just getting here, and you been here for a year . . . " He trailed off, stood from the table with his hands inside his pants near his crotch as if to keep them warm. He seemed dissatisfied with his answer: "It's more than that though." Parenthetically, it is only now, as I write this, that I'm struck by how casually he said, " . . . you been here for a year . . . "—like it was reasonable and to be expected. He never told me how he became the rep, but he had described the simplest path.

In Providence 16D, the lone wood was a resident everyone called Hacksaw because he looked a little like what some imagined the wrestler "Hacksaw" Jim Duggan to have looked like. Hacksaw was a contagiously cheerful guy who was too busy getting along with anyone who got along with him to care much about being the wood rep. Most often, he was huddled in the "black corner" of the dayroom laughing with us. He once offered a black resident some chips, and Carter half-heartedly intervened, reminding Hacksaw that there were rules against interracial sharing.

"Shit man. I don't fuckin' care," Hacksaw said.

He really didn't. My sense was that if not for his harmless, affable disposition and the childhood-*WrestleMania*-doppelganger nostalgia he generated, his frequent violations of GENPOP rules would have been taken more seriously. It was just too hard to be upset with him about anything. He woke laughing and joking and kept that same energy throughout the day. He certainly didn't bother affecting the level of seriousness his black and southsider rep counterparts displayed.

The rep role had been foisted upon Hacksaw by virtue of his being the only wood in the unit, so when a new wood finally entered the dayroom, Hacksaw jumped at the chance to abandon the position. "You gonna be the new rep now!" Hacksaw declared with a big smile. He didn't even give the new guy a chance to put down his bedroll or property box. Hell! He didn't even wait to learn whether the new wood had any experience in jail.

In addition to rep by default, there were at least two other paths to becoming the rep. In Z-4, D-Double returned from one of his court dates sure that he would soon be released. He was completing his fourth consecutive year in Golden County jails when I met him in Sunland. He once told me, "*Everybody* is new to me." The news that he might be leaving set in motion a series of informal discussions about who might replace him.

I asked him directly who the new black rep would be, and he said, "I don't know." He was completely unbothered, and I became annoyed at how little concern he had for how we would fare after he was gone, but in hindsight, that was a terribly foolish and selfish thought. Being the rep wasn't D-Double's calling or life responsibility. His commitment to the role was only as long as his penal time in that housing unit. How invested could one really be in the goings on in a jail housing unit? Jail time was indefinite in multiple ways. The next hour could be your last hour among those residents. You could be transferred to a different housing unit or a different jail. You could make bail. You could quickly wrap up, and you could be sentenced to prison time or set free. The uncertainty of it all worked against anything like a deep commitment to making jail life sustainable for others. He rightly could not have cared less when he pointed at me and said, "Somebody smart."

I was caught off guard and felt worried that he had mistaken my question as a bid to be the rep. I protested, explaining that I didn't know enough about jail. I suggested Toll may do it.

D-Double nodded and said, "But he prawly don't want it."

I later had an exchange with LK who told me, "I'm finna be the rep when D-Double leaves." He was the only person I ever heard express interest in being the rep. He was in his early 20s, and including "about six years in YA," he had been in and out of penal facilities since he was 14. Prior to our meeting, he had completed a few months in jail and then just 10 days of freedom before a fight landed him and his older brother in Sunland. LK was built like a running back, his corn rows were always fuzzy, and he gave me the sense that even when he laughed he could switch over for a fight in an instant. He definitely understood jail culture, but his temper was short, and his primary skill was fighting—not diplomacy. I ignored LK's excited statement about maybe becoming the rep. He just didn't fit the bill.

At the next opportunity I asked Toll about his interest in being the rep if D-Double left. He nodded his head downward in acknowledgment that he had been thinking about it or discussing it with others. "I mean," he began slowly, "I just don't wanna be responsible for niggas, ya know? I guess if it comes down to it, then it what it is." That was enough for me. At only 20 years old, Toll, 6'2", 200 lbs, was nearing his third consecutive year in jail, so he understood the vagaries of jail life better than most. He was a well-respected and level-headed resident who was as diplomatic as he was skilled with 10 toes down in a fight. Toll could throw hands with the best of them.

Days went by, and our conversations about replacing D-Double died down. Toll's reluctance never waned, but it didn't matter. Neither transfer nor release came for D-Double—not while I was there.

A third path to becoming the rep was in deep contrast to Hacksaw's rep by default and the informal committee discussions around D-Double's possible replacement. The southsiders in Z-4 were far more business-like choosing their rep. About a week into my time at Sunland, the southsider rep, Listo, settled his case for prison time: seven years to life, a span I didn't know was even possible.

I never had a personal interaction with Listo, but he had a formidable presence. Deputies let him walk around the dayroom with his shirt off—something I never saw before or after him. He had an elaborate tattoo that traced his broad, muscular chest, but he wasn't otherwise particularly big. He was perhaps 6' tall and about 170 lbs or so. He mostly wore a wartime-serious countenance; however, in the days leading up to his transfer to prison, he spent nearly all his time cupcaking on the phone, swinging a leg and tracing a finger on the wall while talking. Early one morning, a deputy summoned him from his cell, and Listo walked to the sally port in his boxers, socks, slippers, and T-shirt while carrying his oranges, property box, and bedroll. Later that day, D-Double told us that Listo had appointed his celly, Beast, as the new southsider rep. So that was it: rep by appointment.

Months later, when Beast was transferring to Providence, the southsiders held two meetings, one for each tier. Having been appointed by Beast, Reaper conducted both meetings like a chairman of a board of representatives. He stood at the head of the southsider tables and referenced notes as he set out the agenda.

Beast had been a respected and relatively relaxed rep. In fact, the name "Beast" was a curious misnomer in my estimation. He was heavyset, and that might have contributed to his name, but he was kind—ignoring the occasional sanctioning of a beating for an out of line southsider—he was always in control of himself, and he was never visibly worried. Southsiders were required by influence of the Mexican Mafia to carry themselves in particular ways while in jail. One requirement was that they perform a set of exercises "to keep your wind up," as a southsider explained to me. They needed to be physically fit in case an interracial fight broke out. After each set of exercises, southsiders were supposed to announce their completion. Those announcements were infrequent during Beast's tenure. However, Reaper, who I never saw smile even when other southsiders joked with him, was far stricter. When Reaper took over, we regularly heard the call and response: resident name, cell number, and the set completed followed by "Gracias!"

The response came from all southsiders in unison: "A ti!"

Given the ways I knew one could be become a rep, default, informal committee, or appointment, the best man didn't always get the job. That was my worry with LK. A good rep needed to be judicious and not given to empty threats. In one instance, Carter complained that he had been skipped for his turn to read the newspaper. At about 5'7", he was a 20-something-year-old with a dad body. No one responded to his open complaint about the newspaper, so he decided to raise his voice to no one in particular: "I guess I'm gonna have to start whoopin' ass in here." The threat was totally ridiculous, and I remember thinking with a chuckle, *Whose ass is he gonna whoop?* I respected him in the position of rep much less because of the pump-faked threats. Apparently, I wasn't the only one, because no one did a thing about his complaint, and that was that.

The most effective reps were diplomat-warriors with a healthy measure of jail cultural competence. It helped to be a skilled fighter, but it was better to be respected and legitimated by the members of one's racial group. That way, others could be organized to enforce the rules. A rep risked mutiny if he allowed himself to become beguiled by the allure of his authority and lose sight of how tenuous and dependent that authority was. I'm reminded of the way Chief Justice John Roberts[14] once described the role of the Chief Justice on the Supreme Court of the United States: "[Y]ou hold the reins of power, but if you tug on them too tightly, you'll find out they're not attached to anything."

Maintaining Social Order

So, some took to the role more readily than others, but it was everything that reps did that made them so useful to deputies and their racial groups alike. The *kind* of tasks they performed fit into one of three categories: order maintenance, information filtering, or caretaking. So inextricable from each task is a privilege (or set of privileges), that it's necessary to describe both at the same time.

I begin with order maintenance, and it's worth acknowledging that *social order* does not mean that social life is free of violence or conflict. It only means that because social interaction at the micro, meso, or macro-level is stable, regularized, and patterned, you can reasonably expect certain outcomes under certain conditions. Given a serious enough rule violation, reps were sometimes obliged to do or organize *functionally violent* acts by which I mean *violence in the service of maintaining social order*. In some cases, reps were functionally violent to avoid an incident report and more work for deputies; in other cases, reps were functionally violent in adherence to informal rules of no particular benefit to deputies and how they managed the housing units. Either way, deputies imbued reps with the latitude to police GENPOP residents as reps saw fit, and most of the time the threat of functional violence was sufficiently effective and far more common than the act.

One particular incident stands out against the rest. It was late in Z-4— long past 10:00 p.m., "lights out" time, and I was staring into the darkened dayroom against the brightly lit backdrop of my cell. Three deputies escorted a southsider into the dayroom. He was carrying his property box and bedroll. Instead of going to his cell as he should, he took a seat at the southsider tables without saying a word. I could not make out everything the deputies said, but one in particular kept shrugging his shoulders and tossing his hands up in exasperation when the southsider refused to answer any questions or respond to any commands. Soon, the trio of deputies gave up, and, standing at the slider just inside the sally port, they had a brief discussion with the three deputies running the pod that night. The first three walked away—one shrugging his shoulders, again with his palms in the air and head slightly cocksidedways while looking back at the three deputies running the pod as if to say, *This is your problem now*.

Actually, this night was doubly memorable because, in addition to the wild disrespect the southsider showed, I had never seen three women running Z-Pod. I had seen women deputies before, but never three, and none had been the pod primary. "Bear" took first crack at getting the southsider to comply. I cannot say whether she knew it, but residents had given her that nickname because she was a stocky, quick-tempered woman who was once described to me by one of her peers as "bitter and unhappy." She spoke to the southsider via the dayroom speaker. If anyone had been asleep, she surely woke them. Still, the southsider didn't respond, so she ordered him to walk to the slider, where he was met by another deputy's voice.

Nicknamed "Boy" because of her haircut, she tried to speak with the southsider via the intercom but with a softer tone and a smile in her voice. The southsider kept his silence, so Boy stomped into the dayroom to approach the southsider who had, by then, walked back to the southsider tables. He turned his back to her! My celly and I were shoulder to shoulder giggling as the scene unfolded. Boy spat a mixture of commands and questions to no avail before returning to the pod.

Clang! A cell door opened down the walkway to the right of us. Reaper sauntered downstairs in his T-shirt, passing the southsider in the dayroom without saying a word. He walked through the opened slider and stood in the sally port where Bear and Boy questioned him. Apparently, that conversation didn't go well because they quickly sent Reaper back to his cell and just as quickly summoned Beast to the sally port. He strolled through the dayroom to the slider with a sly smile, and after a brief discussion, deputies returned Beast to his cell.

Finally, all three deputies entered the dayroom. My celly and I were punching each other's arms with childlike excitement. The deputies demanded the southsider go into his cell. He refused and remained still. "Then who's your rep?" Boy demanded. "Who do I have to talk to?" That was a level of desperation I would never again see from deputies, but it was then clear that deputies had called upon Beast and Reaper to get the southsider to comply. When that didn't work, they fruitlessly searched each other's foreheads for an answer before going with, "I'm gonna put you in rec' [the recreation area]," Boy said. "Cuz I'm tired of your shit." If that threat was supposed to be the coup de grace, it missed its mark. The southsider wore a blank face and no emotion in his shoulders or stride as he willfully followed them to the rec yard.

I still think about that night from time to time—how reckless it was for deputies to question a resident in front of the entire dayroom. I later learned that the southsider had been assigned to cell with Insincere, who had been given the green light to dole some violent discipline—for what I didn't learn, and I suppose it kind of didn't matter.

That beleaguered southsider was in an impossible situation. Explain to deputies that your wellbeing is under violent threat, and be forced to PC'up to avoid a beating by southsiders in any housing unit deputies placed him. Keep quiet about the threat and hope deputies are discerning enough to try to protect him without requiring the southsider snitch. Or, enter the cell and hope the beating is a one-time event. Deputies, however, chose a fourth option in seeking counsel with the very men who had sanctioned the violence in the first place.

Chippy's short stay in Z-4 is another useful illustration of the reps working with deputies, order maintenance, and the threat of functional violence. When he entered the dayroom, the new black resident was immediately dubbed "Chippy" because he had a badly chipped front tooth. He claimed to have been a trustee, and one of his favorite pastimes was regaling us with details about how much better trustees ate—how they had "real food" and drank Ocean Spray products instead of the skim milk we had. I'd been in a trustee pod, and though I was never a trustee, I can confirm the quality of living there far exceeded any other jail conditions I'd experienced. I never had Ocean Spray drinks, though. If he were once a trustee, his being in GENPOP made no sense unless he had gotten in enough trouble to lose his job in jail and be sent to a GENPOP unit. Chippy was fuzzy on the details of his transfer, and no one pressed him. It seemed obvious he was hiding something, and like most things in jail, it would eventually come out.

Pretty quickly into his time with us, Chippy and his celly, TJ, started to have problems, and we got a clue about Chippy's past. During dayroom time, I saw

D-Double and Chippy off to the side. D-Double was going between pointing at a kite in his hand and pointing at Chippy with a look of feigned parental confusion—the look I've given my own children when I know the answer to a question but ask anyway, *Did you do* A, B, or C thing that has me irked and waving proof of your bad decision in your face? Later, I overheard D-Double tell TJ, "Just wait, and if he does it again . . . " but I missed the ending.

It turned out that Chippy had stolen something—"a piece of candy," TJ said. D-Double confirmed it—mostly likely on TJ's word. Apparently, TJ had shared with Chippy, as cellies often did, but then Chippy went back for more without asking. Stealing anything from another resident—no matter how seemingly petty—was a serious issue. A resident felt well within his rights to respond with violence.

A few days later, Chippy headed to the sally port with his bedroll and property box. D-Double had him rolled out. That is, D-Double worked with deputies to have Chippy transferred to a different housing unit. D-Double explained that the kite I'd seen him shaking earlier was from a resident who knew Chippy and wanted to get the word out that Chippy had been transferred from the trustee pod for stealing. The Jail News Network (JNN) was more efficient than its free society counterparts. Having stolen from TJ, D-Double gave Chippy a choice: roll out or get "DP'ed." A "DP" or to get "DP'ed" is to be violently disciplined for a violation of some kind. On the street, your gang might DP you for failing to respond to a challenge by a rival gang member, for instance. It could be several members of your gang or just one exceptionally talented fighter. Though not always tied to gangs, the DP was a common form of intragroup order mainte-nance in jail.

Chippy chose to roll out, which was the right choice. Having stolen from others, Chippy was a pariah whose presence in the unit would only be aggra-vating to other black residents. With time, a frustrated black resident would find a reason to attack Chippy, potentially leading deputies to put us all on "lockdown," meaning no dayroom time for an extended period. That would be work for deputies and a major disruption to the daily social order in the housing unit. To avoid that, D-Double arranged for deputies to have Chippy sent elsewhere.

That was not the end of Chippy's story, however. A few days later, we got an update about Chippy from Havocc, a black resident on the bottom tier of Z-4. Havocc said he ran into Chippy during an in-custody court appearance. That meant Chippy must have earned a new charge, or he was a witness in someone else's case. Either way, Havocc claimed that Chippy was in the court holding cell boasting about how D-Double had tried to DP him but that he had turned the tables. Supposedly, he had all of us on the top tier afraid of him. Instead of being offended, the news turned into a joke series in which we took turns pretending to be Chippy when the news of his lies inevitably caught up with him.

On the issue of order maintenance, though, these kinds of experiences and observations taught me that deputies leaned on the reps for their intimate knowledge of what could disrupt the social order of the dayrooms, and that sometimes necessitated giving the reps influence over who was in which cell.

During a conversation about cellies, Toll explained that he used to be D-Double's celly, but "We just butt heads on everything." They agreed that they were better off not being cellies, but Toll did not want to leave Z-4, so D-Double worked with deputies to have Toll moved several doors down to cell with Lee, an Asian American resident classified as black.

That kind of authority was nearly exclusive to the reps. The average GENPOP resident had almost no hope of having another resident or himself moved to a different cell or unit. In general, a resident wanting to move had only two options. He could contact the deputies and explain that his well-being had been threatened in which case the resident would have to explain who had threatened him and perhaps why. This was an especially challenging option in open dayrooms. He might wait for mealtime or one of the biweekly clothing exchanges, but he would still need to find a way to slip his kite to a deputy in the presence of everyone in the unit and hope the deputy showed discretion. A lot had to go right. If the transfer happened, news of that would spread throughout the JNN, and then the resident would either need to PC'up or perpetually look over a shoulder for an attack he knew was coming. The other option would be to go through his rep in which case, the rep would need to make the case to deputies that removing a particular resident would ensure order in the housing unit.

Before I learned this, I assumed, more or less, any resident had the capacity to get himself or others moved to a different unit or assigned to a new bed. During one of my earliest stints, I met a wood named Bill in a court holding cell. Bill furtively passed me a kite to give to another wood. He thought there was a chance—however vanishing—that I might bump into a wood known to have "pull with the deps." Bill was hoping to be moved to housing unit 4A, and I was a bit surprised—though I didn't say anything—that he figured the move was possible, that another resident could make it happen, and that

I would somehow meet and be able to pass a kite to that influential resident. That Bill passed me, a black resident, the kite to give to a wood evidenced his desperation to be moved, but worse, Bill never told me the guy's name. He only described him, and there was nothing distinctive.

I suppose I could have had done what I once saw a black resident do in a court holding cell: "Eh wood! Wood," he yelled from about 25-feet away at the opposite end of the court holding cell. He caught the attention of a young and muscular version of the actor Sam Elliott. "Where you get that tat' at?" The Sam Elliott lookalike had several visible tattoos, including an exceptionally well done and colorful depiction of a famous movie scene. The wood responded in too low a tone for me to catch what he said. "That shit is nice," the black resident concluded loudly.

Sure. I could have done that for Bill: blindly addressing random woods and hoping not to offend anyone. But I knew in the moment he handed me the kite that I wouldn't even attempt such a thing. Bill's request, though, led me to think that any resident could get himself or others moved to a preferred housing unit or cell.

However, every example of a resident-initiated transfer of which I learned or observed began with a rep, and none were unique to the blacks. At one point, Henry, the white power comrade and wood rep for Z-4, had a celly we all called Michael Knight for his passing resemblance to the lead character of the television show *Knight Rider*. When speaking to or about him, everyone always used his full nickname: Michael Knight. It was hard to say whether Michael Knight was in his 30s or early 50s—though he was surely older than Henry, who was likely in his early to mid-20s. I had heard that Michael Knight was taking psychotropic medication for a mood disorder. I never confirmed that, but he did everything slowly, as if in a dream state. His eyes had no spark and seemed mismatched against his warm smile.

He was well-liked among southsiders if for no reason other than he was easygoing, harmless, and didn't seem bothered by being the butt of light-hearted jokes. Tiny or some other southsider would yell across the day-room: "Michael Knight! Michael Knight! You aight?" He would smile or wave or say something softly.

My assumption was that Henry preferred a comrade for a celly—or at least a celly he could vibe with, so he decided to have Michael Knight rolled out. When his new celly arrived, a young Huntington Beach surfing type, southsiders were merciless in their teasing. Tiny led the charge: "That's what you get!" he yelled at Henry who had an embarrassed smile. "Eh! Ha! Ha! That's what you get, Henry." Henry had the authority to get a new celly, but deputies didn't send him the kind of celly he had hoped for.

Beast had a similar experience. Following a visitation hour, a few of us chatted while awaiting a deputy escort. Beast complained that "deps" were "fuckin'" with him, sending cellies that didn't speak English. I never figured how it was possible, but Beast, a member of a nearby Indian nation and the southsider rep for "all of Z-Pod," was not conversant in Spanish. His previous, English-speaking celly had been transferred for adjudicatory purposes, and every time deputies sent Beast a new celly with a weak handle on English, Beast expressed his displeasure and deputies sent another. That went on for a while until Beast arranged for Tiny to move in with him—a move he later confided he had been "working on . . . for a while."

In addition to order maintenance through threats or acts of functional violence and working with deputies to get residents moved to particular cells or transferred from the units, order maintenance sometimes meant being a mouthpiece for deputies. Sometimes deputies called the reps to the sally port and gave them instructions to give to us about how to behave during dayroom time. Other times, deputies used reps like ventriloquist dummies.

In one prominent example, the pod called D-Double to the sally port. When he got there, a deputy announced over the dayroom speaker which rules he wanted enforced, but he instructed D-Double to repeat the rules to us. "Eh y'all. They gonna give us extended dayroom." D-Doubled turned to face the pod and then back toward us to parrot more instructions. We were to wear our wristbands and oranges, and horseplay was prohibited. "And no going to different tiers." Clang! Clang! In succession, top tier cell doors popped open, and we filed out into the dayroom.

To be clear, hearing a rep give those instructions didn't incentivize us to adhere to administrative rules. We wanted time out of our cells, so we more or less behaved accordingly. One interpretation of a deputy turning D-Double into a parrot, is to see that as more evidence that deputies relied upon the reps for lots of things—even giving basic instructions. That may have been true, but it was no less true that making D-Double parrot instructions that we could hear clearly from the pod was a crafty way of demeaning the reps who were still GENPOP residents, and perhaps, deputies wanted to remind us of that.

Information Sieves

One of the key privileges reps had was access to information. Chatting with D-Double one day, I mentioned that my celly, Scott, had received five letters the night before. "Yeah. I always see 412 [our cell number] on there," he said. I just stared back: *Why does he know how many letters my celly got?* He said it so naturally—so matter-of-factly—that I didn't question it. It turned out that deputies frequently shared private information with reps, and D-Double's response confirmed something that Beast once told me.

A casual conversation veered into a discussion about snitching, and Beast assured me: "I check everyone's shit. They can't hide anything." We chatted for a while longer. He stood from leaning on the top tier railing, shook my hand, and told me, "If you need anything, let me know." (The gravity of that statement wouldn't really occur to me until many years later. As I would discover, social relations in jail depended, in part, upon a system of favors, but no favor was for free. Had I taken him up on that offer, there was no way to know what he might ask of me in return.)

The reps knew who was getting mail. I settled that in my mind. They performed (or could if they wanted) a kind of background check on each resident's reputation. And then there was a second conversation with Beast a few weeks later. I'd had a small dust up in the dayroom with Lee, who, like me, also had an approaching release date. Beast asked me if things were OK between Lee and me. I didn't actually know, but I said things were cool, and Beast seemed pleased to hear that. He recounted his first response upon seeing me and Lee that day: "I was like, not Mike!" He said he was disappointed because Lee and I would be getting out the following month—it wasn't worth it. Here again, I didn't say anything, but I'd only told Scott and Lee that I had a release date. The three of us had agreed to keep that information between us because we had heard that envy led some residents to start fights to ruin someone's release.

Maybe one of them told someone and it got back to Beast—one of those situations in which everyone swears others to keep the same secret that soon enough everyone is "keeping." Maybe. But I didn't then, and I don't now think that's what happened. I don't know how Beast knew my release date, but it was clear that reps were privy to GENPOP residents' private information.

Now whether their access to that information was part of an official transactional relationship with deputies, reps and deputies behaved as such, filtering what we were told and what we could tell deputies. In my view, the most anxiety-inducing kind of information filtering reps did was from deputies to us.[15] Whether in open or closed housing units, if deputies learned of growing conflict or if pending transfers that could upset the social order in a unit, deputies called the reps to the entryway (in open dayrooms) or the sally port (in closed dayrooms) to discuss the matter.

Whatever the news was, deputies did not think it necessary or proper to make an announcement we could all hear, and in most cases, reps did not share the news widely either. In a Providence open dayroom, 20D1, the southsider rep, Joker, openly shared with Big Guapo after meeting with deputies. In 16D, Carter generally told all the blacks, but there were only four of us. In Sunland's Z-4, Beast usually talked with Reaper and sometimes Tiny after speaking with deputies. Henry rarely told any other wood in Z-4—not openly, at least. D-Double usually (and not always openly) only told Toll and Ken.

I resented D-Double for hoarding information, but more than that, I worried about being in jail with people sharing information around me that could change the character of jail time for me. Thus, I was relentless in asking the content of those meetings. "Nigga!" D-Doubled raised his voice in annoyance. "Don't worry 'bout shit. I'll let you know when you need to worry." Other times, he would say, "Need to know basis, nigga. Need to know."

I didn't like the vulnerability of not being able to see what might be coming. "Oh. Aight. Damn," I chuckled, but nothing was funny. "What would we do without you?" I asked sarcastically.

"Prawly get into a riot."

Not that it mattered to me, but he really believed that. Of course, there was little reason to believe that social life would deteriorate into mass interracial violence and disorder without reps,[16] but that was the beside the point.

When it was clear that D-Double would nearly always stonewall questions about meetings with deputies, a few us starting joking that D-Double just liked knowing something—anything—that the rest of us didn't know. Lee and I sometimes bet on D-Double's likely responses following those meetings. "He'll just lie," Lee sometimes concluded.

But Ken sometimes told me what was going on. He thought D-Double wanted to make himself seem more important than he was by keeping the rest of us in the dark. "Some shit went down in another pod, and they [deputies] wanna be sure nothing spreads here," Ken once explained. I appreciated his openness.

Following one deputy–rep meeting, I watched Reaper and Tiny's face change at hearing what Beast had to say. I had to ask D-Double what was happening.

"I don't gotta tell you niggas anything that doesn't concern you," he shot back.

Later that day, Scott asked Beast for a *Smooth Girl Magazine*, and Beast responded, "I gotchu tonight, if I don't get transferred."

"Transferred?" I interjected with shock.

"Yeah," Beast started. "I'm prawly going to Providence."

I pieced things together. The meeting with deputies earlier was about ensuring a peaceful transition of power among the southsiders. Beast leaving was serious enough that we all deserved to know about it—even if D-Double didn't agree. A day later, Reaper stood at the southsider tables explaining the new rules.

Part of what determined who the reps spoke with had to do with a resident's jail cultural competence, where the higher the cultural competence, the greater the likelihood of the rep sharing information with a particular group member. With years of jail time under their belts, Ken, Toll, Reaper, Tiny, and Big Guapo were all competent in the *doing* of jail time. Indeed, each of them sometimes performed the role of "helper"—a kind of auxiliary position to reps when the rep had court, a health visit, a visitor, or sometimes just didn't feel like doing the job. It was therefore important to keep those residents informed about changes in unit dynamics.

But for the average GENPOP resident, the reps dammed the flow of information, and while I thought the trickle of information from deputies to reps to us was vexing, the reps were an information barrier in the opposite direction, too. Suppose you wanted to submit a kite for a bandaid or new sandals or pain medication. You first had to give your kite to your rep, who then showed it to the other reps, and if they all "thought it was cool," Ken explained, then your rep gave it back, and you could try to give it to the runner during the scheduled security checks. These extra steps and sets of eyes looking at a kite meant two things: we were careful about what we put in kites, and not every kite made it past the reps to deputies.

"Who's Dying?"

That some GENPOP kites didn't make it passed the reps was frustrating and infuriating to us but to the benefit of deputies. As that deputy above complained, it could be overwhelming dealing with a lot of requests from different residents, and so "everyone just gets a 'No.'" In open dayrooms, this was much less an issue. Deputies didn't have direct sight lines into the housing units. Sure. They could watch us through the monitors, but we knew deputies didn't stare at monitors continuously—unless, of course, deputies were just ignoring the occasional DP session. Even when they performed security checks, they did so with as much enthusiasm as a child retrieving his own switch. Sometimes they barely peeked into a tank on their way to the next one. If you were bold enough, you could ping the deputy through the one intercom button—in front of everyone. That, was rare. Usually, it was during mealtimes and "pill calls," when deputies distributed medicine, that residents formed a bottleneck of hands trying to pass kites and verbal requests. Deputies often made little effort to hide how uninterested they were in our wants and needs. In short, deputies working open dayrooms could and often did simply ignore us.

Things were somewhat different in closed dayrooms, where the runner entered the dayroom frequently and regularly to perform security checks. Most often those checks amounted to a deputy glancing inside a cell while walking the tiers. Between security checks, you could hit your cell intercom button to get the pod's attention. That was access not available to GENPOP residents in open dayrooms. Greater access meant more bidding, more cons, and more frivolous requests. Consequently, deputies often operated in *no-mode*,[17] *responding to requests as if they were insincere or less than urgent,* which put the onus on residents to prove otherwise.

How could you prove that you *really* did need someone to fix the toilet in your cell? Relentless will and thick skin. The runner entered the dayroom with an announcement: "Walking!" Sometimes, residents made the announcement before the deputy as a warning to prepare for a possible serious security check. Along the way, residents peppered the runner with needs and wants: toilet paper, a missed visit, a missed court date, a new indigent kit, dayroom time, new slippers, new boxers, a new blanket, a broken table or light fixture—whatever.

Deputy responses ranged from slow fulfillment to polite indifference to no-mode to vitriol to total disregard. My favorite response to mail requests was "Next shift," as in, wait for the next 12-hour shift of deputies. It was a deputy's way of passing off the work to the mythical deputy who was always coming forthright but who never arrived. Just as often, the runner refused to accept outgoing mail, which was especially infuriating. It was one thing to not receive mail, but the inability to get a letter out meant we were truly alone, and that, to me, felt very different—like I was trapped in an unreachable place.

But if you needed something, you needed to be steadfast in your requests and to accept some measure of mortification.[18] Residents put in three days of requests for indigent kits; some spent days asking for medication or a visit with healthcare staff to potentially get a new prescription or a renewal. Sisqo had more than his fair share of incidents of begging. Because his cell neighbored my own, I had a front row seat to his encounters with deputies.

He once foolishly tried to flush apple cores, resulting in he and his celly spending the next several days hitting their intercom button, hoping for an amenable deputy to escort them to the toilet outside in the recreation yard. As the days rolled by, some of us speculated that deputies were slow to get a plumber to the cell because it was Sisqo's fault. That was believable—that deputies took a relaxed attitude toward problems that, in their estimation, were our fault. But deputies could be just as merciless if blame could not be laid at our feet. During our discussion about Sisqo and TJ using the rec yard toilet, Ken reminded us that Z-4 had once gone six months without hot water. "Guys put in a grip of kites over that shit, too," he said. "I think that's why don't fix it. Too many complaints, so they wanna make us wait to prove a point."

Perhaps the "point" was that some deputies wanted us to know that we were a bother to them—that we should not ask for anything—even if that meant taking cold showers, wearing torn slippers, and suffering in a tiny cell with a deposit from your celly's unflushable bowels festering in the commode. Maybe deputies wanted us to cut down on the number of frivolous interactions we were having with them. I certainly initiated a few.

It was the audacity with which they showed us so little regard that quickened my desire to disrupt their fun—most often a movie night in the pod. For instance, one evening, just after lights-out, the pod made a typical announcement: "Don't hit your buttons unless you are dying or we tell you to." Standing in front of my cell door, I saw blue-white lights dancing in the darkened pod: *They started their movie.* I hated movie night because I could be sure that the runner would actually run through the security checks, and then you would have to be bleeding to get a deputy's attention. It was no-mode for sure, so I decided to ruin that a bit. I hit my cell intercom button.

"Who's dying?" the deputy asked.

"No one. I just wanted to know what you're watching."

"It's called, 'go to sleep.'"

Another deputy chimed in, eager to engage: "It's called *Kingdom*, and before that it was *Jumper*." He asked me if I'd ever seen *Jumper*.

I was reminded of an earlier encounter with a deputy who vaunted that he "might get Pizza Hut for lunch" and what was I having? I regretted having asked about the movie. I didn't have the upper hand, so I said that I'd never seen it, and that was that.

I can't say with any confidence how often residents mashed an intercom button for something that could have waited, but whose definition of frivolous is important here? The newbie asking for time to make a phone call was a serious matter—as was his request about how the mail system worked. Too often deputies behaved toward us as if everyone in jail knew exactly how everything in jail worked, but that was nonsense, and being without clean clothes was serious. It was no small matter to not have a toothbrush or soap and being passed over for prescribed medicine was dangerous for some and subjected others to unnecessary pain. Did deputies really expect us to just go without toilet paper between Sundays? Would they have justified those degradations for their loved ones? More than a few times I wondered whether deputies felt good about their treatment toward us or maybe it was by criminal objectification that some deputies justified an uncaring attitude toward us.

How else should we make sense of, "Hey assholes! Stay off your buttons!" at the start of a shift? What was clear was that deputies regarded caring for residents as the least desirable kind of work they could do, and again, if given the chance to lean into care or into punishment, deputies generally chose the latter. But caretaking was part of the job, so what were they to do?

Another of Sisqo's interactions with deputies is one that sits with me even now, but it's important here because it illustrates deputy attitudes toward caretaking. During an early evening, Sisqo tried to stop a quick-stepping runner to pass a kite through the doorjamb, but the runner moved on too fast, and the written request fell to the floor. Later, sometime between 1:00 a.m. and 2:00 a.m. of day one going into day two, Sisqo stopped a different runner who told him that he needed to submit a kite for an indigent kit. Sisqo pointed to the floor and tried to explain how the kite was at the runner's feet and why. "Do I look like your fucking nigger?" the deputy responded sharply. That is, *Do I look like your servant—like I'm subordinate to you?*

They exchanged a few more words, and Sisqo supplicated for help, adding that he had " . . . never been in any trouble, sir."

The exchange was going nowhere when the runner ended the conversation with, "Fuck that fish kit," and continued his rounds.

Sisqo persisted. He pestered the runner at every chance to no avail. Hours later, a new shift of deputies was onboard. Using a softened tone, Sisqo stopped the runner and asked for an indigent kit.

"Huh?" the deputy responded loudly. "Who's your rep?" Sisqo murmured something and the deputy ended the exchange with, "I'm not your rep."

Hours more would pass before a deputy set an indigent kit outside of Sisqo's cell door to be retrieved at the next mealtime or dayroom time. But what struck me then as it does now is that the reps were so integrated into how deputies managed the housing units that the runner felt comfortable referring Sisqo to D-Double to procure an indigent kit—something that no resident expected of his rep. But you wouldn't be in a closed dayroom for long before deputies taught you that your rep was indispensable to some of your basic needs—not of necessity but because deputies made it so.

Servants of All

Reps settled intraracial conflict and neutralized interracial conflict. They filtered information between deputies and GENPOP residents such that only those kites that reps deemed inconsequential to the social order of the housing unit were permitted to reach a runner. But the mediating management model paid its greatest dividends to deputies when reps labored as caretakers, doing the work that would otherwise fall to deputies. In my estimation, this was the main point of there being reps in GENPOP housing units, and caretaking was far more consequential in closed dayrooms than in open. Remember: there was a single source of hot water in both kinds of dayrooms, but in closed dayrooms, the hot water spigot was outside of the cells—as was the television, the newspaper, any books, checkers, or chess board games.

We spent an awful lot of time locked away in our cells in closed dayrooms. During those frequent and long periods in the cells, deputies cut on the television and sometimes the phones, as they permitted the reps to roam about the dayroom freely. That wasn't bonus time out of the cells; there was work to be done. Your rep might find himself changing the channel on the television in accordance with whichever racial group had control that day. He might make several trips to top and bottom tier cells, dropping off books, the newspaper, and race-specific checkers and chess board games to be retrieved later. He almost surely passed kites and verbal messages to residents on either tier. As the number of requests from a rep's racial group increased, so did the number of his mini-caretaking missions.

Suppose you wanted hot water for coffee or "a soup" (sic) that you had purchased from the jail's commissary. If you hit your intercom button (see Figure 2.1) to ask a deputy to get hot water, you invited one of three responses: nothing—no acknowledgment that you had hit your intercom button at all; a deputy might remind you that they flashed the overhead lights at end of dayroom time, signaling to an opportunity for hot water (something you might not have learned just yet); or a deputy might tell you to ask your rep. Instead, you banged on your cell door or yelled through the doorjamb to get your rep's attention. You signaled that you wanted hot water by pointing at your empty cup or at a soup package. Your rep then took a race-specific cup, filled it with hot water, and met you at your cell where you needed to know to spread open a potato chip bag and slide it through the doorjamb, so your rep could pour hot water down your makeshift funnel into your cup or soup bag. *Voila!* Jail Grubhub—of sorts. In these ways, reps attended to the mundane needs that residents would otherwise pester deputies about.

And crisscrossing the dayroom as caretakers was only part of the way reps relieved deputies' workload. At the start of every "feed" or "chow" time, deputies summoned the reps from their cells to provide a count of their respective members to a deputy waiting in the sally port with the trustees whose job it was to deliver food to the housing units. "Wake up, bitches!" a deputy announced before breakfast. "Trustees[19] [reps] hit your goddamn buttons." Seconds later three loud clangs tore through the morning's silence, and each rep went about their normal count. Of course, deputies knew how many residents were in every housing unit, and they could have just ensured that each resident was given a food tray. Instead, deputies added unnecessary uncertainty into mealtimes by relying upon a count provided by the reps. I don't know that it ever happened, but I wondered whether a rep ever decided not to count a tray for a resident he didn't like—and if he did so, how would deputies handle that? Might they refer the hungry resident to his rep? After all, during mealtimes, the body of each racial group sat at their respective tables while the reps and helpers carried over the appropriate number of trays. But without the reps, deputies would have to distribute the food trays themselves. Better the deputies subject GENPOP residents to needless jeopardy.

Finally, and it was never clear to me whether the task would have fallen to deputies or facilities management, but once a week, usually on Sundays, deputies let the reps out to clean the dayroom. Sometimes, however, the pod made a game of who would get to clean: "Gentlemen. If you do not have court tomorrow and you would like to volunteer to help clean, hit your button." The word "volunteer" was deceiving. I never saw or heard of a deputy helping to clean a dayroom. Perhaps the "help" they offered was in the form of cleaning supplies. Either way, announcements to clean the dayroom found no shortage of volunteers: anything for time out of the cell. Scott and I always raced to hit our intercom button but were never chosen. Herc and LK once moseyed from their cell with giant smiles and silent taunting. They had been chosen, but they gloated just a little too long, and the pod sent them back to their cell, much to our enjoyment. "You guys were bullshitting," a deputy added. The "privilege" of cleaning the dayroom fell to the reps. Deputies popped open their cell doors, provided two mops and buckets and a couple of spray bottles and rags. Reps set about cleaning the dayroom: servants of all.

There is yet more to learn about the reps and the role of race relations in organizing what residents were permitted to do. Explaining any one part of daily life requires a large amount of background knowledge. I've covered a good chunk of that here, describing the structure of relations and hinting at how race was mapped onto jail amenities. I've had to issue a few promissory notes, alluding, for instance, to a set of rules that reps enforced, and in the next chapter, you will be able to cash in those notes. As much as I want you to be clear on how social life proceeded in GENPOP housing units, I also want you to experience the same dizziness to which newbies were subjected.

Hot Plates and Prada

"If you have to do time, prison is where you want to be." No one was even talking to Chino, but there he was butting in again to tell us how much better prison time was than jail time. Insincere once told me the same thing after a visiting hour. It was a theme connecting residents who had been to prison. Having stolen the floor, Chino continued: "You get a pillow and three blankets." He said the bed mat was thicker and more comfortable. "Medical is better—fix ya whole grill for $5. Everything is $5–fix ya back—scoliosis." He paused to bite an apple. "Fix ya legs. Mufuckas get they whole jaw fixed." He said in prison, most cells came with a hot plate, a wall socket, and residents could get Prada and Nike shoes in care packages with CDs, and DVDs—"the latest shit, too!" He talked down on jail food and what we could get from the commissary, saying the prison commissary is far superior. "And y'all don't be out. Rec[creation] is regular in the pen."

At 30-years-old, Chino had a wife, three kids, and a sister that he frequently talked about, and he wasn't advocating for prison, of course. He was "sick of prison." It was lunch time in the Sunland Detention Center, and we had been given an ice cream scoop of peanut butter clumped on a hot dog bun, two small teaspoons of jelly, and a child's-fist size of chopped salad mixed with mayonnaise. Chino just wanted us to know how bad we had it in jail.

3

The "Politics"

Because I entered my final stint in jail having been sentenced to 180 days, I was eligible for the trustee pod, but as the deputy conducting the classification interview hedged, there needed to be space in that pod. I wrongly assumed he meant race-specific space like in GENPOP units.

My deputy escort summoned me from pre-housing holding, and along the way, we stopped so I could get my property box, bedroll, and something called a "boat": a body-length, blue, plastic sleeping apparatus shaped like a canoe. I assumed I'd be sleeping in it, but the deputy didn't explain that or where we were going, and I worried that picking up the boat meant that I was being taken to someplace particularly uncomfortable.

Instead, we entered the Providence trustee pod. If the average GENPOP housing unit was a working poor neighborhood, the Providence trustee pod was a beautiful, gated community. Not all trustee housing units were like the one in Providence. Later, I would pass by some in Sunland, and while they looked clean, they were small, open units holding 10–15 trustees. The Providence trustee pod was grand in comparison. You never forgot you were in jail, but it was a special place—a standalone unit, not attached to other dayrooms like Sunland's Z-Pod. It held more than 60 residents, and some of the cells had windows to natural sunlight! In the dayroom, sunlight shone through a few well-placed, albeit metal-grated, windows, brightening the shared space. It was glorious because you could stand at the windows and feel the sun's warmth on your face. And if you looked out those windows, you could see State St. below. You could see people—real people—walking around downtown, handling their personal affairs, all without knowing you were looking down upon them from a carceral world that was literally hidden in plain sight by the building's architecture.

I used to wonder what those people were thinking about. Were they headed to the Wells Fargo branch that I used to go to? Were they eating at the nearby sandwich shop county employees liked? I bet they were fussing in their minds about something frivolous like: "Should I continue strolling down State St.—maybe take in a movie with salty buttery popcorn? Maybe

I'll have sex later or listen to a favorite playlist or combine the two." Who could know? They were free.

The tables and chairs in the dayroom were fixed in place but not in ways that permitted a natural grouping by race. Every amenity in that unit worked! It was common for clocks in GENPOP units to be broken—hands frozen in place as a metaphor for the indefinite nature of jail time. In the Providence trustee pod, the clock ticked and tocked in conjunction with the rising and setting of the sun. I didn't know how poor my quality of life was inside artificially lit units until I could watch sunlight beam into the trustee pod. The hot water spigot was always on—and hot! There were four showers with water hot enough to sting your back and steam the area. There were a variety of books, a few decks of actual playing cards, and more than one set of checkers. Downstairs, there were three phones and one more on the second tier in an area that can rightly be described as a resting nook where there was another table with four chairs under a sunlit window.

Deputies running the pod were noticeably nicer—calm and unprovoked by an image of us in their minds. Sometimes, deputies let us prop open our cell doors during dayroom time, so we could go in and out of our cells as we pleased—something unthinkable in GENPOP units. When it was time to clean, deputies gave us sufficient supplies to do the job. They offered dayroom time more frequently and for longer periods. When they referred to us as "gentlemen" or "gents," it didn't feel like condescension, and they weren't calling us "criminals," "assholes," or "dickheads," the way the GENPOP deputies sometimes did. At lights out time, deputies cut off the dayroom lights *and* the cell lights. Sweet darkness! There was something calming and soporific about seeing moonlight in the cell. I knew another day had passed—that I was closer to going home.

I was in a bottom tier cell that was larger than normal. Instead of being stacked, the bunks were on either side of the cell, and I slept on the ground, in my boat, between the bunks. During waking hours, I stored my boat under one of the bunks. No one told me how long I'd be in that boat, so I figured it would probably be for the entirety of my sentence. I was happy that my cellies didn't seem to be bothered with a third man in the cell. Casey, a redheaded, White American, and Alex, who was Latino: we were like racial Neapolitan ice cream in that cell.

Prior to my time in the trustee pod, I had experience in other Golden County housing units: three were GENPOP units in Providence, on e in the Barracks Jail, and one in the Cardinal Detention Center. All of them were open units—the largest of which was in Barracks. Deputies assigned residents to beds in all those units according to race, and they used the rep version of the mediating management model to regulate social life, so I naturally expected the same while in the trustee pod, but nope! There was no talk of "blacks," "southsiders," or "woods," and there was no racial pattern to how residents used unit amenities. There was the occasional conflict between residents in the trustee pod, but those episodes remained interpersonal and disconnected from race. Also interesting, not every resident in the trustee pod started out there the way I had at the beginning of my sentence. Some transferred from GENPOP units, meaning it wasn't as though residents in the trustee pod were unaware of how race structured social life in other parts of the jail. Nevertheless, it seemed that somehow, race wasn't so important in the trustee pod, but I didn't trust that I was understanding matters properly. Maybe my interracial cell assignment was an administrative mistake. I needed to be sure.

During dayroom time, I approached Lamont. He was a Black American trustee with broad shoulders, a lively personality, and big hands nearly always wrapped around cards in a game. He was playing against Hunter, a White American trustee who rarely spoke. "So, I can use whichever phone I want," I asked from the clear blue with uncertainty in my voice.

"Yeah," Lamont said with shrug. He played a card and pointed around the room. "You could use the one up there or the one back there or whatever."

"Cool."

"Yeah. We don't have that shit in other pods—that race shit. Mufuckas in here can do what they want. Just don't be disrespectful, but it's not about race." Hunter nodded, and Lamont continued, "I mean, Mexicans kick it with each other, but they don't have to. Shit. I play cards with whoever, ya know?"

I made it a point to shower in all four showers. I sat at different tables in different parts of the dayroom during different times. During mealtimes, we lined up by tier and not by race to get food trays. And then I was invited to a "spread." I'd seen spreads among southsiders in other units. It was a potluck-styled meal in which residents pooled their personal food items, each contributing soups [sic], soup flavoring packets, cheese squeeze, Doritos, hard-boiled eggs, mayonnaise and jelly packets, off-brand Slim Jims, and sometimes a few other ingredients from the jail's lunch or dinner that someone had saved. Those food items were gathered into a pile in one of the heavy-duty, clear plastic bags in which our commissary orders came. Add hot water, twist and tie closed the bag, shake and massage it around to mix the ingredients, and let it sit for about 10 minutes. After the food "cooked," the bag was untied and cut so that it spread open on the table. Residents dug in from their vantage points.

I'd only ever seen intraracial spreads; they were community building events that often fed the indigent, but I contributed to and toughed down a couple of bites from a spread that included residents from a variety of racial and ethnic groups. It wasn't that the food was bad. It wasn't—surprisingly. Rather, I couldn't overlook that men were licking their sporks and digging in again.

"Greens Only!"

I was only in the Providence trustee pod for about eight days, and nearly every day was one of discovery. There were no reps, but there were plenty of discussions about how much everyone hated the rep system. Casey and Alex always started their rants about the work they did and ended up talking about reps, GENPOP residents, and race. Casey worked in the kitchen, which meant deputies roused our cell at 2:30 a.m. to get him up to cook and distribute breakfast for the jail by 4:30 a.m. "It's slavery!" he would say. It most certainly wasn't that, but supposedly trustees earned $.50/day. "They make us do their work," Casey said of deputies. "Real talk. We're doing the work they're supposed to be doing."

"If we weren't here," Alex said, "they would have to clean this fucking jail up, and they don't wanna do that, so they shit on us." Alex floated as a worker, sometimes doing janitorial work and other times working in laundry. "Meanwhile, you got every-fucking-body begging for better clothes and more food and shit. Yo! I hate that shit! That's why I hate dealing with them [GENPOP residents]."

During a different rant session, Lamont had a similar sentiment: "Do these mufuckas know that the messes they make gotta be cleaned up by us? And then they wonder why the fuck we don't be fuckin' with them like that. Mufucka cuz you nasty."

However, not every trustee expressed resentment of GENPOP residents. Months after my time in the Providence trustee pod, I stared down the line of residents at the trustee manning the clothing bin under the supervision of a deputy. Z-Pod residents were as likely to be denied an opportunity to make exchanges for clean bedding and clothing as we were to be left with items that fit no one in our unit. On this day, the deputy announced that clean towels would soon run out and that only "shit stained" and torn towels were left. *Great.* And looking down the line to guestimate my prospects of getting a clean towel, I caught the trustee signaling to Tiny that he was putting aside a clean towel. The fix was in. The line moved along at a quick pace, and the trustee made two mistakes: (1) he tried to toss the clean towel past me to Tiny, who was, well, tiny compared to me; and (2) he underestimated how badly I wanted a clean towel. I intercepted the pass and moved on to the next bin like that's how it was supposed to be.

Some trustees didn't play favorites. "I can't do that for you," one explained to a GENPOP resident who had asked for a clean shirt—in front of a deputy, no less.

Even if a trustee was inclined to help us out, he couldn't ensure that everyone got clean clothing items. *Someone* was going to have wear the shirt, boxers, and socks with the mysterious stains. "Get your fucking chonies and get going!" a deputy we called "Deputy Dog" commanded bitterly. "Keep the line moving, gentlemen."

But whether they helped out or not, many GENPOP residents held antipathies against trustees. Part of the resentment was rooted in the inconsistent favoritism some trustees showed. And part of it had to do with privileges deputies accorded trustees relative to every other resident classification. Nearly every clothing exchange, D-Double referred to the trustees as "house niggas." Having enjoyed the comforts of the Providence trustee pod—the "Big House," as it were, and having toiled in the proverbial fields of GENPOP housing units, I never argued against D-Double's analogy. "They don't want no problems," D-Double continued under his breath. I could tell he was in an imagined argument with the trustees manning the clothing bins, and apparently, he was winning the fights in his mind. He said they performed their duties with a sense of superiority—like extensions of "massa's" power.

"They think they're better than everyone else," Ken added. "Like, they think they're deputies and shit."

Managerially speaking, division between trustees and GENPOP residents was useful. It meant the two groups never formed a unit to challenge the exploitive power deputies held.[1]

As to why there were no reps in the trustee pod, I can only guess, and I don't suppose there will ever be a revelation of a coherent philosophy by which deputies determined when to institute race in the housing units, so here's what I know, because I observed and lived it: When deputies decided race was useful and significant, it was; hence, the rep version of the mediating management model in GENPOP units. And when they decided otherwise, it wasn't; hence, social life in the trustee pods wasn't organized around race relations. It was clear that the whole racial project[2] in Golden County jails was arbitrary. But, of course, all social behavior is emplaced,[3] and all it takes for some patterns of behavior to take hold in one place and not in another is the establishment that it *should* be that way. So, deputies didn't use race to manage the trustee pod, but there still needed to be an efficient way for two deputies in a command pod to manage over 60 residents, and I am reminded of Jane Elliott's "Blue Eyes/Brown Eyes" exercise.[4]

Following the assassination of Martin Luther King Jr. and during something called "National Brotherhood Week," which, whatever value that week once held, it is now reduced to a parody song by Tom Lehrer, Elliott, then a teacher in Iowa, asked her all-White third graders who is not treated very brotherly in the United States. Several students quickly noted, "The Black people," which always stuck out to me because I have long believed that despite White tears, empty apologies, and pleas of ignorance, White America is informed enough about the plight of Black America to know they would not want to trade places.

Having discussed the matter further, Elliott had a classroom of students eager to learn a lesson about racism in the United States. She divided the students into two groups: blue-eyed and brown-eyed students. She proclaimed one group to be superior in every way; she ridiculed the students in the downtrodden group; she allotted extra privileges to students in the superior group; and not only did the students participate in the exercise, some of those in the superior group came up with creative ways to better track, manage, and punish students with the devalued eye color. That was one day. The next day she made the opposite proclamation, and students eagerly accepted the new set rules: privileged in a moment; oppressed in the next.

The exercise was a small-scale, precise demonstration of the central argument in sociologist, Charles Tilly's book, *Durable Inequality*.[5] Even the most arbitrary and intrinsically meaningless differences become durable when resources, privileges, and punishments are consolidated and differentially distributed according to those differences. Such is the brilliant tyranny of institutionalizing status differences.

Recall, now, that trustees wore green uniforms, were scheduled for release, and held jobs in jail. But the Providence trustee pod also held residents like me: dressed in county oranges, scheduled for release, and *not* employed by the jail. Some of us "oranges," as deputies and residents in the trustee pod referred to us, were happy not working, but most of us would have gladly accepted a job because, aside from eating better in the kitchen or wearing cleaner and better fitting clothes while working laundry, deputies privileged "greens" over "oranges."

I'd be in the cell listening to Casey and Alex feed on each other's complaints about being trustees when the call came: "Bottom tier! Bottom tier! Greens only! GREENS ONLY! Dayroom time." The pod popped open the cell doors on the bottom tier, and we began to file into the dayroom. Some of trustees wore their white T-shirts and green bottoms, leaving their green tops in the cell: something prohibited in GENPOP units. I heard the announcement clearly, so I sat silly-faced in my boat, as Casey propped the cell door open on his way out.

But there were always a few overly eager oranges who entered the dayroom with the greens. It was obvious who hadn't heard the announcement clearly and who had heard what they wanted to hear. The former entered with their orange tops and bottoms, not attempting to blend in with the background of green uniforms. The latter had on their orange bottoms and only their white t-shirts. The strategy was to quickly take a seat and let the table cover your orange bottoms, so you could hang out in the dayroom with the greens. Success depended upon how stealthily you entered the dayroom, whether deputies were actively watching everyone in the dayroom, and whether the greens kept quiet about your hustle.

You see, deputies nearly always gave greens extra dayroom time. They would let us oranges out, too—perhaps 15 minutes to an hour later. It just depended upon how the pod felt. In some cases, greens were given twice the dayroom time of oranges, but quite frankly, we thought it stupid to have oranges and greens in the same cells and then privilege greens because, from our viewpoint, it wasn't having a job that kept misconduct at a minimum. It was that each of us had a scheduled release date, and no one wanted to mess that up. And because deputies usually let greens and oranges mingle together in the dayroom eventually, there was almost no point in privileging greens to oranges—almost.

In most cases, deputies spotted the obvious orange and repeated part of the announcement: "Greens only, gentlemen."

Then a chorus of greens joined in: "Greens only!"

"Not yet! He didn't say oranges," Lamont said as if personally offended by an orange wanting extra time in the dayroom.

Typically, greens policing the oranges in the service of deputies was enough to send every hustling orange back to his cell. But sometimes one of us tried to hide—or we didn't appear to be moving quickly enough to the cells. "I said, 'greens only' unless no one wants dayroom time at all!" the pod threatened.

"No oranges!" green voices surged. The deputy's threat hit its mark, and lingering oranges quickstepped to their cells.

Now, you might have been an orange with a green celly. You might have had good rapport with a bunch of greens. Maybe you even enjoyed a spread with greens, but none of that was worth losing dayroom time over. Deputies pulled on that proverbial lever, the greens shouted you back into your cell, and there was never a serious discussion of greens and oranges uniting against deputies and the needless division that they stoked—not while I was there. And like relations between deputies, reps, and GENPOP residents, greens policed oranges to the benefit of deputies who had fewer residents in the dayroom to watch at one time.

The "Politics"

In the middle sleeping hours, a deputy's voice tore through night's silence: "Walker."

The voice startled a "Yes!" out of me before I was fully awake.

"Roll up."

I thought I was being released, so I fought back feeling despondent when it turned out I was just being transferred to Sunland over an hour's drive away. There was no explanation, and I'd not done anything wrong, but life events need to make sense, so I told myself that race-specific space had opened elsewhere—that *obviously*, I couldn't stay in that boat as a third man in a two-man cell. And *obviously*, I wasn't going to be given a job in the jail, so I was being moved. I don't know if any of that was true, but that's what I told myself.

It was emotionally taxing to leave the Providence trustee pod—especially the way I did. I'd come to know who I was in that place, and I liked the stability that came with being able to name my place in the social world—despite it being a damned jail. I understood the schedule even as I hated it. I was used to Lamont playing cards, shit-talking, and passionately defending green privileges against oranges. Alex and Casey complained a lot, but their complaints were part of the landscape of social living that made my time in the trustee pod stable. I learned the pathway that two oranges took in making circuits around the dayroom. They never ran out of conversation as they walked. That place was my reality, and it is underappreciated how emotionally and cognitively disruptive a move between housing units and jails could be. Such moves were common, and they felt like rips in the fabric of one's sense self in the social world.[6] It made life in jail all the more uncertain; it made your present moments more pronounced. You could not escape your vulnerabilities. I hated those dead-of-the-night moves.

A week into my time in Sunland's Z-4 unit, I knew the rules, I had learned them when I was in GENPOP open units, but they were still so damned counterintuitive—especially in a closed dayroom. Initially, I made a few mistakes. I hung up the phone near the hot water spigot by the southsider tables. The black tables were on the opposite end of the dayroom where the television was, so I headed over there. Without thinking, I cut through the southsider tables and was approaching the wood tables. "Eh! Yo! Watch out!" black voices warned. I high stepped on the tips of my toes and arrived at a group of frustrated black residents.

"Don't cross between they [sic] tables, nigga!" D-Double said in a chastising tone.

I apologized and took a seat. A few days later, though, I was talking to Toll from afar. I started to cut through the wood tables and was halfway through before I remembered the rule. *Shit!* It was one of those moments when your mind makes calculations faster than time, and things slow while you process everything that's about to happen. I saw a few wide-eyed woods and a southsider, and time resumed its normal pace as I heard black residents registering their public protest. "Damn! This nigga dumb as hell!"

"'Fuck is wrong witchu?"

"Nigga stupid!"

I didn't try to defend myself, as they kept up their complaints—both because they were annoyed and because they needed to appear that way. More on this shortly. D-Double approached to emphasize the collective disgust at my *faux pas*. "You don't—cross—between—they [sic] fuckin' tables," he said while making and breaking an "X" with his arms near his waist. I hung my head, and he explained that he didn't want anyone to say "some shit came up missing" because then we would have to "deal with that." I said that I wouldn't take anything, and he shot back that it didn't matter. He wanted to avoid the potential accusation. As the black rep, he had final responsibility to ensure black residents didn't create problems—that we adhered to "the politics."

In jail,[7] the politics was a set of race-based rules by which social behavior was governed, and there were three broad principles: *we all ride*, meaning an attack against one' member of a racial group necessitated full racial membership participation in a fight; no interracial sharing—not even walking lanes; and only minimal interracial communication allowed. These are the rules I was expecting and pleasantly surprised to not find in the Providence trustee pod.

It was by racial classification that deputies gave meaning to race; in GENPOP housing units, residents subsequently racialized resources; and in the politics were the codes to how it all worked. As I explained in the previous chapter, to create racial categories is to establish normative boundaries and resource claims by race. Thus, there was, for example, the "black phone," the "wood tables," the "southsider showers," and even walking lanes were policed along racial boundaries.

Baked into that kind of resource distribution was a hidden inequality that made jail life more difficult for residents in larger groups in a given unit. Jail amenities were distributed equally—not equitably—at the group level. You might be the lone black resident with a shower unto yourself in a unit with 12 woods and eight southsiders. You would have far greater access to your race's amenities than any single member of the other two racial groups. Also, you wouldn't have to contend with status[8] differences, whereas the southsiders and woods would have to work through their intragroup hierarchies based upon esteem and respect. I call this arrangement a *flat hierarchy*: *a set of relations characterized by intergroup equality and intragroup inequality.*

For instance, there were several single-item amenities to which each racial group was given equal access. If the television worked, residents created and affixed to a wall a calendar and marked each day with an "S," a "B," and a "W" to indicate which racial group had control over what was watched on that day. Deputies participated in the politics, too. If a deputy let me use the fingernail clippers, all the blacks who wanted to use them did so in succession before a southsider or wood could. Deputies handled haircuts the same way.

It was different, however, when there were only two of a given amenity. In those units, southsiders and woods shared. It wasn't that black residents dominated and claimed facilities or even an issue of who had the largest membership in a given housing unit. Rather, it was familiar anti-Black racism[9] that joined wood and southsider butts at the toilet, hands at the sink, and soap scum in the showers. We find the same racist rationale at the heart of patterns of residential segregation in the United States and preferences for neighborhood racial composition.[10] This is not to say that woods and southsiders didn't hold each other in mutual contempt. No doubt, except for their comrades, white supremacists don't have friends—only temporary transactional arrangements, but speaking as an African American man, if the world has taught me nothing at all, I know that I am as envied as I am despised,[11] and members of other racial and ethnic groups have, from time to time, demonstrated their resolve to avoid being contaminated by me[12]— if not while trying to take a piece of me for themselves. So southsiders and woods made life harder for themselves by sharing to avoid sharing with blacks. It is what it is.

To summarize, the politics were the rules that made the flat hierarchy functional. The stricter the adherence to the politics, the more stable the flat hierarchy, the lower the likelihood of interracial conflict, and the greater the intragroup pressure to find ways to develop a fair system to make amenities available to members. By way of the flat hierarchy, the strongest didn't determine which showers or phones they used and for how long. Small cadres of interested residents didn't band together to control resources. Your group got what it got, and any single interaction between residents was as much—if not more—a person–group interaction as it was a person–person interaction. You wanted to avoid racial norm violations because the consequences stirred conflict at the group level.

In fact, a story about a mayonnaise packet is useful here. Well, the incident wasn't really about mayonnaise, but that's how it lives in my memory: *the mayonnaise packet* story. Like so many conflicts involving property, the actual issue had less to do with the property than the sense that one's status was being challenged. It began with a lighthearted dispute between Ken and TJ over who had claim to a packet of mayonnaise. Ken wasn't serious at all, which I suspected angered TJ all the more. It didn't help that the rest of us interjected jokes about how TJ looked. TJ was about 40 years old. He wore what we thought was a ridiculous ponytail, his belly was near perfectly round with skin stretched tightly over it, and he had short arms.

TJ was the frequent victim of a "bagging" session where we piled up jokes about everything he did and how he looked. Truthfully, everyone had their time in the fire of everyone else's jokes, but something about the mayonnaise, the bagging, Ken's demeanor, and most likely the fact that he was in jail just didn't make the moment funny to TJ.

Ken could not have been more different from TJ. Ken was in his early 20s; he was Korean American; and he was "wit' the shits." It turned out, in fact, that he and I had attended the same university at the same time. In jail, Ken was a good-natured person. I never once saw him somber or with anything other than a positive attitude. I certainly never saw him appearing fearful.

"I was just joking with you," Ken said to TJ in a serious tone that signaled Ken's willingness to address with more aggressive energy. "We can handle it no problem," he added. Ken was so calm, and it looked like he half hoped that TJ would opt to solve their disagreement with a fight.[13] If TJ would have agreed to a fight, they would have chosen a cell to meet in, and most assuredly, TJ would have been beaten up. Staring at each other in suspense, TJ must have seen that future beatdown in Ken's eyes, so whatever TJ wanted to do, he was too afraid to do anything. He looked away, and Ken blithely moved on. We all did—except for TJ, who immediately gave away his food and tantrumed up the stairs toward his cell. In that same moment, the pod flashed the dayroom lights and popped open the top tier cells.

As misfortune would have it, deputies had smashed an egg on the ground inside TJ's cell earlier that day as punishment for his celly, Sisqo, having violated the clothing exchange rules. TJ kicked the egg out of his cell and onto the walkway. Some of it landed in front of the nearby southsider cells.

As we—me and Scott, LK and Herc, D-Double and Ken, Toll, and Lee, and Sisqo—headed to our respective cells, we saw what TJ had done. "What the fuck? Nigga, did you kick this shit all over the place," LK demanded of TJ.

TJ appeared in his cell doorway, claiming only to have "moved it" with his foot, but LK pressed him.

"You can't be kickin' shit all in front of their [southsider] doors." Whatever TJ said in response was unsatisfactory because LK continued angrily: "Aight. If they [southsiders] fuck you up, we ain't helpin' you." LK stomped off, and Scott and I decided to start cleaning the mess. It was partly in front our cell, but we wanted to avoid the potential conflict of leaving crumbles of hard-boiled egg in front of neighboring southsider cells. LK returned, pushing his way passed onlookers and passersby to deliver one final threat to TJ: "Eh! You better watch yo' attitude." I detected in LK's voice a wish that TJ wouldn't watch his attitude, so LK had a reason to put hands on TJ.

D-Double appeared on the scene seconds later. TJ apologized to him while closing the door behind Sisqo. "You can't be doin' this type of shit at all," D-Double warned loudly. The statement seemed performative—a way of letting southsiders know the matter was being handled before it became an issue. My celly and I were on our hands and knees, cleaning the mess for the greater good. TJ insincerely yelled through his cell door that he would clean up if the deputies let him out of the cell. Then in a strange twist, TJ offered D-Double a mayonnaise packet. (That offer sustained Scott and I with jokes for hours after that.) Of course, the mayonnaise wasn't the issue, and in any case, it was Ken, not D-Double, who had the back and forth about the condiment, so TJ offering D-Double some mayonnaise was comedy. D-Double waved TJ off like a dismissive parent, we finished cleaning, and shut our cell door.

That event was quite the web of potential violence. First, TJ wisely backed down from a challenge and avoided a beating from Ken. Then he narrowly avoided a beating from LK, who declared that TJ would be on his own if the southsiders decided to retaliate with violence for the disrespect. How real was LK's threat of abandonment? It reminded me of my grandmother promising not to take me to the hospital if I disobeyed her by riding my bike in the street and getting hurt. I assumed LK's threat was just frustrated bluster, but it may not have been. Though I never witnessed it, I imagine that it was possible for a single resident to be so problematic that his racial group could cut him loose for punishment by a different group. I can imagine that, but it seems more likely that the rep would have that resident rolled out long before matters deteriorated to that point.

In any case, the mayonnaise packet story is a window into how the politics worked to neutralize between-group violence while increasing the likelihood of functional violence within groups. TJ got away with a series of threats, but he may well have been DPed had D-Double had the inclination—especially if doing so would calm interracial tensions.

We All Ride

Whether the police, political parties, sororities, gangs, neighborhood associations, or one's immediate friends and family, the mandate is the same: if one is threatened, all are threatened, and the more serious the threat, the larger the group-based response. Any differences in this proposition are mainly a matter of degree.

But just because *we all ride* was familiar to me didn't mean that I was automatically ready to help a random black resident in a fight with a random wood or southsider. Sitting in a court holding cell after a skirmish between two black residents, I made a provocation to a nearby black resident who had also watched the fight: "Muthafucka's be fightin' each other so much. I'm supposed to fight for these fools? They'd just as soon jump me."

"But those are your people," he said calmly. "You wouldn't help your people?"

I immediately knew I'd said the wrong thing, and we sat in silence with that comment hanging out there.

Other interactions solidified how serious *we all ride* was in Golden County jails. One of the first things Charlie B, the black rep in Providence's 31C3 tank, told me had to do with the mandate to fight at the group level. Charlie was soft-spoken and ever vigilant. I thought it was his demeanor, but his watchfulness was situational: "We don't really fuck wit' southsiders," he said during the orientation. I'd entered a housing unit in the midst of growing tensions between blacks and southsiders. "If they get it crackin' over there," he said, talking about the neighboring tank on the other side of the Jack-and-Jill shower area, "we gotta get it crackin' over here." I looked around: there were only four of us and 12 southsiders. I tried to imagine Charlie and the other two guys beating up southsiders, three apiece, but I couldn't make the image work. Across the way, C-Macc was the black rep in 31B3, and there, too, blacks were outnumbered significantly by southsiders. I nodded when Charlie B told me we would have to fight in our unit if a fight started in C-Macc's unit, but really, I wanted nothing to do with that. No one did.

A few days into my time in that unit, tensions remained unchanged, and deputies offered us rec time. I was half asleep, but I heard Charlie B being turned down by the other two black residents before he tapped my bunk, and I agreed. As I got myself ready, he told me never to go to rec as the lone black resident. Always go with at least one other.

More than half the southsiders lined up for rec time with Charlie and I bringing up the rear. He must have known we would be paraded through hallways because as soon as the line got moving, he pulled his bottoms down to a comfortable sag, and he swayed his shoulders heavily, added a noticeable pause and small skip on his left stride, and pulled his right leg forward slowly like it couldn't be bent at the knee. He was pimping so hard, and when the Black vernacular style of walk was done right, a man appeared to glide effortlessly. Charlie wasn't gliding. His exaggerated stride struck me funny. He kept his head low and chucked up the peace sign with a "What's up?" nod to residents we passed along the way, communicating to anyone with the concern that jail had not robbed him of his swagger or his dignity.

I was surprised to see that the Providence rec yard was on the roof of the building. I was more surprised to learn that we were going to rec at night. The clock in the dayroom was broken, and there were no windows. I didn't know it was dark out. It had to be after 9:00 p.m. judging by the inactivity on the streets below, which we could see despite the tall gate and net to keep the balls from falling off the roof. The night air smelled so differently than the recycled metallic mildew smell in the tank, but Charlie didn't let me revel in the pseudo-freedom. He told me to follow him to one of the side courts, and he said we needed to pay attention while shooting around.

We were *bracing*—that is, we were in a *state of near sustained tension in expectation for an unknown harmful event*. It's an all-too-common state of mind in neighborhoods and places with high rates of violent crime. We barely spoke, and after about 20 minutes, the southsiders left the main court, and we took it over. I kept waiting on a fight that never came.

For some residents, *we all ride* was strictly enforced or else. Near the end of another uneventful dayroom time in Z-4, we herded up the stairs to our respective cells. At the top of the stairs, one of the new woods stood fidgeting with himself and darting his eyes here and there while standing outside Henry's cell. Henry was exceptionally pale, about 6'1" of lean muscle, and he walked strangely erect with a slight bounce, like he might break into a skip at any moment. At one point, he had an undercut of blonde hair, but he later shaved it all off. His tattoos were a mix of Nazi symbols with death scenes among other images. Most importantly, Henry was a comrade who was "wit' the business" or "with the shits," which is to say, he was a skilled fighter nearly always prepared for physical conflict.

Approaching the cell, I heard the unmistakable sound of fists dashing against flesh. The herd moved a little slower, trying to get a glimpse, but no one actually stopped to watch so as not to call unnecessary attention to the pod that something was happening—a way of "dry snitching" or indirectly informing law enforcement of misconduct.

"They don't tell me shit," D-Double complained as he realized what was happening. *Reps share these kinds of things with each other beforehand?* As I passed the cell, the DP session concluded with Henry pushing a cowering and wincing wood onto the top tier walkway. There was so much confusion in his face. I imagine that Henry delivering blows to his head must have struck him sober with a question as to how his life had come to that moment. Surely he hadn't planned that into his day.

It turned out that as the rep, Henry had explained that all woods needed to be in the dayroom during dayroom time to give the woods more numbers in the case of an interracial fight. The new wood and his celly had not taken the rule seriously. They chose to sleep; perhaps they hoped they could get through their jail time by retreating within their cell, but Henry wasn't having it, so he chose one of them for a DP.

Similarly, paisas in Z-1 tried to reject the southsider moniker, saying they were unwilling to "ride" for the southsiders who degraded them, but their resistance was summarily put down by homies given the green light to issue a series of DPs. The, ride or else, threat seemed to travel down status hierarchies more easily than it did up.

Race, Sharing, and Communication

Following the rules staved off interracial conflict, not following the rules might lead to functional violence, but no sharing across racial boundaries and minimal interracial communication put extra teeth in the pang punishment. During my earlier stint in Providence 20D1, a deputy appeared at the security gate. An anticipatory quiet fell over the conversations residents were having. "Walker!" the deputy said. "Roll up. You're being released." (I'd hit the "gov-boot" lottery! The Golden County sheriff ran a program to relieve overcrowding in accordance with a federal ruling that set the limits for how overcrowded the jails could be. Gov-boots were never guaranteed, but to be eligible you couldn't have any holds, and you couldn't have a violent charge.)

When my name was called, I hopped off my bunk with a hundred-tooth smile because let me tell you: I've dived into deep pools before I knew how to swim and nearly drowned before reaching the surface with frantic kicks and arm flailing; a street soldier from a neighborhood gang approached me with bad intentions until an OG yelled the order to stand down; I was days from eviction when a friend unexpectedly paid my whole rent. But none of those events matched the feeling of staring down the endless road of indefinite jail time and being rescued from the journey just as I was giving up hope.

I dug through my property box to get notes I'd written and snacks I'd not yet eaten. I offered the sundry leftovers—toothpaste, paper, stamps, pencils, and deodorant—to the blacks. They picked over what they wanted, and I headed to the trashcan to dump the rest.

Before I got there, I offered the twos and fews to Big Guapo, one of the high status southsiders in the unit: "Eh. You want any of this? You can have all this shit if you want it."

Big Guapo had regret in his face: "Aw, naw, Mike. I would, but I can't, ya know?"

I nodded and dumped usable creature comforts in the trash because blacks didn't want them, southsiders couldn't take them, and had there been woods in that dayroom, they, too, would have been forced to decline my offer.

Thus, no interracial sharing and minimal interracial communication might mean you watched someone throw away exactly what you needed because you were in different racial groups. Those same rules made fun less fun by restricting whom we could have fun with. If none of the blacks wanted to play dominoes, I couldn't just ask a nearby wood or southsider.

During a rec period, Z-4 top tier blacks and southsiders were in the small area. It was first come–first serve in determining whether your racial group started on the basketball court, the pull-up bar, or the handball court. We switched activities after it *felt* like 20 minutes had passed. On this day, two southsiders finished a game of one-on-one and, as they headed off the court, one complained aloud, "Well, I'm ready to play another game, but we can't play with you," pointing in our direction. It was an indirect way of asking whether an interracial game could be had.

I grumbled about the politics being stupid. TJ and LK nodded.

"Could we pick them up?" TJ asked aloud to anyone willing to answer.

LK said the southsiders wouldn't be able to play, "but ask if you want."

"Yo!" TJ blurted at Reaper who appeared to be lurking in the shade within earshot just to ensure the politics were being followed. "Can we pick them up?"

Reaper shook his head and walked away. The two southsiders left the court and headed to the pull-up bar. There would be no interracial games.

Peculiarities and Variations in the Politics

Adherence to the politics could also mean suffering unnecessary indignities because we weren't free to share with whomever we wanted, but residents often skirted the politics in large and small ways—often because it was the humane thing to do. As an example, in Z-4, there were so few of us who took prescribed medication, that deputies called top and bottom tier residents from the cells at the same time for "pill call."

Pill call was twice a day. In open units, deputies stood at the security door or gate and yelled, "Pill call!" In closed units, deputies sometimes announced the pill call, and residents hit their intercom buttons; other times, deputies called directly into the cells to see if you wanted your pills; and in other instances, deputies just popped the cell doors of the residents scheduled for medication. Standing in line for a nightly pill call, I overheard a wood complain to another that he didn't have toilet paper. He had put in several kites, but deputies hadn't delivered any. Generally, deputies gave each cell a roll on Sundays, and while residents asked for more if they needed it, deputies slow-walked responses to that request if it wasn't Sunday.

"I can't even wipe my own fuckin' ass properly," the wood grumbled.

"That's some bullshit," I said over my shoulder. It was a risky interjection, but I said it without thinking it through entirely—one of my bad habits.

"Yeah man," the wood responded in a clandestine volume. "Fuckin' rules they got here." He added that he was offered a roll by "this one Mexican" but that accepting it put him at risk for a beating by his rep. No doubt. His rep, Henry, was a white power comrade and a bit of a bully toward other woods.

I told the wood I'd see if I could get him a roll, and he nodded. I wasn't sure whether he would accept the toilet paper if I brought it to him, but I decided to try. I checked with D-Double who said with a laugh, "Nigga! I don't care give a shit about that." It was possible that he would say no, and that would be that.

Next, I checked with my celly at the time, Flip. We had a stash of toilet paper, and I couldn't unilaterally decide to give some away. "GyaaaAAaat damn!" Flip exclaimed. "Now they want mufuckas walkin' 'round here wit' shitty asses and shit? Man. Shits fucked up, man." Flip agreed to let me donate a roll to the wood.

I'd done my due diligence with the blacks, but I still couldn't be sure that offering a roll of toilet paper to the wood wouldn't get him in trouble. Ultimately, I figured if it was a problem, it would be *his* problem. *I'm trying to do a good thing*, I rationalized to myself. I carried a roll with me to the nightly pill call, risking an excited deputy asking me to explain the toilet paper or worse, labeling it "contraband." On my way back, I dropped the roll in front of the wood's cell. He nodded and mouthed "thank you" through his cell door window, but we never spoke of it.

I wasn't the only one driven by empathy to violate the politics. I listened as Dago, a new black resident in Z-4, conversed with LK near my cell. Dago explained that he had been having an earache and that a southsider gave him some aspirin. "I hope no one is mad, but I can't wait on them [deputies] all day." He had put in a kite for pain medication but hadn't heard anything about it.

Rules against interracial sharing didn't have to be about goods; nor did violating the politics have to be about helping a man to maintain human dignity. Residents sometimes violated the politics for a harmless favor. It seemed to me that every housing unit had at least one southsider who was an exceptional artist. In Z-4, a paisa tended to sit in the same spot at the end of the southsider tables, so I passed him whenever I walked to and from the phones. I started by glancing at his work and offering praise without stopping my stride, but when I saw him standing outside his cell on the top tier I asked him whether he would draw something for me. He asked me what it was, I told him, and later I met in the same spot with my crude version of what I wanted.

Someone had abandoned *A Long Walk to Freedom*, Nelson Mandela's autobiography, and I'd been reading it. I wanted the phrase "uMkhonto we Sizwe" (Spear of the Nation) and "amandla" (power) drawn in some artistic way. I thought I might get another tattoo when I got out. "I can do it, ya know," he began. "It's just some guys think they're politicians." He added that we're all the same color on inside. I asked him what he wanted for the drawing— soups were the usual trade—but he said he didn't want anything. A day or so later, during breakfast, he slipped the drawing under my cell door. It was outstanding (see Figure 3.1). Later that day, during clothing exchange, he strolled by me furtively and asked what I thought of the drawing. I told him it was better than what I'd hoped, and again, he declined any payment when I offered. Nevertheless, I dropped a few soups outside his cell door the next time I had the chance.

Despite our clandestine efforts, we were making exchanges in the day-room, and most likely, others knew of it. That we got away with interracial sharing is not totally shocking—though I would not have been surprised if he were DPed for the drawing. Absent functional violence as a coercive measure, most residents would likely ignore the politics altogether. And yet, what a resident could get away with wasn't totally random. In general, southsiders were stricter than woods who were stricter than blacks, but even that continuum was only a loose generality. Beast lent out installments of his cache of *Smooth Girl Magazine* to southsiders, woods, and blacks without prejudice. Hacksaw in Providence 16D primarily hung out with the blacks.

In fact, there were some variations in how deputies racialized bed assignments and how residents responded to those variations. While sitting in a mental health holding cell, a wood named Paul-Bunyan (we said the name fast like it was one word) revealed: "I had a Korean celly for 14 months.

Figure 3.1 Amandla! uMkhonto we Sizwe

He slept most of the time, but we got along OK." Surprised, I commented that I didn't know woods could have Asian cellies. "Well, I can't," Paul-Bunyan responded. "The rep we had had before was kinda relaxed, ya know?" He explained that when a different wood became the rep, "He rolled my celly out . . . He complained to the deps, and they rolled him." Apparently, the new wood rep was more committed to white supremacy than the rep he replaced, but the important point here is that deputies had classified an Asian American resident among the woods.

Indeed, it may have been the case that Asian American residents could opt out of being with the blacks depending upon how they answered questions during the classification interview. Some evidence to support this came when David entered the Z-4 dayroom on his way to a cell on the top tier.

He looked to be Vietnamese American to me. D-Double immediately recognized him and tried to jog Toll's memory about him. I was dismayed that a resident had been in jail, left, and returned to the same housing unit to find D-Double and Toll in the same place. As David neared his cell assignment, Herc approached him and asked, "You ride with the blacks?" I'd never seen

Herc or anyone else ask that question. David said he did, they chatted briefly, and D-Double approached with a smile and handshake. Herc's question, though, suggests that how an Asian American resident was racially classified was not a foregone conclusion. At the same time, David was heading to cell with TJ, following Chippy's transfer, so it struck me strange that Herc asked about David's allegiance. David could not very well cell with a black resident but ride with a different racial group.

An exchange following a visitation hour further complicates this issue. The Z-Pod visiting room was in the hallway, just outside the pod. It was about the size of a small pre-housing holding cell, and deputies gave us visiting hours without regard to race. On this occasion, it was me and Scott, Henry, Beast, and Insincere. We had finished our visits and were awaiting the runner to escort us back into the dayroom.

As usual, there was some light conversation—far more than there would ever be in the dayroom. It was very much like being in pre-housing. Apparently, Beast's new celly had transferred in from the Cardinal Detention Center because he had gotten into a "race riot" between southsiders and woods. Almost immediately, Insincere was excited, shadowboxing and boasting how he would have been beating on woods if he were there. There was tension after that.

Insincere's demonstration could have been taken as a threat or a challenge to Henry—a way of saying, "Here's what I would've done to your wood brothers, but I can do that now, too." Hell. I certainly took it that way. It reminded me of an interaction I'd had with Insincere weeks before after a visiting hour. He intimated to me that state prison had stricter politics with more serious consequences for violations. He said he was "unimpressed with these fools." But was he looking for a fight with Henry?

Our collective attention was pointed at Henry to see what he would do next. "Don't look at me," he said, feeling our eyes on him. "I'm not a wood. I'm a comrade." He sounded afraid to me. Was this the same Henry who had DPed a wood for not coming out for dayroom time? There he was, shying from the responsibility of white supremacy and the politics. The tension dissipated, and I'm fairly sure the "race riot" at Cardinal hadn't happened. There may have been interracial conflict, but that's a far cry from a "race riot."

I couldn't quite make sense of what Henry had said, though. I talked with D-Double about it, and he was unequivocal: "[Henry] would get his ass whooped later," he said with his usual stutter in response to me asking what would happen if Henry refused to help other woods in an interracial fight.

"You're either a wood or a southsider." In other words, there was no choosing when to adhere to the *we all ride* principle. Thankfully, I never learned what would happen in an actual race riot, but my guess is that most would avoid fighting if they could.

I should point out that the degree to which politics were instituted and enforced varied by place.[14] The politics were a nonissue in trustee pods, pre-housing holding cells, and we violated the rule against minimal interracial interaction while in the visitation room. There were other examples.

Periods of waiting in mental health holding cells usually came with lively discussions about a wide range of topics without regard to race or the politics. There were never more than four residents on any one trip to mental health, and usually there were exactly three of us—the same three: me; Paul-Bunyan, who was in a different pod; and a paisa from Z-1. Deputies had us wait in holding cells across from the booths where mental health staff held appointments. While we waited, our conversation topics jumped from our cases to developments in our respective housing units to our evaluations of the staff to our home life to news about the way the prosecutors were handling certain charges.

On one occasion, we got on the subject of gang enhancements, and a new guy, a wood, chimed in to say that deputies had tried to "put" a gang enhancement on him. I asked him how he avoided the enhancement to which he bitterly responded, "Cuz I'm not a fucking skinhead." He apparently mistook my question for an accusation, but we moved on without tension, and that was the point. It was much like being in pre-housing holding. We conversed and ate and shared food across racial boundaries.

But in no place was the emplacement of social behavior more evident than in "church." Z-Pod held church in a space called the "program room" or just "program." It was an empty box, about 20' square, with concrete benches that ran the length of the walls. Program was brightly lit, just inside the hallway to the left of pod and just before the nursing station. The door to the rec yard was across the hallway. From Z-4's top tier, you could see directly into program—especially if your cell was closer to the center of the housing unit.

When the pod announced church over the dayroom speaker, the first 10–15 residents lined up at the slider, if we were out for dayroom time, or hit our cell intercom buttons if church was offered between dayroom times. The number of attendees changed based upon who ran the pod, but there was always representation from each of the three racial groups.

In program, usually the same two Christian volunteers greeted us. They were always a bit disheveled, and their bodies bore the wounds of hard lives. Frequently, they used testimonies to tell the tale of how hard their lives once were, and I noted to myself that they never said they were doing much better. They usually began the service with prayer: heads bowed and eyes closed. I remember feeling strange about the profound situational trust that sprung from adjusting our behavior and expectations to being in church. After the opening prayer for peace, understanding, and god's presence, one of the volunteers read a scripture and connected it to something that any one of us might have been dealing with in our condition as residents. Sometimes that was enough to inspire a resident or three to share something personal. Other times we had to be prodded with a call to speak on how the scripture might apply to our lives.

Church was a remarkable experience. The same residents who walked carefully past one another in the dayroom, were in church holding hands in prayer, offering words of encouragement, nodding in support of one another, telling empathetic stories to build community, and commiserating about nightmares, terrible sleep patterns, and the girlfriends, wives, or mothers of children who purportedly made their lives unnecessarily difficult. During that sweet respite, we were not southsiders, blacks, or woods but just a group of men chatting about politics, family, jail food, and the food we craved. We laughed together without concern for "politicians."[15]

After an hour or so, a deputy escort had us line up to reenter the dayroom. We code switched reflexively: back to the politics. The turn was dramatic. I sometimes wanted to check on a man—that is, a resident—who had shared some awful news about his family or his case, but seeing them in the dayroom was like seeing strangers. Maybe it was me; maybe I was seeing them through the lens of the politics while in the dayroom, but I suppose they saw me the same way because none followed up with me. We had gone from residents to individuals and back to residents, and I couldn't find a way to reconcile those transitions. It just was what it was.

What I learned, then, was that some racial groups got along better than others depending, in part, upon the housing unit in question. In Z-4, southsiders and woods had closer ties to each other than with black residents. The closer the association, the more likely were violations of the politics between the membership bodies. When Chris, a white power comrade, joined Z-4, his apparently higher level of commitment to white supremacy caused tension with Henry. Going back in the dayroom, there were other matters.

As was common during dayroom time, the black and wood showers were unoccupied while there was a line for the two southsider showers—there being so many more southsiders than woods and blacks in Z-4. Cutting lines to the showers or the phones (for that matter) was generally prohibited—even for high-ranking southsiders. Tiny figured he would get around the rule by asking Henry for permission to use the wood shower. I have to assume that Tiny first got permission from Beast, but either way, it would have been unconscionable for a wood or southsider to request use of the black shower in Z-4. Henry gave the OK, and Chris immediately protested—loudly. Henry tried to offer a rationalization, but Chris wasn't OK with the decision at all. He stomped off, barking over his shoulder at Henry, "This is bullshit!"

I viewed that event as one that revealed something important about the potential for mass interracial conflict. Because members of different racial groups could be dragged into an interpersonal conflict between just two residents, the threat of large-scale violence was widespread but not evenly distributed. That Hacksaw, a wood, enjoyed the company of black residents over southsiders was an anomaly. And remember that young black resident who had earned a red tag in court holding cells for fighting? He claimed his carryover beef from YA was with a southsider. I didn't ask him whether he and the southsider were alone in the cell when he launched his attack, but it's hard to imagine news of that fight not spreading throughout the jail news network (JNN).[16] That it apparently didn't spread was a major aberration from what would have been expected. In general, southsiders and woods tended to have a stronger relationship than either had with the blacks.

Before Chris threw a fit about Tiny using a wood shower, there had been a history of positive associations between southsiders and woods. That it didn't may have been a matter of luck, but Still, *that* skirmish didn't erupt into mass interracial violence,[17] either.

Southsiders and woods were far more likely to maintain alliance—however tenuous it might have been. In Z-4, southsiders and woods had a nightly call-and-response solidarity ritual[18] that went like this:

SOUTHSIDER CALLER: "Homies, sure ños, y paisas, ye todo, Buenas noches!"
SOUTHSIDER RESPONSE: "Buenos noches!"
SOUTHSIDER CALLER: "Gracias!"
SOUTHSIDER RESPONSE: "A ti!"
SOUTHSIDER CALLER: "And to the woodpile and the comrades, goodnight!"
WOODS: "Good night!"

SOUTHSIDER CALLER: "Thank you!"
WOOD CALLER: "Thank you! Woodpile; comrades; good night!"
WOOD RESPONSE: "Good night!"
WOOD CALLER: "Thank you!"
WOOD RESPONSE: "Thank you!"
WOOD CALLER: "And to the homies, the paisas, Buenos noches!"
SOUTHSIDER RESPONSE: "Buenos noches!"
WOOD CALLER: "Gracias!"
SOUTHSIDER RESPONSE: "A ti!"

There was no such call for black residents, and neither the woods nor the southsiders acknowledged us.

I asked around about why we didn't have a unity call. Herc and D-Double said there used to be one, but neither could say exactly why the ritual had stopped. Herc implied that no one wanted to lead it, so it just died off. After I pressed a bit, he agreed to write the call-and-response down for me:

BLACK CALLER: "Africans, keeways, damus, others, and nonaffiliates, asante!"
BLACK RESPONSE: "Much respect!"

The words "keeway," "damu," and "asante" are Swahili. "Keeway" has come to mean "crip" in English, referencing the crip gang, and it may be an English interpretation of "kiwete," which means "crippled." "Damu" and "asante" are straight translations: "blood" and "thank you," respectively. So, had we been doing it, the call would have been a shout out to crips, bloods, other gangs, and non-gang-affiliated Black people.

That nightly call and response was a serious matter. For whatever reasons, some deputies really disliked the "good night" calls, and they often threatened to put us on lockdown if the calls didn't stop. Some deputies made preemptive threats: "No chants . . . if you chant, I will leave the lights on all night." That was hardly a threat. The lights in the cells stayed on all night, so no one cared whether the dayroom lights were on.

One deputy in particular seemed to feel personally offended by the chant: "Stop yelling!" No one listened, and we could hear the chant coming from Z-1 to Z-2 to Z-3, so the deputy repeated himself but with beg in his voice: "Gentlemen. Stop yelling." When it was time for Z-4, he announced something about a last warning, but woods and southsiders gave their good night call loudly and without pause.

Each night, I took those calls as reason to keep bracing because it was possible that southsiders or woods would jump in a fight to support the other against blacks. I couldn't use the unity calls as evidence of a strict alliance against blacks, but like so many other matters in jail, the threat was enough to shape emotions and behaviors.

Other peculiarities in the politics were less threatening but more jarring—rendered less disorienting through repetition alone, but they never made sense. Visitation meant going from politics to relaxed politics to politics again. In the dayroom, we walked along racialized paths, stuck to our racialized tables, used race-specific phones and showers, stole moments of interracial interaction, and when the call came, we lined up to go without thinking about race. After our visits, we relaxed the politics to near insignificance. Then we returned to the politics as we reentered the dayroom.

Solutioning

All the variations and peculiarities in the politics—the fact that deputies didn't always institute the rep system—it all felt like nonsense to me. I wasn't alone. The reps performed their role, but with few exceptions—Reaper, Henry, and Chris come to mind—I only ever met residents who thought the politics made life unnecessarily hard. Deputies instituted and sustained the rep system with the dubious argument that they were solving a potential problem. And yet, by managing residents through the rep system, they created the problems that they claimed to be addressing. This is what *solutioning* looks like: solve a problem you created in a self-congratulatory way. That way, you muddle the relationship between your solution and your problem and give yourself justification to continue with your circular reasoning.

Standing at the fingerprinting machine on Providence's production line, a deputy gave me a response that summarized administrative thinking on the matters of race, the politics, and punishment. I baited him by making a complaint about the jail's use of racial classification. "These rules don't work in the world, but they work in here," he said. I wondered who he thought the rules worked for.

Even more direct, I used to visit with Nurse Bee, a Sunland Detention Center mental health nurse. During one of our meetings, I told her I was stressing out, trying not to violate the politics. I told her the politics did more harm than good. "Well, I read in the Golden Press," she started, "I think not too long ago that people were blaming the jail for segregating inmates. Don't they know they'd be killing each if they weren't kept apart?"

Tell me: What can anyone do in the face of such obviously untrue thinking?

Sensory Deprivation

Yesterday I received a letter with a woman's perfume on it. I can't stop smelling it. When I close my eyes, the fragrance sends me to bodies intertwined, interlocked fingers, ear whispers about the feeling, candlelight shadows dancing on a far wall, and the buildup of pressure.

The image dissipates as quickly as the perfume generates it, and I'm on my bunk under relentless lights in a sweaty, fart-smelling cell with Flip.

I wish I had a window to see outside. Professor Ward sent me pictures of leaves and of sunlight breaking through a tree line. I miss the diversity of natural colors.

4

Deputies

One of my initial interests in jail was to learn why a person might choose to work custody. In California, sheriff's deputies have custodial responsibilities in jails, but whether deputies are required to work custody before patrol depends upon the county. The Archway County sheriff, for example, permits deputies to work custody or patrol depending upon what's available. Golden County deputies, however, were required to work custody before getting a patrol assignment. As a result, for some deputies, managing jail residents was a mere stepping-stone to a preferred job assignment. I learned that long after I was released, and looking back, my understanding of how deputies treated residents is colored by the knowledge that some deputies likely didn't want to work custody at all.

My usual curiosity led me to ask deputies about their decision to do that work, and the most common answers had nothing to do with an abiding commitment to law and order or some similar disposition. A deputy would be escorting me to or from a mental health visit, standing watch during the pill call, guarding while I visited with a nurse, and I always asked some version of the same question: "What made you become a deputy?" A physically fit and even-tempered deputy at the Providence fingerprinting station explained that his sister went to take "the test" to become a deputy, "and I just went along with her. I passed all the tests," he said with a shrug. At the time, I didn't have an expectation as to his response. I half thought I wouldn't get a response at all, but if there is an expectation that more forethought than "I passed all the tests" goes into becoming a deputy, you may be in for disappointment.

A nearby deputy, obsequious in his manner, found his opening: "Yeah, sir. And there were a lot of tests, too."

This was the most common response to me asking deputies their motives for doing the job: a set of unambitious incidences resulted in someone passing tests and being offered a job in law enforcement. Deputy Brown in Sunland, who I had quite a few interactions with, was most forthright: "Honestly, I just kept passing the tests," he said with a laugh. "I don't really have a reason."

Deputy Burke was the only Black woman deputy I ever saw. When I asked her why she decided to become a deputy, she explained, "Well, my parents wanted me to become a lawyer, and I rebelled." She said she took both the exam to be a probation officer and the exam to be a sheriff's deputy but that the latter called back first.

Deputy Rodriguez had a similar story. She said she had taken time away from school and ended up taking the test to be a probation officer. While waiting to hear back about that, she passed the exam to be a sheriff's deputy. The sheriff's office was quicker on the draw, so she became a deputy.

In some ways, these answers are unsurprising. My mother retired from the United States Army after 22 years of service, and when I asked her if she thought people joined the military from a sense of patriotism, she said, "Hell no! I mean, I'm sure there's a small percentage—'I wanna serve my country.' I wouldn't say it's 50%; I'd say maybe 20%. It depends on who's in office— who's the president and if it's wartime." She said none of her friends and most of the soldiers she met didn't join because they felt a duty to do so. I asked her why she joined when she did—in 1973—and she said she was 18 and that a girlfriend convinced her that the military would be an adventure they could share. She added, "That's not how they sell the military: 'Come save your country.' It's just a bunch of kids, they're poor, and they want a better life. Recruiters sell the benefits not the idea of serving your country. You know you could fight 'cause no matter what your MOS [(military occupational specialty)], they could put a gun in your hand 'cause you're infantry if needed."

What strikes me about my mom's perception of most peoples' motives for joining the military and what some deputies gave as their reasons for joining law enforcement are the similarities in decision-making. Popular culture would have us believe that law enforcement and military service are callings, and perhaps they are for some, but they're also jobs with income and benefits. Interestingly, many Golden County deputies were ex-military personnel. I suspected as much by the militaristic demeanor that some deputies carried, but a Providence deputy told me plainly that most were ex-military, and while awaiting a court liaison in Sunland, I overheard two deputies commiserating on their military background: "Yeah man. All but like one or two deputies was [sic] in the Armed Forces."

I think it's edifying to imagine a person at home after completing a few years of military service, finding themselves not in school or on a preferred career path, and faced with the question, "Now what?" Several of my friends became excellent teachers because teaching answered that question for them.

One of my cousins passed all sorts of city and county exams, and he hoped to be a fireman or to work in waste management. In the end, he became a correctional officer. To whatever extent my friends and family have come to view their careers as callings, many started out with the basic need for income. My point is that deputies were no different.[1] They were people working jobs—not necessarily their callings—and it's worth keeping that in mind as I describe some of the events that typified deputy–resident relations.

Code Switching

You may be wondering how I got deputies to talk to me, because I was, after all, a penal resident. When I was 10, my brother and I lived with my grandmother for a year while my mother did her first tour of Army service in South Korea. About a week before my mother was to leave, we piled into my mom's white Pontiac Trans-Am, our "Knight Rider," and drove from El Paso, Texas, to Los Angeles. When we pulled into my grandmother's driveway a day or so later, the first thing she said to me was, "Hug my neck." Then she held my face and said, "Michael. You don't be cussin' like these lil' foul mouthed kids I see runnin' 'round here, do you?"

I put on my most serious 10-year-old face for a lie: "Grandmother, I don't cuss."

"I knew my number one grandson didn't cuss," she said with genuine happiness.

I wasn't particularly good at it, but I used profanity just like every other kid my age—not in front of my mother, grandmother, or grandfather, though. When in the presence of any adult, really, I automatically code switched to a diction appropriate for a respectful child speaking to or within earshot of an adult, and I never slipped.

I didn't have the same reverence for deputies that I did for my mother, but I code switched to speak with them, just the same. In fact, my experience in trying to engage deputies in conversation taught me several tricks. The first thing I learned was that deputies were more likely to chat if there were no more than four residents around. This seemed to me a practical matter. The more residents there were, the more vigilant a deputy needed to be, so a conversation could be distracting. Through trial and error, I learned that more than four residents tended to put deputies into no-mode. A deputy would just stare forward without acknowledging whatever I'd said, or they instructed me to be quiet. In general, the fewer the residents around, the more in-depth the conversation could be.

Also, I didn't try to force myself upon deputies. I struck up a conversation when they had no choice but to be near me instead of seeking them out for an unwanted interaction. I'd tried to make random or what I thought to be insightful observations to get deputies to react, but I failed more than I was successful, so I landed on asking them why they chose the job, because I wanted to know, but it also gave them an opportunity to talk about themselves and that seemed to catch deputies off guard. It was undoubtedly better than asking for a favor or a service of any kind.

Finally, I affected a diction commensurate with the year of graduate school training that I had at the time. The signals were subtle but impactful. I would say "in order to" instead of "because" or just "to." I sprinkled in words like "structure" and "process," and I avoided almost all slang. In short, I spoke as if I were giving an academic talk, mixing in a lot of abstract terms that give the sense that something smart is being said. That wasn't my normal way of speaking—not around residents. There is a strange misconception born of ignorance, wishful thinking, and/or a fanciful understanding of life in Black communities that there is no room for the gangbanger, the college-bound person, the hustler, the parent, the hooper, and the 9-to-5 worker to be in the same communities interacting.[2] That simply isn't true. In some cases, one person might embody all or several of these types of people, but the point is that I didn't need to be anything less than what I was while talking with residents. I could mix California slang with my standard use of African American Vernacular English with college-educated phrases without worrying that I'd be rejected.

But as a penal resident, I had more to overcome if I wanted to converse with deputies. Keep in mind that I'm a 6'4" Black man, not skinny, and at the time, my beard, mustache, and receding hair were growing wildly. Also, I've been told that the shape of my eyebrows gives others the sense that I'm angry when I'm really just concentrating or squinting because of a bright light. Now dress me up in county oranges. I knew that I might live as the "criminalblackman"[3] in the minds of deputies, so I figured expensive-sounding diction would shock them out of no-mode and permit them to hear Michael—not just an orange. And to the sprinkles of graduate school vernacular, I added a smile and soft shoulders to appear less threatening. More than a few times, deputies turned to me as if to say, "Who is this guy speaking like this?" When I saw that look, I knew I'd hit my mark.

In one conversation, a deputy told me he preferred custody to patrol because the former was "calmer." We shared a few exchanges about military service, and then he observed: "You're obviously a smart guy—not like every other knucklehead in here. Why are you here?"

His question likely came from a genuine place because I presented differently from other residents he had spoken with or observed, but I hated that question because my experience taught me that the answer didn't matter. I still don't know what anyone expects from a question like that. It reminded me of why I was starting to understand jail and custodial deputies as analogs for slums and slumlords.[4] The general circumstances were hairs from the same beast. In both communities, the poorest and most sociopolitically defenseless subpopulations reside in deplorable living conditions, under the control of people who have found some way to justify imposing those conditions. Both subpopulations become inextricable from the places in which they are trapped. Both are pathologized as social objects. For, in free society and the penal slums of jails, the subpopulations are thought to be justifiably there, having both constituted the slum and being constitutive of it. And that question, it felt to me, was akin to asking why I lived in a slum. I had to give him a response. "I'm here for the same reason any so-called 'smart' person would be: I made poor decisions." I've settled on that response for quite a while now.

"Yeah, but you're guilty—your charges—did you do it?"

He said that in declarative form with a question mark at the end. Honestly, I wasn't ready for that. Until that point, I saw us as two men walking down a hallway having an adult conversation, but his question reminded me of my unkempt hair—that I'd been doing push-ups, that I was wearing a county jail uniform, and that I had several inches of height over him. What I mean is that I felt hyper aware of myself in that moment. "I'm certainly guilty of poor decision making, but the charges don't reflect the circumstances," I said. I've settled on that response for a while now, too.

"Hmm."

Obviously, code switching had its limits. I had a similar experience with Deputy Brown. He was slender, White, and in his mid-20s. He often escorted me to and from mental health visits and visiting hours, so we chatted and developed something of a mutually respectful rapport. At some point, he started calling me "the writer" because I'd told him that I was writing down what I saw in jail. We typically had lighthearted exchanges, so I expected nothing less when I hit my cell intercom button and discovered he was working the pod that day. "Did you say hit the button if you want some music?" I asked. No one had made that announcement, but I figured I'd ask for music in a somewhat clever way.

"Oh. The writer," Deputy Brown said. He chuckled and suggested that I buy him an iPod so he could play music for us. I told him I'd work on it. "I see all the money on your books," he said. "I see y'all laughing and having a good time." (Parenthetically, I rarely had more than $40 in my commissary account at any time, and sometimes, I had nothing.)

"Laughing to keep from crying," Scott said.

"Yeah. We're stressing in here," I added.

"You guys are taken care of," Deputy Brown said. Then he thought it funny, I suppose, to say, "I wish I were in here sometimes."

"Man, I have a son, a car note, credit card bills. I did have a life before I came here—"

"What the fuck could you do with a credit card?" Deputy Brown asked with a laugh. "You're already a criminal!"

I'd never been called a "criminal" outright like that. Like I said, code switching had its limits. But I think it's telling that for Deputy Brown, my being in jail—that is, being a "criminal"—was incongruous with having credit or paying bills or being an active father. It's hard to imagine "the criminal" having prosocial behaviors or positively contributing to society. Later that day, Deputy Brown chimed into our cell: "Walker . . . you have a visit, my man." When I met him at the sally port, he greeted me with a smile: "The book writer."

"Yeah," I said with a holdover of bitterness from our earlier exchange. I suppose he got over the emotional whiplash of calling me a criminal quicker than I did.

A few days later, he was working Z-Pod again, and it was the night pill call. He asked me if I'd gotten a lot of writing done. At that point, it was annoying to be asked about writing every time I saw him. Obviously, it was his way of connecting with me, but I saw him differently after he called me a criminal, and I didn't want to chit chat about my writing. I told him I'd gotten some writing done, and the nurse suggested that I write about how nice the nursing staff was. I said something about the nurses being the best staff in jail to which Deputy Brown threw up his hands as if to ask, "What about us?"

"In general," I said, "y'all seem to forget that we're humans."

He mumbled something in response and seemed disappointed.

Typing Deputies

Despite my feelings being hurt in the interactions described above, I thought of Deputy Brown and that older Black deputy as "cool deps." There was a lot of talk from residents about "cool" and "asshole deps." The line demarcating the two was situationally thin. In most cases, cool deps met the standard by referring to residents as "gentlemen" when declining a request for creature comforts like commissary slips or by answering a question about the mail or by permitting sufficient dayroom time for us to shower. It didn't take much. Asshole deps, by contrast, might still use a formal greeting in addressing you and declining your request, but encounters with asshole deps meant being treated with condescension that shaded into cruelty when deputies felt like it.

Distinguishing between cool deps and asshole deps was rarely a productive enterprise—at least, not for me—though I certainly understood the value of the characterizations. We have a series of interactions with a particular tone over time that becomes patterned and regular enough to build expectations for how things will go. We act on the expectations preemptively because the history of our interactions inform how we feel and what we do. These expectations can give the illusion that *your* interactions with a person or group represent *the* way that person or group essentially is.

This is partly how we come to objectify others, and we experience these misapprehensions all the time in our romantic relationships. Your partner mistreats you, and the longer that goes on, the more likely you are to conclude that your partner is a bad person. But then you notice that they bend over backward for others, so you can see that your partner is capable of treating you better, but that's not the pattern of your relationship. It can take incredible forces to break you two from the gravity of your interactions. So it was with some deputies. At the extremes, the cool and asshole deps could be relied upon to embody those characterizations, but there were plenty of deputies who exhibited cool behavior at time one and were the assholes at time two.

Still, residents used the characterizations like tags to explain the likelihood of a deputy doing or not doing a thing and to explain why a deputy did or didn't do a thing. Tactlessness was, perhaps, the baseline character of deputy–resident interactions, but sometimes deputies were noticeably kind or exceptionally cruel. In either instance, we let the tags "cool" or "asshole" stand in as a shorthand for the treatment, which circumvented the need to discover a deputy's motives. Did we know whether deputies hated us—whether they took pleasure in our suffering? Did they tell us that they had forgotten—through routine or by some other factor—that we are people? Barring an admission on those matters, we couldn't be sure of the internal interests of any deputy, but we were confident in the generous, unprovoked hostilities and vitriol that some deputies heaped upon us—that some smiled and found humor in the indignity of dressing us in filthy clothes or getting around to clogged toilets eventually. We knew they referred to us as "oranges," "assholes," "court bodies," and "gentlemen" with equal meaning and that their term for our breakfast, lunch, and dinner was "feed." We also knew that some deputies seemed aware that we were already in jail, so there was no need in worsening our circumstances—even if only because doing so required more effort on their part. We didn't know with certainty the innerworkings of deputy minds, but we knew their behaviors, and it was on that basis that we labeled some "assholes" and some "cool."

"Asshole" Behaviors

There was a wide range of behaviors a deputy might exhibit to be called an "asshole," but really, the label applied to any contempt deputies showed residents. That included appeals to the mythical other, polite indifference, and no-mode responses to resident needs.

One of my earliest experiences with contemptuous behavior from deputies came during my first opportunity to submit a commissary order in Sunland. Residents were in the dayroom filling in commissary slips, and I had no idea how they got out. I was searching for something that obviously linked the ones who were in the dayroom. They weren't all black residents. They weren't all from the top tier. *Did they put in a request to put in a request earlier? How does this shit work?* Time was passing, and some residents were already returning to their cells after having submitted their requests. I anxiously hit my cell intercom button and walked away from it as if the voice on the other side might come get me. "What's your emergency?" the deputy asked. I stumbled through an unformed question about how to get and submit commissary slips. She didn't respond, and time was passing. There were only a few residents left in the dayroom, and I was scared that I was about to miss my chance to order food. I'd been so damned hungry relying on jail-issued meals, so I hit the intercom button again. "What?" the deputy asked with a bitterness that made me regret hitting my button.

"When would I turn in my commissary sheet?" I asked meekly.

"Uh, now," she said sarcastically.

"How would I do that when I'm locked in here?"

She didn't respond. She just popped my cell door, and I felt such relief and confusion as to why she seemed bothered by me wanting to place a commissary order on the day and time that orders were being submitted.

Later, but still early in my time in Sunland, I was laying on my bunk while Flip paced as he normally did. He had his back to the cell door when I noted in a low, conversational tone, "The deputy just passed. He only looked at the lights." We had covered the cell lights to dim the cell and ease the difficulty of sleeping under constant artificial light. It was a nightly effort, and deputies didn't always permit us to do it.

Well, the deputy heard me! He backed up to our cell door window: "What? What'd you say?" I knew the look and that kind of conflict energy. He was hoping for some action—for a reason to escalate the situation. In nearly every fight I'd been in or seen, there was a "What? Whatchu say?" moment. The strange thing was, normally we had to yell to get a runner to hear us, but that guy heard my voice after he passed our cell.

I didn't want a problem with any deputy—let alone one wishing for a problem, but before I could say anything, Flip interjected with a *please don't hit me, sir* tone: "*I* didn't say anything." The deputy stood there waiting on my response. I told him what I'd said, and he stood there for a long stare. He appeared to be trying to come to a decision about whether to push the action or simply move on, but I wasn't going to give him a reason to be hostile. I stayed still on my bunk as if in the presence of a grizzly bear. After what felt like an entire minute of staring, he left.

Flip and I looked at each other, acknowledging that we had dodged a bullet. Then he told me a story that he would eventually retell a few more times during our time together. It was the end of dayroom time, and the pod flashed the dayroom lights to signal that residents should head to the cells. Normally, residents waited until the end of dayroom time to line up for hot water, so that it would be hot when they got to their cells. On this day, Flip and his previous celly were the last in line, and so they were the last inside their cell. Just as they closed the door, Flip explained, the pod ordered them to the sally port and then put them "in program." After a little while, "About eight deps came! We thought we were gonna be chicken-wanged [sic], for sho,'" Flip said with a laugh.

Sunland was known as "chicken wing central." The "chicken wing" was a maneuver in which deputies forced your arms backward so that the backs of your hands were flat against the center of your back and your elbows bent outward like wings. The move sent you to the tips of your toes in pain.

One deputy, who Flip used to call "Herman Munster," asked, "What do you think it means when I flash the lights?"

Flip and his celly said they hadn't seen the lights and that, "Normally, you give us five minutes before lockdown, so we can get water." Now, obviously, they saw the lights. That's why they lined up for hot water, but I would have given a similar response to that question if I were Flip.

"I don't have to do nothing! I'm the boss," Flip mimicked the deputy. " 'I'm the boss!' That's what he said."

I sat on my bunk wide-eyed. He said the deputies made them apologize and then left them in the program room "from 10:00 p.m. to 2:00 a.m." During that time, he said, they decided to pray. At some point, deputies threw two Bibles on the floor outside the program room door. Flip said the deputies wanted to be seen doing it. Apparently, deputies had retrieved the Bibles from Flip's cell. When deputies finally opened the door to escort Flip and his celly back into the dayroom, Flip said they were told they couldn't have their Bibles back and then the deputies chucked them into a nearby trashcan. The story sounded crazy to me, but the story never changed, Flip didn't have a Bible, despite requesting one nearly every other day. I'd seen deputies do unnecessarily mean things, and while I was able to confirm with others that they had seen Flip and a previous celly in program, none of the black residents remembered why—though none thought the story implausible.

It wasn't always what deputies did; sometimes it was what they didn't do. Early one morning, the toilet in my cell backed up. I told the runner, who laughed and made a smart remark, but he said he would put in a maintenance request. The entire day passed with Flip and me in that tiny cell. The toilet water was connected to the sink water, and we couldn't run the sink water without spilling some onto the floor. As the day progressed, we asked deputies for help, and finally, around 2:30 a.m., I stopped the runner during his security check. "It's kind of a bad time," he said. "We gotta take care of court." I asked for something to clean up with—maybe the mop we normally used for the dayroom on Sundays. He said he couldn't do it right then. The smell of urine and feces filled our cell for another day.

It was common for deputies to tolerate that kind of neglect. As another example, commissary orders were delivered on Tuesdays and Thursdays between 7:00 p.m. and 8:30 p.m., but one night the pod announced, "For some reason, commissary has been canceled." We groaned our complaints. "Personally, I don't think you should get commissary," the deputy added. We generally read such unnecessarily mean comments as "asshole" behavior and moved on.

"Remember, gentlemen: Stay in school," a muscular Black deputy with a booming voice said to us as we reentered the dayroom to see how malicious and spiteful deputies had been in "tossing" (searching) our cells for contraband. He was mighty pleased with himself, and he won a few chuckles from his colleagues with that remark. Ours was a collective shrug and a series of looks to communicate that we recognized the deputy's comment for what it was. But while our ability to endure breakdowns in facilities management waxed and waned—while we chalked up willful neglect and polite indifference as typical asshole behavior, it was much harder to endure jail when deputies went out of their way to be mean and vindictive.

Few deputies had more contempt for penal residents than Sunland's "Deputy Dog." He might have been in his 30s or 40s. His pudgy stomach protruded farther than his underdeveloped pectoral muscles. He wore glasses that didn't sit right on his face, and he was as angry as he was dimwitted, surviving the tasks of his job, it seemed, by being slavishly devoted to enforcing any rule he was given. We had a love–hate relationship with him, and we openly mocked him whenever we saw him. "DEP-YU-DEE Dog!" we would yell out whenever he entered the dayroom. He was reliably mean as hell, and I sometimes wondered whether it was his love or hatred for the job that made him so angry all the time—maybe it was that we mocked him.

I remember when I first encountered him. It was the smile in resident voices as they yelled out "DEP-YU-DEE DOG is here! Deputy Dog!" Flip ran to our cell door window to see Deputy Dog make his way around the dayroom as the runner. I asked why he was called that, and Flip said he was like the character Barney Fife but much meaner.

"Look at'em! Ha! Ha," Flip said with a laugh. "Don't he just look like he should be Deputy Dog? Deputy Dog is on the scene! He's on the case!"

I laughed at how happy Flip and others were to see Deputy Dog. I didn't quite get the nickname, but nearly everyone—residents and deputies alike—were known by a nickname, and usually (but not always) the nickname highlighted a quality or habit that could make you the butt of jokes. Some entered jail with a nickname from the streets: D-Double, Toll, Herc, Havocc, Tiny, Big Guapo, Beast, and Reaper are examples. Others earned a nickname in jail. "Flip" had been given his nickname by D-Double and Toll. Apparently, Flip's mood changed dramatically, and he was said to "flip out" over inconsequential matters. I was called "Mike" as often as I was called "Egypt." The latter was a reference to my tattoo of Egyptian hieroglyphics on my neck.

I learned I'd been given that name within days of being in Sunland. I was standing on the top tier, and I heard a voice calling "Egypt! Egypt!" I didn't know the name, so I ignored it at first, but I kept hearing the voice call the name, so I looked around, and I saw Beast standing at the bottom tier calling up to me. I didn't question my nickname, and I accepted "Deputy Dog" as his name, too.

Usually, Deputy Dog was accompanied by a deputy we called KGB because he had an accent that someone had decided was Russian. It didn't sound Russian to me, but I went with it. If KGB wasn't there, then it was a deputy we called "Marine" because he kept a high and tight haircut and spoke with a choppy military cadence. Whoever was with him, when Deputy Dog was on the scene, we knew we were in for laughs and disrespect.

Deputy Dog was never the pod primary. We used to joke that his superiors didn't trust him with the controls. As the runner, he was one of those who enjoyed kicking our cell doors and yelling at us about our lights or doing push-ups or whatever else. But he truly shined with "asshole behavior" during biweekly clothing exchanges. On Wednesdays, we could exchange razors and whites (shirts, socks, and boxers). On Sundays, we could exchange razors, whites (including sheets and towels), and our oranges. As was often the case, Z-Pod residents were offered scraps of clothes—the least well-cleaned and most ill-fitting of the clothing bins. On one occasion, I was in line with Scott, plotting our move if we couldn't get clean or properly fitting boxers when Marine raised his voice: "Why don't you speak English?" At first, we weren't sure whether he was serious. His face was stern, but the question was ridiculous, so we waited for more information. "Why don't you speak English?" he repeated. He was yelling at a confused, heavy-set paisa with badly bowed legs. "Say George Bush one time! Say George Bush!" The dayroom was silent, as we all stared to see what would happen next. There was nothing. Marine chuckled to himself and permitted the paisa to get a new shirt and boxers.

"Asshole," Scott murmured to me.

During a different Wednesday clothing exchange, Deputy Dog had KGB with him. They entered the dayroom and stood behind the trustees manning the clothing bins. Each bin had different clothing items, but for some reason, KGB told us that we needed to say aloud what we were exchanging instead of just moving along from bin-to-bin in near silence the way we usually did. The lined moved along, and as usual, Deputy Dog sniffed out an issue. He barked at a paisa: "Where's your wristband?" We were supposed to wear our identification wristbands at all times and especially while interacting with deputies, but most residents hated their wristbands, and many found ways to slide theirs off and on at will.

A black resident we nicknamed "the Minister" constantly forgot to put his on, and when I suggested he just keep it on to keep from being yelled at for not having it, he was offended: "I'm not an animal."

In this case, as was his wont, Deputy Dog was waiting on an answer. "He doesn't speak English," a southsider behind the paisa spoke up.

"Where the fuck is your wristband?" Deputy Dog persisted.

The paisa threw his hands up, and Deputy Dog miserly gave him a pair of boxers. At that same moment, the paisa must have realized what Deputy Dog was referring to because with boxers in hand, he gestured that he had left his wristband in his cell. Then he tried to move on to the next bin.

"Did you hear him?" KGB said, stopping the paisa who nodded. "Then don't walk away! You answer him when he's talking to you."

Not one to be outdone, Deputy Dog said of the paisa's wristband, "You forgot it? Maybe we should forget to fuckin' feed you for two days!" The paisa moved on, and a few residents later, LK tried to do an exchange without his wristband. "No!" Deputy Dog yelled. "No wristband. You ain't gettin' shit!"

LK had his hands in supplication, saying "C'mon man. I need—"

"You don't have your wristband? You ain't gettin' a fuckin' thing. It's the fuckin' rules!"

Here's another *rule* according to the "Inmate Orientation" document we had been given: "You have the right to expect that as a human being, you will be treated respectfully, impartially and fairly by all personnel." That, there, is a slippery "right." The word "expect" does a lot of work. Our right was to expectation—not result. But with Deputy Dog, KGB, and Marine, we learned to expect disrespect. It was all germane to jail time—not that it needed to be, but it was.

"Cool" Behaviors

Earlier, I recounted a senior deputy's explanation for why he became a deputy and the nearby junior deputy's eagerness to jump in with his two cents on the matter. Our conversation extended beyond how they came to be deputies, and I felt a strange sense of accomplishment—like I was fortunate that they would speak with me like a person instead of a criminal object.

As the conversation died down but still felt successful, I told the senior deputy that a couple of guys had been skipped over for meals, and I pointed them out. He responded by telling me his shift was ending, which I took to mean that he was about to leave and that a mythical other would have to feed whoever had been skipped. Instead, I saw him get meals for the two guys before leaving. On the one hand, it was basic benevolence to feed someone; after all, his job was to care for us. On the other hand, it was an extraordinary kindness, and he could have left without feeding those two residents. He leaned into care instead of punishment. That was the mark of "cool" behavior.

We tended to see the same deputies over and over. Deputy Brown once explained to me that deputies didn't know where they would work until the start of their shifts. "They choose for us," he said. But given how frequently we saw the same deputies, it seemed to me that an administrator took the shortcut of reassigning deputies to units in which they had previously worked. Consequently, residents learned to identify the "cool" and the "asshole" deps. We knew we were in for a hard work shift when an "asshole dep" was the pod primary, but "cool deps" established something of a contract for mutual cooperation, and the reps enforced our side of the agreement.

"Chill. They gon' take away the extra dayroom," D-Double said in response to Scott and Lee playfighting during a cool dep's shift.

In general, cool deps gave us extra dayroom time in exchange for residents keeping their requests to a skeletal minimum and refraining from activities that might force deputies to intervene. In open units, cool deps kept the phones, television, and hot water on longer than most other deputies. In closed units, we were rewarded with plenty of dayroom time.

But the main difference between more caring and more contemptuous deputies was how vigorously they enforced mundane rules that made life harder for residents. In their pure types, cool behavior was diametric to asshole behavior. With a cool runner and pod primary, we knew the mail would be delivered and done so in a way that respected us. We knew outgoing mail would be collected. You could stop the runner to pass a kite. They just had more patience—even for somewhat frivolous matters. With a cool dep at the helm, I decided to hit my cell intercom button because, why not? A deputy respectfully asked how he could help me. "It occurred to me that when I signed my deal," I began, "I was told I'd get a gov-boot." I was being a bit insincere.

I knew deputies didn't control who got a "gov-boot." If I'm being honest, I was just bothering the pod to have any kind of interaction other than what I normally had with my celly. "That was two months ago. Where's my gov-boot?"

The deputy responded with such even-handedness that I was taken aback. He said he didn't have any knowledge of how the program worked—a damned lie—and that gov-boots "are handled by the business office." That was true. He said, "This pod is pretty full, so maybe soon." That's it. That's all it took for me to think of him as a "cool dep." He answered a question faithfully. This is why I thought of Deputy Brown as a cool one. He answered my questions—a lot of questions, in fact, and I suppose that's why he felt safe bagging on me by calling me a criminal. Had we been friends, I might have read that differently, but I wasn't his friend any more than he was mine. We had a rapport that mostly stayed decent, and that was that.

There was, however, a deputy in Sunland who regularly worked Z-Pod and who was consistently nice to everyone—uncomfortably so. We normally knew deputies by their surnames, but we knew Araceli by her first name. Latina, about 5'1" with her boots on, she always wore red lipstick and she sometimes wore her dark curly hair down instead of in a ponytail. I first met her as my escort from a mental health visit. I said something about the way some deputies mistreated us, and she responded: "I can be fair, and I can be a bitch." In the dayroom, I never saw her be anything but cool. She was always the runner, and she made it a point to greet residents and exchange pleasantries, insisting that we call her by her first name. I never saw her angry or even annoyed with us. There was a time when some southsiders got into trouble, and her male counterpart took the lead in angrily tossing cells while she shook her head and poked out her bottom lip with loving disappointment. It was—weird.

Beast used to say, "She's at the zoo," and we're "her favorite animals."

One night when the pod cut the lights off, Araceli got on the intercom, affected a sultry voice, and said: "OK boys. It's time for nighty-nighttime."

That earned howls and whistles, and whenever she came up in conversation, the discussion started and ended with an obligatorily blunt question and answer: "Did you see Araceli? I'd fuck." I never saw anyone make openly sexual overtures toward her, but it's hard to imagine that no one did. We had all heard stories of correctional officers having sex with prison residents. But more in line with Beast's evaluation of her, I just didn't trust Araceli. I was put off by the strangeness of her behavior toward us even while appreciating that she was always cool.

The coolest behavior I experienced from custodial deputies, though, was when they played music. I first heard Lil Wayne's "Lollipop" while in jail. I never heard any music in open units, but in Z-Pod, you would hear the faint rhythm in a cell off in the distance. If you hit your intercom button, the pod didn't ask what you wanted or needed; they just pumped music into your cell through the intercom. I always wondered what would happen to the resident who hit his button because he was truly in need, but instead of help, the pod hit him with the song "Sexual Eruption" by Snoop Dogg. For, while we got to hear music—and we generally appreciated it—the deputies got to ignore us.

Different deputies played different genres of music. One played contemporary hip hop for hours. Others mixed in pop and R&B. No one ever played any subgenre of metal or country music. Some deputies played music over the dayroom speakers instead of the cell intercoms: "Gentlemen! I'm in a good mood, so don't fuck it up," a deputy announced. Then he played hip hop and upbeat R&B from lights out until about 2:00 a.m. The runner did his security checks with a bop in his step. The pod shuffled between Prince, T-Pain, Tupac, Phil Collins, and R. Kelly. It was nearly 2:30 a.m.—when deputies summoned residents for in-custody court appearances—and the pod played E-40 songs and his partner bobbed his head in the dayroom. They ended their shift a few hours later with a song and an announcement: "Gentlemen. It's been a pleasure." Indeed, it had!

I have to assume that some residents felt disturbed by hours of music. Sleep was hard enough to get, but no one dared complain.[5] Music broke through the vacuity of jail time, introduced something new upon which our minds could latch, and gave us something to talk about during meals. We welcomed cool deps and their playlists.

Scott

Scott and I talked about our families tonight. It started as one of our perennial arguments about Blackness. Scott was a slim-built brotha with vibes and a look that reminded me of "Bud" from "The Cosby Show." He seemed to have a real problem being a Black man. He said his father was "a light-skinned, blue-eyed Indian" and his family could be traced back to Ireland, and he was proud enough of that to claim it all the time. He said his father, whom he admired greatly, was "a pimp" that had kids with lots of women other than his mother. I didn't ask, but he named a few of the women. Scott said he and his brothers "don't date Black women"—that he prefers to have a "White girl or a Latina" to have his "heir."

I had heard that from him several times. "Heir to what?" I used to ask.

He and his brothers wanted "light-skinned kids" to look like their father, but at 23 years old, Scott didn't have a single thing worth leaving to a child. Whenever I asked about his very Black American mother, Scott dismissed the question—sometimes adding that his mother "got a mouth" that justified some of the violence she had experienced from men she had dated.

In our early days as cellies, I argued with Scott quite a bit about Blackness and domestic violence. I brought all the judgment and condescension I could muster. This time, however, I mostly listened and asked earnest questions. In Scott's eyes, his father lived a relatively lavish life. Scott's mother, however, was living a hard life. These realities somehow mixed in Scott's mind, and he reasoned that the darker you are, the harder your life is, so he and his brother wanted to have kids with lighter skin tones and presumably better lives. It was hard to argue with that logic—even if I felt awful about how he had come to it.

Scott's father was "always around," but it seemed he didn't play a central role in Scott's life—or that of his siblings. At some point, the state took them from their mother and placed them in various foster and group homes. Scott said he used to run away from the foster homes and, while in a group home, he contracted a disease that temporarily robbed him of his ability to walk. (Because neither of us knew the spelling, I wrote "micitosis" in my field notes. I actually thought he was making it up! But I've since done some digging, and it's likely "juvenile dermatomyositis.") After a couple of weeks in the hospital and several weeks of rehabilitation, the court sent him back to his mother. He had been gone from ages 5 to 12, and he was the last child to be returned to his mother. Scott had seen so much, so young.

5

"Court Bodies"

I was zombieing through a game of checkers with Herc when the slider opened and all eyes turned toward the sally port. I hadn't noticed how noisy it was until the din settled just then. The "court bodies," as deputies called them, were tottering in. It was nearly 5:00 p.m., and they had been gone since 2:30 a.m. They looked emaciated—robbed of normal sociability—the five or six of them. As usual, their legs shuffled their bodies straightaway to their cells, skipping the never-guaranteed chance to shower, use a phone, or hang out. None of us troubled them about what had happened. There were a few "what up" head gestures, but we kept our questions to ourselves: Did you get to eat? Who did you see? When do you go back to court? What happened? Were there fights? Who was involved? All of that would come out eventually. In the meantime, the court bodies retreated to their respective cells for chrysalis and, hours later, they would emerge again as jail residents. Anyhow, the moment passed, and my partner in opposition to tedium was looking down, waiting on me to take my turn. We picked up where we left off, thrusting round plastic pieces at each other without strategies.

Preparation

The rule was, if you had court the next day, you were given priority for phone time and haircuts. This was no small matter. Everyone wished to cut the line to use the phone, and deputies generally permitted residents to shower after haircuts. It was extra time out of your cell—time to revel in your relative freedom, joking and pointing at others with their jealous faces pressed against their cell door windows. Give up your bid to use the phone, and you might have to wait until the next day. Give up your chance at a haircut, and it would be you looking longingly at others enjoying extra time in the dayroom. It was never an issue though. Residents abided by the rule, and sometimes, in fact, made considerable concessions to help others.

Quite a bit of effort went into presenting the least blameworthy self in court.[1] You are, in essence, trying de-objectify yourself—to put the flesh and complexity of self back where it once was. Residents shaved, showered, clipped their nails, and cut their hair with purpose. "I've got court tomorrow," so went the refrain from southsiders, woods, and blacks. It was a community effort—mainly by racial group. Someone might point out that your orange bottoms looked dull or wrinkled, so they would tell you or teach you to "iron" your clothes. If, for example, you wanted a crease down the center of your pant legs—and I can't imagine why you would, though some did— first fold your pants as if you were going to iron a crease into them. Then lay them under your bedroll and either sit on them for a long while, or sleep with them pressed between the metal frame and the weight of your body. After a few hours, you would have a crease—or you will have removed the major wrinkles, if that was your goal. You could do the same with your orange top. I sometimes saw southsiders trading tops among themselves to get a color match with the uniform bottoms and maybe look marginally better in court.

Interestingly, I never saw black or wood residents share clothing like that. Following one Sunday clothing exchange, LK lamented: "All I wanted is a set a that matches; I have court tomorrow." None of us offered to help him out with that.

Like nearly everyone else, I did all that primping, but consider for a moment what seems like the magical thinking involved in cleaning ourselves up for court: We apparently believed—enough to make the effort—that a haircut could be the difference between freedom, an unwanted continuance, or an unfavorable outcome. In our subconscious minds we imagined a court teetering on the edge of throwing our lives away only to be convinced of our inherent worth because our oranges matched. We understood—as anyone honest with themselves does—that there is no more formidable stigma than appearing in court hampered by ankle cuffs and handcuffs linked to a waist chain while wearing a county jail uniform—especially as a Black or Brown person. The situation renders the presumption of innocence as hollow as an empty roll of toilet paper—and of equal utility, too. Court isn't church, where people do you the favor of pretending that you can "come as you are." Show up as you are in court, and you will find Lady Justice wearing her blindfold like a cute headband while judging you not exclusively by the truthfulness of the evidence in your case but very much by all the status[2] markers of a society deeply rooted in categorical inequality.[3] Our thinking wasn't magical. The way race, ethnicity, gender, age, and general countenance come together in the minds of court personnel—that was dark magic. Our response was practical: Best cut your hair.

Preparing your body was one thing. Preparing yourself emotionally was another, and it was clear that pending court dates weighed heavily on resident minds. "Fuuuuuck! I got court," was a common exclamation to anyone within earshot who cared to take up the issue. Toll used to freestyle before court appearances about his lawyer being a "truck"—slang for a dimwitted person. He rhymed about his lawyer's bumbling virtually guaranteeing an unfavorable outcome.

One morning before a court appearance, LK asked me to look over his case documents. I might have taken his ask as a compliment, but it felt burdensome. I couldn't interpret legalese, and I was as worried that I wouldn't be able to help as I was that I would. I imagined that if I somehow bullshitted a strategy that worked, I'd become some sort of jailhouse lawyer.[4] The thought sent me down a rabbit hole of what ifs. I wouldn't be able to help everyone. If I asked for something in exchange, I'd need to establish the value of my efforts, and I'd need a way to handle grievances. But there I was accepting what LK was handing me without being completely free of the thought hole. I told him the obvious: "I'm no lawyer."

"So? Nigga, just tell me whatever it is you think," he said.

I looked through his file between dayroom times. That he allowed me to look into his case was a tremendous show of respect and trust. Since I'd arrived in Z-4, LK had been sharing bits of his case here and there, but with paperwork in hand, I could potentially disconfirm some parts of his story, and if I said anything about it, that would create problems for him. It wasn't an issue though. I didn't see any incongruities, and I wouldn't have said anything anyhow. My legal career came to an end at the start of the next dayroom time. I handed LK his documents. I couldn't tell him anything he didn't already know. With a sagging face and weak shoulders, he thanked me for trying.

The Call

At 2:15 a.m., deputies cut on the dayroom lights in open and closed housing units. Until that moment, you might have been in the throes of a nightmare, maybe you caught a restless nap, or maybe you had been lying awake on your bunk. None of that mattered. You may be in a jail that's more than an hour's drive away from the superior court in Providence, where your case will be heard. The farther you are, the earlier they wake you, but by 5:30 a.m., deputies roused every "court body" for an exhausting day.

In open units, a deputy appeared, hollering instructions to the last names of residents scheduled for court. In closed units, deputies buzzed into cells and popped cell doors. In either case, you had no more than three minutes to line up before deputies threatened to leave you behind to suffer the consequences of missing court that day. That was no idle threat.

Scott had been looking forward to a court date, in part, because his mother and girlfriend would be there. He thought there was a good chance he would be given community service for discharging a BB gun in an open field. The call came, but not for Scott. He was frantic on our cell's intercom button, but the pod said that he wasn't on the list; otherwise, they would have called him. We knew that wasn't true—that deputies never made administrative errors— because the same thing had already happened to Herc who once pleaded with the pod to look at his paperwork, proving that he had court that day. They ignored him, and he missed his scheduled court appearance. Someone caught the error—probably when the judge called Herc's case—and deputies sent Herc to court the next day. Still, the pod was final that Scott was not going to court.

That was a particularly difficult day for him. He couldn't call anyone. He couldn't request to see someone. He couldn't change his situation in any way. I tried to lighten the mood by joking that he would get a "failure to appear" (FTA) complaint for missing court. He didn't find it funny, and sure enough, he was in court the very next day. The court had issued the FTA! Scott's mother was there raising hell.[5]

Presuming you were called on your scheduled day and you made it to the line within three minutes, deputies marched you into the hallway and gave the instruction to face the wall. Remember to stand inside the red line painted on the floor, or a deputy would have to remind you. One or more deputies walked the line, frisking each resident for contraband: paper, pencils, food, an extra pair of boxers, a kite for someone in another dayroom, a weapon. In effect, they were all the same to deputies who confiscated whatever wrong things residents had.

Next came the chains, and depending upon where you were in line, you heard them before you saw them. It was scary—especially if it was your first in-custody court appearance. You're facing a wall, and thoughts scramble in your mind. Maybe you think, as I thought, that you're in a line of residents, so nothing too bad could happen to you. You know that feeling of relative safety that comes with being in a crowd? It's the nonsensical thought that somehow a bad thing is less likely to happen because there are so many people gathered together. Fish swim in schools for safety, and still when the predators come, the school is destroyed. But that's what I used to reassure myself in that moment. You hear the metallic tings of chains being gathered behind you, but the atmosphere doesn't match what's happening. You might expect this to be carried out with serious minds, but deputies were a thousand emotional miles from what they were doing. It was a routine, and they executed it as they normally would. One chain went around your waist, and for larger residents, deputies connected two chains. Your wrists were handcuffed and then tethered to the waist chain, restricting your movement. You couldn't touch the back of your head, the tops of your shoulders, and if your waist chain was low and tight, you couldn't scratch your face. Your legs were shackled at the ankles, and those cuffs were connected by a chain that shortened your natural gait, so that you scooted and shuffled while leaning forward slightly to keep your balance.

The system of chains locked the body up, and the metal hurt, but experienced residents had a strategy to help them endure the pains of being shackled. If you let deputies put the ankle cuffs directly on your skin or only over your socks, your ankles would be cut and bruised by the end of the day. Every step would hurt, and it would be harder to keep your mind sharp and to stay vigilant because your thoughts would be occupied with pain. So, before walking into the hallway, the savvy resident pulled his socks up and pant legs down. If lucky, your pant legs were too long, and you could tuck them under your heels. If you were unlucky, you had "high water" orange bottoms and "drunk" socks that wouldn't stay up. Then it didn't matter whether you knew the endurance strategy. You were in for a long painful day.

Likewise, deputies tended to apply the waist chains with just enough room for you to breath, but if you were clever about it, you could poke out your stomach when the chain was going on. Wait until the deputy walked away; then relax, and you'll have more space around your waist than you would have had. You may even be able to scratch your face if you hiked the waist chain up your torso. This move required skill and a bit of luck. Poke your stomach out too far, and you would be caught.

If you were caught, some deputies just laughed at your efforts to get a little extra wiggle room. Cool deputies understood the hustle, but they weren't going to give you that benefit, so they would laugh while having you stand with your stomach at its natural girth. Then they applied the chains as they normally would. "Asshole deps," however, seemed personally wounded by the strategy: "Suck it in!" a deputy commanded. "Tighter." Another deputy chuckled while the first latched a tight string of waist chains around the southsider who had been caught trying to get a little extra comfort.

For some residents, waist chains and ankle cuffs were the least of their worries. Some, like Toll, had a reputation for fighting in the court holding cells, so deputies cross chained them. It didn't too much matter who started the fight. Toll had more than his fair share of enemies, but in defending himself, he was identified as someone who fought a lot. Days after every court visit, Toll would complain of shoulder pain. Whereas deputies normally tethered your cuffs in line with your body, being cross chained meant having your right wrist tethered to your left hip and your left wrist tethered to your right hip. It made you defenseless in every important way.

In any case, with everyone properly shackled, deputies trooped the line to the next housing unit to pick up more residents for court. It was so strange. Since kindergarten, we have all been lining up and walking without talking under the authority of one person or another. We stand silently or quietly in public lines, moving up as the lines move. By adulthood, we're professionals at waiting and walking in lines. Doing so on the way to court, however, was just a different matter altogether. There was incredible tension in just walking along: the sounds of your thoughts racing, the quiet anxieties in each of us, the sound of radio chatter from walkie-talkies, the tap-shh of jail slippers smacking and sliding along the ground, the arrhythmic percussive ting-pings of chains echoing in hallways, the cold air conditioning mixed with the heat generated from your effort to manage the discomfort in your body, the vascularity in hands that held pant legs up because not every resident had bottoms that fit at the waist, the efforts we put into grooming ourselves, and the black nitrile gloves deputies wore so you wouldn't contaminate them. Walking in line should have been easy, but it wasn't.

Having made several stops at different housing units, deputies put lines of residents in holding cells without regard to race. Almost no one spoke. The trip from the housing units to the holding cells was tiring and aggravating. Everyone found a place to sit or stand and wait. Once the appropriate residents were aggregated in holding cells, deputies marched everyone to the bus bay to be shackled in pairs—again, without regard to race. That's how you rode the bus to Providence where your case would be heard: with your body shackled and shackled to another person.

Court Holding Cells

There was a relatively steady stream of residents entering Providence court holding cells, as deputies amassed us from throughout the jail system. They distributed us across the cells, you guessed it, without regard to race, but unlike our time in pre-housing holding cells, we had been exposed to the jail's flat hierarchy and the politics. Race mattered on court days.

Being in a court holding cell was significantly different from being in other kinds of holding cells. The cells had all the normal trappings of any other dingy holding cell, but the main difference was that there was a temporal arc of *conflict energy*,[6] by which I mean *charged up intersubjectivity and emotional energy toward potential conflict*. During the morning period, when residents were first arriving, everyone was groggy and the energy was low. Few residents spoke or made eye contact. As the day progressed, deputies sent groups of residents "up" for court, and the remaining numbers were small enough to permit a comfortable conversation without being heard by everyone in the cell.

The middle period was marked by residents returning from court to one holding cell or another. They were wide awake, active, and mostly soured by whatever court disposition they had just gone through. The conflict energy was highest at this point, and you could feel yourself and others bracing in the presence of residents from the far reaches of the jail system—some with gang-related beefs, others with various allegiances, and plenty of residents with individual issues that might be worked out violently. There were always fights. Always. And when no one was fighting, the threat of a skirmish loomed over every social interaction.

Moving toward the end of the day, we entered the closing period, when deputies escorted some residents back to their housing units and bused others to different jails. The conflict energy reduced considerably, coinciding with how tired everyone was. By 4:00 p.m., a good number of residents had been shackled for nearly 14 hours and, in many cases, residents were not returned to their housing units until closer to 5:00 p.m.

As far as I could tell, the only meaningful division deputies enforced in court holding cells was between PCs and GENPOPs. Aside from that more fundamental separation by classification, first-timers summoned for arraignment were in the same court holding cells as the resident hoping to accept a deal, the witness in someone's trial, the resident hoping for trial, and the resident in the midst of trial. There may be one black resident in a cell full of woods, or there may be a sprinkle of woods among a relatively large number of blacks and southsiders. Deputies didn't appear to care much about the racial composition in the cells. And they were either unaware or unable to manage the group and interpersonal beefs that were given life by court days. When the inevitable fights occurred, deputies just separated the fighters into different holding cells. Sometimes that worked. Sometimes not.

One time that it didn't work sticks out in my mind. It was the middle period of the day, and I was on sitting on the bench when a black resident at the door announced, "Oh! They finna get down." I hopped up to see over his shoulder across the hallway into the holding cell where two black residents were locked in the pre-fight ritual: sizing each other up, bluster, and attack.[7] (You can always tell who is better trained for fighting: "Bomb first"[8] is the rule. If you sense that the fight is on, be the first to attack.) One of the two, a heavy-set resident, had only one arm chained to his waist. The other was in a sling. Suddenly, he pulled his arm from the sling and started throwing full punches at his stunned opponent. Residents crowded behind me to get glimpses of the action.

"Daaaaaamn!" a voice from behind me said.

"He was fakin' that shit, yo!" another voice said.

Like most fights, it was over after a few seconds. A group of deputies rushed into the cell to separate the fighters, and the crowd behind me dissipated. The cell buzzed with energy after that. Residents reenacted the fight and some jokingly complained that they had not thought to fake a broken arm. That fight sustained us with laughs and a story to tell as deputies summoned some residents from the cell and put others in it. Middle period energy transitioned into closing period energy, and I was staring out the cell door window. The one-armed man was still in the cell across the hallway when deputies added a black resident dressed for church to the mix. (Small world: Months later I would see that well-dressed resident, C-Macc, as the rep in Providence 31B3, adjoining the open dayroom I was in.) Almost immediately, the one-armed man started jawing at C-Macc. The fight was imminent, and in an instant, C-Macc hiked his waist chains up to his chest and rushed the one-armed man with hooks. Out came the healthy arm for the fight. They tussled out of view, and in came a rush of deputies to separate the two, putting C-Macc in the cell I was in.

He was still huffing and puffing with a smile. We stared at him with eager eyes. Story time! Someone asked him what happened, and C-Macc explained, "That nigga was like—as soon as I got in that bitch, he hit me up: 'You from

Midtown Ridahs?'" C-Macc said he wanted to know who was asking, and the one-armed man said, "'I just got down witcho nigga'... And I'm like, aw cuhz—in my slacks? BIP! BIP! BIP!" C-Macc made the sounds of the blows he threw while demonstrating his curtailed punching range.

Smaller world still. Later, during my time in Sunland, I was in a circle of black residents sharing crazy stories that were true. I gave no names, but when I told the story of the one-armed man, D-Double paused for half a second and said: "Oh you talkin' bout C-Macc. I know him. He wit' the shits." News traveled quickly and efficiently in the Jail News Network. It was yet another reminder that lying about who you are in jail is not a smart move.

In Court

When deputies came to take you to court, they first took you to a smaller holding cell—a staging area—so you would be within arm's reach when it was time for you to enter the courtroom. I'm convinced our presence in court was mostly ritual because residents rarely spoke, and judges mostly addressed their conversation to the lawyers. A large portion of the legal discussion seemed designed to keep the average citizen from knowing what was being said.[9] Judges and lawyers spoke in legalese shorthand and seemed annoyed when they had to translate that to English. Sometimes, the judge would speak legalese insultingly slower the way I'd seen Americans do in conversations with South Koreans who didn't speak English. If a resident didn't understand what was being said on the second or third attempt at plainer language, judges often reverted back to standard legalese and legal process in asking for some official response. Then you had to offer an answer without fully understanding what it would mean. The resident who tried to explain anything was immediately shut down and forced into one position or another. His public defender helped things along by encouraging him to enter a response in accordance with legal process. No one wanted to hear your story. Court appearances, we surmised, weren't about justice as much as they were about process.[10]

Part of that process meant it was common for residents to meet their public defender for the first time while appearing in court. Sometimes a public defender from a different case was assigned on the spot. Other times, a public defender rummaged through a stack of files and an accordion file folder to glance at the formal statements on what brought you to court in shackles that day. This meant you weren't prepared for court, and neither was your legal counsel, but legal process required that there be representation, so that box was checked.

The apparent focus on process in court proceedings was not without consequence. Ninety-five percent[11] of criminal cases are settled by plea deal, which is, in large part, a function of the fearmongering that goes into plea bargaining. In discussions about their cases, residents frequently talked about the number of penal years they were virtually promised if they didn't accept a plea deal for some significantly shorter period of penal time. The difference between the threatened time and the time you could do if you accepted a plea was your clearest sign that your potential punishment was disconnected from your charges and that it was not the public's interest or yours that mattered. Caseloads need to be processed, and whether you did a lot of time or a little time was of little concern. Thus, when Chino told us he had heard a public defender bargaining with a prosecutor in the halls, we believed him: "C'mon. I gave you the last one," the prosecutor reasoned. "Look how many priors he has. I gotta give him some time." One thing is for sure: When you're told your charges carry over a decade of prison time or you can sign for under a "county lid"—usually a year or whatever is the maximum amount of time you could get in jail before being sentenced to prison—justice takes a backseat to the practicality of the deal: something judges, prosecutors, and public defenders know well.[12]

Of course, not everyone accepted a plea deal—certainly not immediately, and some residents weren't offered a deal. They fought for their day in court, instead. Toll once told me: "This the [sic] only place where people say: 'Man. I'll be glad when I go to trial.'" Indeed, many residents hoped their trial would begin sooner than later, but in waiting, they became evermore cynical about court processes.

"They should be ready for trial when they arrest you," D-Double complained. "Or the district attorney should have 60 days to go to trial." I asked him why he thought residents languished in jail for years, but it was Toll who interjected an answer.

He said the prosecution "keeps filing a bunch of stuff that I don't even understand that just gives them more time to lock my ass up!"

"Violating peoples' rights," D-Double added flatly.

During one of my early short stays, I was in a Providence court holding cell with a southsider who strolled around the cell calmly while I sat on the bench nervously. I noticed that he had changed quite a bit from the picture on his wristband. The person on the ID had a skinny neck, slim head, low cut hair, and an unconfident face. The southsider moseying about the cell was something different: unbothered; short, shiny, and slicked back hair; and a healthier build. I made a comment about how he had changed since his picture. He paused for a second and looked down at his wristband. The picture looked old, and so did the wristband with its tattered edges. "How long you been here?" I asked.

"Two-and-a-half years."

I was shocked. Before he said that, I didn't know how long someone could be in jail. During my many court appearances, no one ever said, "Mr. Walker. Just so you know, you could be in jail for years and years while everything is gathered for a trial." In hindsight, court actors seemed to think that involvement in legal cases gives defendants a working understanding of how the system operates. Imagine assuming that hospital patients know and understand the potentialities within healthcare *because* they are patients and then using that presumption to forego explaining the intricacies of treatment plans and contingencies. That's jail.

Two and a half years! I started calculating the days in my head. "For me though," the southsider interrupted my math, "it's worth it cuz of the time I'm facing."

I summarized what he had said in my own words, and he nodded and gestured with his hands like, "Now you understand."

A related consequence of process-focused criminal justice had to do with the frequency and vigor with which public defenders sold residents the dream of the "gov-boot." Of course, getting a gov-boot was like winning the lottery, but it turned out that public defenders often told guys that they were likely to get a gov-boot as encouragement to accept a plea deal.

Following a court appearance, Sisqo entered the dayroom feeling upbeat. He said he was going to sign a deal because his public defender told him, "With the way they've been doing gov-boots, you'll be out in three days." A few of us laughed aloud at hearing him say that. Ken added that he had expected to be out after a weekend. Nearly three years later, there he was in the midst of us laughing at Sisqo. When I signed my "deal" for 180 days, I told a couple of guys in the trustee pod that I'd likely be out in a few days—that my public defender had all but assured it. It seemed believable—or at least, I really wanted to believe it. I'd been granted a gov-boot once before, so I knew it was possible. Trustee pod residents snickered at my faith in a gov-boot, though. One said he had been told that same thing eight months prior and that he would be out in two months. Other residents told similar stories in which they were sure they would get a gov-boot in a "three days" or so.

But public defenders couldn't know if a resident would get a gov-boot, and they certainly couldn't say whether it would happen in three days. That so many of us heard the same phrase, though, revealed how public defenders were using the gov-boot to encourage residents to accept plea deals. Three days passed, and I was still in the Providence trustee pod. After day seven, I was dejected—teetering on hard-timing-it. I hadn't prepared myself to do the whole sentence. I hadn't worked on my emotional endurance. A few residents noticed that I was struggling to deal with my improperly placed faith in a gov-boot, and I briefly became the focus of mockery. Between laughs, Lamont explained: "Man. Everyone is told that. You ain't goin' no-where. Ha! Ha!" He was right, and we were right about Sisqo, too. The thing is, public defenders didn't have to be there in those critical moments of vul-nerability and unrealized faith when it became clear that a magical gov-boot would not save you from indefinite time.

In addition to incentivizing a falsehood about the likelihood of getting a gov-boot, process-oriented criminal justice seemed to deemphasize justice-seeking in favor of caseload reduction, and residents developed the sense that public defenders were either too incompetent to help, or too indif-ferent as to how penal time affected our lives. I cannot speak to the plight of Golden County public defenders—if "plight" is even the right word—but residents had a legion of stories about problems they had experienced with their "public pretenders." Not fighting continuances, not listening to the resident's explanation of the events, not having any time to discuss the case, not showing up to court, pushing against a resident's wishes for the sake of what appeared to be their own convenience, and presenting what appeared to be inept legal arguments. Golden County public defenders were frequently discussed with contempt. I empathized because I had my own experiences.

Previous to my final stint, I'd made bail and was going to court as a free person. On a scheduled a court date, I parked and passed my public defender who was strolling away from the courthouse. He was carrying a bundle of manila folders and casually chatting with a woman. He looked his normal disheveled self: messy hair, an ill-fitting gray suit, and some cheap black dress shoes. "Hi." I greeted him as I passed, and I could see that he didn't recog-nize me. No matter. I wasn't his only case. "Aren't you going the wrong way?" I asked.

"Huh?"

"Yeah. We've got court today—Walker." I pointed to myself. He looked confused. The woman he was with turned to see his response. He gathered himself and claimed that we didn't have court that day. "Yeah. We do," I replied. I was sure of it.

Maybe my confidence jogged his memory. Maybe he faked remembering, but whatever the truth, he said, "Oh. Yeah. Yeah. I'll be there."

My case was scheduled to start 20 minutes from then, and to his credit, he was there on time. I imagined him sprinting to the court division after cursing and having to be consoled by his friend. As sure I type this now, that man would not have been at my hearing if I hadn't seen him walking that day. Months later, at another hearing, we sat in a courtroom, staring down the barrel of a trial that he clearly didn't want to participate in, and I worried about the years of prison time I'd been threatened with. He sat next to me with annoyed energy.

Moments later, a judge appeared at the bench, and the assistant district attorney called a meeting in the judge's chambers. About 10 minutes later, one of the lapels on his gray suit was flipped up as my public defender nearly sprinted back to me. He slammed a document in front of me, shoved a pen toward me, and huffed: "I gotchu a probation offer! Sign this!" I didn't ask a single question. A short while before, that man was upset with me for not having a better defense, but if I signed that document—whatever it said—I would go free. I signed the paper and the judge had me stand so she could castigate me until she felt better.

As we left court that day, my public defender had his chin in the sky. He was proud of himself, and for a moment, I thought he had pulled some sort of reverse Perry Mason move to save me. The "good guy" is always the prosecutor on television. It's the opposite in film. In real life, I was the beneficiary of an overstressed court system. My public defender explained that the assistant district attorney had been newly assigned to the case—that "a bunch of them" had recently quit. She didn't have time or energy to try a case she knew nothing about. She just wanted to process the cases on her desk, so she offered me probation. Voilà! Justice.

For in-custody residents, court tended to be painfully uneventful—especially for arraignments. You had done all this primping. You may or may not have survived the conflict energy in the holding cells without getting into a fight. You fought your anxieties while in the staging area, and then you found yourself sitting in a designated area that was set a bit higher than the gallery. Deputies forbade you to make eye contact or communicate with anyone in the gallery under the threat of having you or your loved ones removed. It was worth the risk, though. Many residents mouthed "hello" and "I love you" to their supporters.

Every court procedure came with some dangers for residents. If a resident had lied about his involvement in a case, that information would come out in court. If he had lied about his charges, that came out during the arraignment when the judge read the charges aloud. For residents with cases beyond the arraignment, there would typically be a discussion between the defense attorney, the clerk, and the prosecution as to when the case could reconvene pending some legal maneuver or another, and then the next case would be called. It was all so perfunctory—hardly the drama you see in television, film, or high-profile cases. Then, a deputy marched the court bodies back to the staging area, and then to the court holding cells, with little more than a mandate to return to court again. For some, years went by just like that.

The Hope Roller Coaster

One of the problems with court appearances was that there was always the small likelihood that something miraculous would happen in a resident's favor, and that potential—however tiny it was—fed a resident's hope, even if he didn't want it to. As a result, residents road the Hope Rollercoaster with its peaks of "maybe this time" and its valleys of "the defendant is ordered to return" in two weeks, a month, or some other date that just meant more jail time.

Scott, for instance, grew increasingly excited before every court appearance. Each time, he was sure—or hoping to be sure—that he would be set free and given probation or community service. His mother and girlfriend wrote him, and they were hopeful, too. He would leave the dayroom with smiles only to return in despair. He would lay on his bunk for hours—withdrawn into himself. Then, he would ride that rollercoaster again at his next scheduled appearance.

LK's hopes were more modest: "I just wanna see my brother" or sometimes it would be his wife or his daughters. I never asked him, but I imagined that he must have felt conflicted about seeing his brother in court for the same charges he was facing. Perhaps LK felt some comfort in knowing he wasn't going through everything alone, but then again, jail time is an isolating experience, and he wasn't in the same housing unit with his brother.

He might have felt awful knowing that his brother was in a unit down the hallway from us and that there was nothing either of them could do to make matters easier for the other. However he felt, LK frequently left court with minor aspirations, only to return emotionally devastated.

It was the same for Toll. He worried about his brother, and sometimes a cool dep would let Toll pass soups to his brother in the adjacent housing unit. Beyond that, Toll had learned not to ride Hope—at least, not for *every* court appearance. Early into my stint in Z-4, he was sure he would be going to trial and that he would be released. He kept telling everyone how it was going to happen during his next court appearance. "They have to release me," he kept concluding after summarizing the merits of his case. Kinsley cut Toll's hair the night before court. Toll cut his fingernails and toenails, and a few of us held a roundtable to discuss the details of his case. We agreed that the evidence and charges didn't make sense, and when the call came a few hours later, Toll walked to the sally port, turned back with an optimistic smile, and he went into the hallway to be cross chained.

When he returned, it was as if his body autopiloted him into the dayroom. He blinked slowly with heavy eyelids and eyes that might have cried if not for pride. He was leaning backward as his feet led him through the dayroom. A gust would have blown the man down. His arms didn't swing. He closed himself in his cell. There was no trial—just another continuance. For days, he was quiet during mealtimes. "You good?" one of us would ask. It may not seem like much, but "You good?" is a caring and non-prying way to acknowledge that something may be the matter but that you won't press into a person's feelings about the issue. It communicates, "Should you feel ready to talk about it, I'll be here."

Toll mostly nodded to the question. After a few days of hardly eating and minimal interaction with us, he explained in a somber tone: "They gave the prosecutors more time. . . Don't really know what the fuck happened." After his next court appearance, he said that his lawyer told him that trial would definitely be soon. "I heard that before," Toll said conclusively with a shrug. I was released five months before he lost his trial.

Thinking on the ups and downs of the rollercoaster, I suppose every continuance and delay was on solid legal grounding. I have to think that because I don't want to think otherwise. The emotional peaks and valleys residents experienced led some to give up hope altogether. Beast, for instance, spoke about his case as if he had come to an understanding about the likely outcome, and so there was little use in being emotionally invested about it. "I'm not afraid to go [to prison]," he said. "Ya know what I mean? It's the process. In court you have to [deal with] all that stuff. Your past comes up, and 12 people are gonna decide what happens to you." I said he seemed resolved to getting a lot of time. "They got all their little ducks in a row with my crimeys snitching and shit."

D-Double's disposition was similar but less convincing. He had told me that he wasn't afraid of prison time, but I'd seen him ride high on Hope's ascent and accelerate to deep misery on Hope's descent. Leading up to one court date, he was convinced he would be going to trial and that he would be released. He was so upbeat that I didn't like his company. He was saying good-byes and talking to us about what he would do once free: sex and food, and the order didn't matter. Like so many others, that court date came, and he was given a continuance of some sort. In the following days, he locked himself away in his cell and Ken took over his rep duties in the meantime.

Most residents, it seemed, rode Hope. Sisqo had a series of continuances, but one stands out in my mind because he had biblical faith that he would be released. In fact, he tried to give away the crummy supplies he had accumulated. He said he had prayed and that god told him he was getting out. Knowing something about his case, a few of us told him he wasn't going anywhere, but Sisqo was adamant. He returned with a "deal": a county lid and 60 days credit. We joked that he "only" had 305 more days to go before he was right about getting out like god had told him. Sisqo was in no mood for our jokes, though. He stopped interacting with us for a while. His celly told us Sisqo was "depressed," and we eased up. Not long after, I gave him some chips to cheer him up, and he soon returned to his usually social self. Such was life between court dates.

Champion

Another soul-crushing Sunday clothing exchange: Scott directed my attention to Henry's shirt. It was a crispy white T-shirt made by Champs Sports. It had the damned insignia on it! "How the hell did he get that in here?"

"He been wearin' that, too," Scott said. "I'on't know if he got a few of them or he just know how to keep it clean, but he been wearin' it."

I was jealous while turning in an ill-fitted and dingy T-shirt. When it was my turn at the T-shirt clothing bin, I pulled a clean one. It looked new, but it wasn't made by Champs Sports. On a whim,

I asked the nearby deputy how I could keep them from taking it from me. "There really isn't any way to hide it," he said.

Someone told him wrong.

6

"Jailing"

Scott started with our toilet-sink, working in a near polish. I moved everything from the table onto my bunk, wet a rag, scrunched a bar of anti-bacterial soap that I'd purchased from the commissary, and I started with the
table. Using a second cleaning rag, I sopped up the excess suds and wetness
before reorganizing my books on the table. Scott slid by me in silence to wipe
down the metal bed frame. I maneuvered around him and tucked my sheets
and blanket tightly around my mattress so I could roll it to the head of the
bed and passersby would know we detailed our cell. I stacked the field notes
I kept under my bedroll into a neat pile. Scott grabbed our slippers from
their spot by the cell door, and I grabbed our commissary bags from under
my bottom bunk, and we set both on my bunk's exposed metal slab next to
my field notes. Scott got on his hands and knees at the cell door and began
"sweeping" with the cardboard back from the paper pad he had purchased
from the commissary. I joined him from the opposite end of the cell under
the bunks and we swept backward, looking over our shoulders here and there
until we met near the center of the cell without bumping into each other.
I wet an edge of a piece of paper to make it stick to the floor, and we swept up
the small amount of dust and dirt we had gathered. I balled up the "dustpan"
and tossed it into a repurposed commissary bag. Scott used a cup he had
purchased from the commissary to make sudsy water, and then he tossed
the water onto a section of the floor. I did the same. We used different rags to
mop the floor on our hands and knees—all in silence.

The top tier cell doors popped open in a sudden cascade of metal
reverberations: dayroom time. We kept working, though, to get the finishing touches done. From two cells down, Toll appeared in our doorway.
He studied us—consecrating our cell: "Oh. So, y'all just jailin', huh?" Scott
replied that we were nearly done before grabbing his orange top and slippers
and heading to the door to put them on. I finished a final spot of mopping
and did the same. We headed into the dayroom.

Jailing

I instinctively understood what Toll meant by "jailing," and I felt a sense of pride about the acknowledgment he gave us. Scott and I were demonstrating one of the strategies for "doing" jail time. That's really what *jailing* is: *the set of endurance strategies residents used to manage the psychic, biological, and emotional realities endemic to jail living.* We can think of this as culture in action—the ways residents made sense of and endured the demands that jail time put upon us. "Endurance" is important here because jail was not a puzzle to be solved. Renewing the effort to keep yourself from being overwhelmed by the buildup of jail-induced frustrations was a daily and sometimes moment-to-moment effort. This is why the term "coping"[1] is inappropriate insofar as it means struggling with and sometimes overcoming difficult circumstances. Likewise, enduring is very different from "adapting"—especially if in any sense "adaptation" connotes residents becoming better suited for jail than free society in some pseudo-evolutionary way. With adaptation there is also the implication that you suffer less *because* you are adapted. That wasn't true, and in the next chapter, I show you what it looked like for endurance strategies to fail—and they inevitably did.

The truth is that enduring jail required constant effort. You would find yourself juggling problems, and if you lost concentration, it wasn't the problem that fell. It was your emotional defenses. Then you would be open to feel the full brunt of being in jail. Thus, you might endure your lack of support one day and find yourself pricked in your mind by feeling abandoned the next. A great conversation helped you forget your hunger one night, but the grumbling in your stomach was all you could think about the next day. You could be racked with loneliness one week, find a way to repress those feelings the next, and then have your endurance fail when your celly smacking his teeth during a meal became too damned much to take.

Jail was a biological, emotional, and psychic assault on the self. For some attacks on one front or another, there were tactile endurance strategies you could use to defend yourself. Other endurance strategies were behavioral, and others still were emotional and psychological. I don't cover them all here: neither the problems nor every available endurance strategy. Rather, I want you sense with your whole self the jail environment and some of what we did to endure jail time a little longer.

Vacuity

Whenever I've been asked what jail residents did all day, my answer is usually some version of, "Nothing." Most of the time, there was nothing at all going on, and residents often talked about being bored, but "boredom" is a misnomer here. *Boredom* is *having something to do but lacking sufficient interest to do it*. It wasn't boredom that confronted residents in the milliseconds of lingering moments. It was indefinite *vacuity—the emptiness of support for social activity*. Listen when I tell you there were hours—seemingly endless vacant hours—in a cell or on a bunk under bright dayroom lights with your mind turned against you in the chasm between time and the lack of activity to fill it. That emptiness of activity is what vacuity refers to, and it was experienced as an emotional assault from the inside out.

For me, vacuity was most noticeable in the loud silence of the dayroom. I didn't immediately register the silence. I'd be talking with my celly or listening to others chat in an open unit, but when the conversations stopped, the quiet snuck up on you. Before you knew it, the quiet in the dayroom turned up the volume in your head, so you could hear more clearly the collisions of thoughts and voices you would be smart to ignore because they didn't have anything good to say to you. There developed in some residents a desperation to hush their own thoughts or be louder than them, and then it became calming to make noise or really any sound.

Our minds found and looped obscure sounds hidden in the crevices of memories. Residents walked around humming and singing and beatboxing bits of songs and melodies that became lodged in the forefront of their minds. I had Jay-Z's first two verses of "Hovi Baby" stuck in my head—that and the wrong lyrics to Sam Cooke's "A Change Is Gonna Come." Toll used to rap and modify Tupac lyrics that he couldn't remember while snapping his fingers and thumping his chest with a fist. There was always a black resident or southsider making beats on a table, a wall, or a cell door. The residue of annoying commercial jingles and songs no one had heard in months or years were on repeat: the Kars4Kids jingle and the earworm parts of "Tom's Diner" by Suzanne Vega—a song that was surely released before most residents were born. Big Guapo sang Rockwell's "Somebody's Watching Me" like a tic. He couldn't help himself: "I gotta get this shit outta my head," he laughed. I volunteered that the song was by Rockwell, but I couldn't help with the lyrics, and he couldn't stop repeating the same part with the same failed high notes: "I always FEEEEL like, somebody's watching MEEEE!" In the cells,

Flip sang to himself, and TJ said Sisqo talked himself to sleep in the quiet of the night.

Sometimes, however, it wasn't music that filled the soundless void. When Z-4 residents didn't get dayroom time as expected, there was, at first, a quiet. Eventually, someone started whistling. Then came animal noises, and a resident from the top tier started a conversation with a resident on the bottom tier. From a cell on the bottom tier, a southsider feigned a woman's voice, yelling: "Yeah! Fuck yeah," as if in the throes of sex. Someone would add boogieman laughs and grunts; someone else bird calls. It was disturbing, and Scott sometimes decided to get in on things by kicking the cell door. Despite threats from the pod to keep quiet, a full cacophony ensued and kept up until a rep yelled, "Radio!" or "Radio that shit!" meaning to be quiet. It was usually Beast, and he would end his command with his cell number, so everyone knew the command was legitimate. It was another reminder of the stabilizing role of the reps, for even the blacks and woods (if they were in on the noise-making) stopped after Beast rose his voice.

Projects

In addition to using sound to stamp out the loud silence, residents got creative with finding things to do. Each racial group may or may not have had a game of checkers or chess, which, of course, had to be shared. Many dayrooms didn't have any books. Some books were missing entire chapters or just the ending or the beginning. We read and reread whatever was there—most of which were commonly referred to as "hood books": fiction tales of young Black men rising up the ranks of illegal drug markets to reach kingpin status only for it all to end in different degrees of tragedy. I always thought it interesting that *those* were the books we had access to.

I was fortunate to have friends and family who sent books to me—a bit of an ordeal in and of itself. The book had to come directly from a retailer, and then deputies wrote your last name, resident number, and housing location on a slip of paper affixed to the books or across the book covers. The latter has become an unnecessary reminder.

But you couldn't rely on having books or board games to fill the time. In fact, there was no *filling* the time because there was always more time than there were things to do. I used to read whatever was scratched into the bunk's metal frame. I once lost count of the cracks in the cinderblocks. Those were instances of *unproductive projects* or *activities in which the central goal is the doing of a thing*. There were many examples of unproductive projects (e.g., those few times I pestered the pod with frivolous requests), and in some cases, an unproductive project came with the added benefit of giving others something to talk about. Sisqo made binoculars from two toilet paper tubes and stood at his cell door looking into the dayroom to give a "blow-by-blow" of everything he saw. That went on for several consecutive nights: Sisqo "reported the news" and his celly, TJ, was entertained—if not slightly annoyed—and we got to hear about it during mealtimes. I must say that it was much easier to tough down jail coleslaw and skim milk at a race-specific table while laughing about a late-40-something-year-old Black man playing "eye spy" with toilet tissue binoculars.

Scott and I used to say anything but our names during the nightly "face card" check. Each night, whether in open or closed units, deputies performed a "face card check," requiring every resident to show his face and respond with his first name to check against an image on a small card the runner held. It was more serious than the typical security checks, but Scott and I noticed that deputies didn't always do that job with any seriousness. We ran with that. "Robinson," a deputy called at our cell door.

"Yah trick! Yah!" Scott replied with lyrics from the rapper Soulja Boy.[2]

"Walker," the deputy continued.

"Egypt," I responded.

The deputy was satisfied with our responses, and he moved on. We tried other responses, too. Sometimes we gave each other's names, but deputies never did anything more than note that we were in our cell before moving on.

For me, though, the pinnacle of an unproductive project was Flip's decision to make a broom. In some ways, the unproductive project was mine while his was more of a *productive project*, meaning a *kind of project in which something of use is created*. The broom was to be in lieu of the cardboard we normally used, and I was immediately incredulous. I asked him how he planned to do it.

"Newspaper," he shrugged.

I laughed and told him it would never work. In hindsight, I shouldn't have been so dismissive. I'd seen residents MacGyver[3] a lighting fixture to light and smoke weed. Flip was undeterred. He forged ahead with his plans, and I mean that. He sat on his bunk—the bottom bunk at the time—and sketched plans for a broom, and when he thought his plans had design flaws, he balled up the paper and started over. Meanwhile, I occupied myself by ridiculing everything he did. Every time he threw away some plans, I offered unsolicited advice to just give up. "Just watch," he kept saying.

After a while, he figured out how he was going to do it. He arranged some materials on his bunk: toothpaste, newspaper, and a razor. Other residents contributed materials to his project during lunch and dayroom time. Once he had what he needed, he cut newspaper into strips and then stood back looking at his plans and the strips. He made some revisions to his plans, paused for dinner, and when we returned, he was single-minded about fashioning that broom. He took his shirt off, showing his skinny and veiny arms, as he rolled some newspaper into a handle. I kept up a healthy barrage of disparaging jokes. He laughed along, but he never stopped working. He used the toothpaste like glue, figuring out how much water and pressure were needed to get maximum hold for the pieces of newspaper. When he completed his model, he put it under his bedroll and waited for the "glue" to dry.

The anticipation was barely tolerable.

An hour—perhaps more—went by and he revealed his project. *Holy shit! He did it!* He held the broom up with pride, and I was shocked that it looked like an actual broom, but I knew it would never sweep anything because the newspaper strips were too flimsy. Still, I was surprised at what he was able to accomplish. "Aight. Let's see you sweep some shit with that," I laughed.

Rightfully, he wouldn't have me steal his moment. He was equally impressed with his work, and he should have been. He strutted like a male peacock with his new broom for a few minutes while repeating with righteous glee, "Niggas always doubt, but I showed ya."

Finally, the moment of truth: he tried the broom, and it was totally useless. The "bristles" were too flimsy. "Gyaad damn," he said with a smile and tone as if he had almost had it.

I burst into fetal-crunching laughter. He couldn't be bitter in the moment; he joined me, and we laughed together until our sides hurt. It was nearly 10:00 p.m.—lights out. He had spent the whole day building a broom, and I'd spent the day telling him he couldn't do it. It was a dual victory.

Some of the more productive projects were clever lifehacks. We made dominos and playing cards from the cardboard backing of paper pads. Recall that in the trustee pod, deputies provided playing cards, but in GENPOP, playing cards were "contraband": just another of the jail's ironies. Using pencil lead and toothpaste, some southsiders fashioned dice that clacked just like real dice when thrown. Nearly everyone removed the blade from their shaver and cut a cleaning rag from the one bath towel we were provided, and those cuts needed to be precise—especially for black residents who, unlike southsiders and woods, always cut out a washcloth, too. (You didn't want to be the black resident discovered to be showering with your hands or a bare soap on your skin.) If your cuts were wrong, you would have an unnecessarily large cleaning rag, an oddly sized washcloth, and a bath towel that was too little. That last part was doubly troublesome because many residents rolled their towels as pillows.

Having made some creature comforts, residents needed to prepare for the likelihood of having them taken away or destroyed in nearly every Sunday's thorough security check when deputies "tossed" the cells. Included among the dangerous and forbidden "contraband" were jail-made dice, dominos, cards, hardboiled eggs or an apple you might have squirreled away to get through the night's hunger, your cleaning rag and washcloth, and basically any material item created to help residents endure jail punishment. There were only two kinds of productive projects that were usually safe from a deputy's intervention: cleaning and cooking.

Voluntary cleaning requires a feeling of responsibility. Residents cleaned their cells from a sense of personal responsibility. We cleaned the dayrooms from a sense of group-level responsibility. Of course, that there was a sense of responsibility at all means that both activities weren't purely voluntary. After all, the standards for responsibility don't spring from thin air. They are built into social relations and emergent goals, and they are enforced through positive and negative sanctions. Cleaning had practical benefits, though. No one wanted a communicable disease to spread. It was common to hear a new resident being warned of staph infections, but in closed units where residents could claim personal space a clean cell was a status marker and source of pride. It also signaled how skilled a resident was at jailing.

Initially, I couldn't care less about cleaning a cell. *It's a damned cell*, I thought—*not my house*. Flip whined constantly about it—how he was the only one to sweep or mop, but I had no problem ignoring him. Two things changed my mind: I did jumping jacks in the cell one day, and my feet were filthy; and around that same time, D-Double showed me his cell for the first time. He made me take off my slippers and socks at the door. The floors—I tell you the damned floors—were so clean that they felt soft under my bare feet. The air was different in his cell, and I'll never forget how D-Double stared at me beaming with pride as I took it all in. The paint in his cell seemed newer than mine. It was a revelation.

For Golden County jail residents, the cell was an example of what sociologist Erving Goffman called "the stall"—a temporary "territory" of the self to which we make personal claims.[4] The cell wasn't home, but for the time that you were there you claimed that cell as your own. In so doing, your cell (or your bunk in open units) became an extension of your ego—your very sense of self. When someone violated your place—when they encroached upon a territory of your sense of self—you experienced the violation as personal disrespect. That could lead to conflict if not made right. This is partly why Flip was so bothered by me not cleaning the cell and, had I entered D-Double's cell with my slippers on, that would have caused conflict. Like fashion, cars, homes, and personal information, our cells (and the surrounding personal space) were extensions of how we understood ourselves. It was, after all, *my* cell.

After seeing how a cleaned cell could look and feel, I cleaned religiously. Seeing how others did it, there seemed to be two levels of clean: basic and detailed. Me and my cellies always stayed at the basic level, which included, sweeping, mopping, cleaning the table and toilet-sink, wiping the bunks down, and rolling the bedrolls to the head of each bunk. I learned that if we mopped regularly and didn't wear our slippers in the cell, the floor felt soft—nearly like D-Double's. Then there was the detailed level of cleaning, which included all the basic features plus cleaning the walls, the vents, and the cell door window. Residents in cells cleaned at the detailed level often bragged and ranked one another according to effort and outcome. That's how I learned to clean my cell better: listening to others brag about what they did and how they did it.

Whatever level of clean residents shot for, they had to purchase their own cleaning supplies from the jail commissary because deputies didn't provide disinfectants. Thus, a clean cell was a status marker, which depended in part on a resident's financial resources. The first thing needed was a cleaning agent: Dial anti-bacterial soap was the weapon of choice, and it could be augmented with shampoo for better suds. Some residents mixed soapy water in cups purchased from the jail commissary; others temporarily stopped up the sink to get suds. Then, using the cleaning rags cut from the bath towel, you could get to work.

It wasn't the same, though, cleaning in closed units versus cleaning in open ones. Once you have been in a cleaned cell, you couldn't go back to one with grime and dust bunnies. But it wasn't just the productive project of having a clean cell. Cleaning put us in meditative states. I didn't have my "clean up" playlist, but the effect was just the same. I used cleaning time to think through problems, draw conclusions, reminisce on my son's laugh, and make new promises for new starts. How often residents cleaned varied (some once a week, some twice, and others cleaned constantly). Whatever the frequency, I often heard residents describe having the same focus of thought that I had.

Contrarily, cleaning in open units was a damned chore. Beyond the immediate personal space of one's bunk and a perimeter of inches thereabout, there was no sense of personal responsibility to clean up. We cleaned because we felt a group-level responsibility to do so, and that was significantly less gratifying. Whereas the cell was yours—at least temporarily—the open dayroom belonged to everyone, so it very much felt like cleaning up after others. We did it though.

Like cleaning, cooking was therapeutic, bragworthy, and residents established a status hierarchy around being relatively good cooks. You needed products from the jail commissary, and not every resident had that kind of free society support. Those who did looked forward to Thursday evenings when commissary orders were delivered. The orders arrived, deputies (usually) let you out of your cell to get yours, but residents needed to double check their original order sheet against what was in the clear plastic bag of goods. Most of the time, you got what you ordered, but often enough, items would be missing or the commissary had run out of something, so someone made the decision to send you nothing instead of a replacement.

At first, I ordered chips and noodles and cookies to bridge the long gap between dinner and breakfast, and I listened to ongoing debates between LK, D-Double, and Toll about who was the best cook. They were always talking about how good their "pizza" or "burrito" was, and curiosity got the better of me. During one debate, I asked if someone would make me a pizza. That kicked of the latest episode of *Top Chef: Jail Edition*. LK, D-Double, and Toll jockeyed to cook my first resident-prepared meal. I went with LK for no particular reason. I gave him the ingredients he asked for, and he made me a "burrito," keeping the leftover ingredients for himself—something I hadn't thought about until I realized I wasn't getting "my change." I reported that the burrito was good, and the responses were a bit like finding out that you had sat in the chair of the bad barber instead of waiting in line for the ones who actually know how to cut hair. Toll, Ken, and D-Double were incredulous about how good the burrito was, and after a bit of shit talking and put-downs aimed at LK, who, as I learned, didn't have the best reputation for cooking, it was decided that Toll would make me a pizza.

In fact, he practically begged me for the opportunity. As before, I gave him the ingredients, and I should say that eating cooked food in jail was a bit of an adventure—at least at first. The recipes weren't written down, but below is a recipe for "pizza" (see Table 6.1). (To make a "burrito," hold the pepperoni slices and use chicken instead of beef seasoning packets. That's literally it.)

I imagine that the list of ingredients doesn't sound delicious to you, but jail pizzas and burritos were so splendid to eat that when I was finally home from jail, I tried and failed to reproduce the meals with free society ingredients from my local market.

Toll's pizza was superior in every way to LK's burrito. I think jelly or mayonnaise was missing. "It just don't taste the same without the jelly," Toll said.

I was in my cell enjoying my pizza so much that I called D-Double to my cell while he was roaming the dayroom with the other reps. I wanted him to get word to Toll that I was loving the pizza. "Lemme see inside it," D-Double

Table 6.1 Pizza

Ingredients	
1 "soup" (Top Ramen®) with beef seasoning package	1 package of pepperoni slices
2 hardboiled eggs	1 Slim Jim® styled meat stick
1 bag of original Doritos®	1 container of cheddar cheese squeeze
1 package of mayonnaise	1 newspaper
1 package of grape jelly	Hot water

Directions

1. Using a small opening in package, pour in hot water until soup is submerged; prop soup up for about five minutes or until noodle curls loosen.
2. Drain the water from the bag; neatly flay the softened noodles atop the package.
3. Sprinkle the seasoning package (I preferred the "beef" flavor) on both sides of the noodles; spread grape jelly on one side of the noodles; spread mayonnaise opposite the grape jelly.
4. Spread a layer of cheddar cheese squeeze over the mayonnaise; using a plastic spoon, roughly chop and spread hardboiled egg pieces over the mayonnaise.
5. Lay down a bed of Doritos® over the mayonnaise; spread a layer of cheddar cheese squeeze over the Doritos®.
6. (Optional) Spread another layer of hardboiled eggs atop the cheese; cut and arrange bite sized pieces of the meat stick atop the cheddar cheese or the hardboiled egg (if a second layer was added).
7. Spread a layer of cheddar cheese squeeze over the egg and meat; arrange pepperoni slices over the cheese.
8. Carefully fold the pizza onto itself so that the ingredients are in the center; slide the pizza into its original package.
9. Wrap the package in newspaper to let it "cook" for approx. seven minutes; unwrap and enjoy!

requested with disbelief. I showed him, and he nodded. "OK. I taught all these niggas . . . When you want a champ to make you a pizza . . . " he pointed at himself.

Eventually I took him up on his offer, but we ended up on lockdown and I worried that he might be tempted to eat the pizza he made for me. To my surprise, D-Double appeared at my cell, waving to the pod, and then my cell door popped open. D-Double handed over the pizza he made, explained how to make it, and returned to his cell. I was dumbfounded. That pizza was quite flavorful, though.

A pizza or bag of chips helped to get you through the 12-hour period between dinner and breakfast. Commissary food items—if you had the money on your books to buy some—meant you didn't have to rely upon jail food so much. You would still be hungry though. You would be hungry all the time. Whatever you cooked got you through moments, not hours. It was the same with projects. They were temporary supports for you to endure the vacuity of jail life, and there was always more. There was more nothingness and more hunger than there were brooms or burritos. And yet, there were biological dangers that needed to be endured, too.

Bodies and Fluids

A sheet-shuffling sound of friction woke me. At first, I kept my eyes closed—partially focusing on the sound, partially hoping to fall asleep again. The sound didn't stop, so I stared at the metal underside of the top bunk, listening to the rhythm of the friction. The sound was unmistakable, but I needed a moment to determine what, if anything I should say or do.

My celly, Flip, was masturbating on the top bunk. *What a sad fucking state of affairs.*

Earlier in the day, Flip had excitedly shown me a copy of *Smooth Girl Magazine* that he had gotten on a time-sensitive loan from Beast. Residents weren't permitted to have pornography, but somehow *Smooth Girl*—light on commentary and heavy on imagery—toed the line. I failed to connect Flip's initial giddiness with what was surely to come on the top bunk. And so, I laid there, disgusted, but I couldn't help but to pity Flip. I wondered: What does it take to construct a fantasy to reach erection and to hold it long enough to reach ejaculation while another grown-ass man—a stranger with very little reason to keep your best interest at heart—sleeps (or so you hope) just beneath you? And in this place, no less! How was he compartmentalizing himself and the fantasy from the cell and me? Was he a deviant or a master of concentration?

Jail creates a tension between bodily yearning and resident living conditions. In many cases, the body wins. Flip wasn't sexually deviant; neither did he have superhuman focus. He was just a mid-40-year-old person chasing a fleeting de-stressor. In jail, residents slept. Ate. Laughed. And yes—masturbated, too.

My pity extended only so far, however. I didn't want to be below a man masturbating as I'm sure he wouldn't have appreciated me doing that while he tried to sleep. We hadn't had a conversation about that sort of thing—assuming that was a conversation to be had. I was early in my 180-day sentence, and we had been cellies for only a short time. While he raced toward a stopgap reverie, my imagination assaulted me with short action clips in which Flip and I fought after I had to dodge his dripping semen. The clip would start over and there would be a gush of semen on my leg, an ensuing fight, more charges because I beat Flip ceaselessly, and with my hands in the hair I pleaded my case to an all-male courtroom: "He jacked-off and got some on me!" *Surely, they would understand!*

The moment grew too toxic. I had to say something: "What are you doing?" The sheet shuffling stopped. We didn't discuss it—ever. Maybe he was as ashamed as I was uncomfortable. On the other hand, maybe the situation was as Flip once said: "That's jail," and being jailed means suffering those kinds of intimate violations.

Most residents preferred to wait until they were alone in the cell to masturbate. If you were lucky, your celly left for church, took mental health visits, and had frequent visitors and court appearances. Or there was the highly coveted windfall: you had no celly for the short period between when one leaves and a new one arrives. In one instance, Herc learned that his celly, LK, had court on a particular day: "Ah shit," Herc said while making a masturbatory gesture. "You know what time it is!"

Toll, on the other hand, didn't see the point in waiting on this celly to leave: "My celly know. He just gotta deal with that shit. I do."

But say you can put it out your mind that your celly will masturbate while you're in the cell—that wasn't even the worst of it. To my mind, the dried genetic deposits that wrinkled the pages of *Smooth Girl Magazines* take that title. Beast had a bunch of issues of the magazine that he circulated widely without regard to race. Each issue spent nights with untold numbers of residents, and there were dog-eared pages, offering unwanted windows into someone's favorite. There was a very real chance of putting a thumb or fingertip in dried semen while flipping through what was colloquially known as "jack-off material." It wasn't as though residents weren't aware of this. I wrote field notes while Scott flipped through an edition on the top bunk. He stopped on a page and noted aloud that it was easy to tell "which page they stopped on . . . Fuckin' nasty!" He said he didn't even want to touch the pages, but he didn't put the magazine down.

Toll offered this rationale: "My nigga, it's not about the bitches. I just need a way to relax. A nigga can't be in here with niggas 24/7 and not go crazy."[5] I said something about some guys soiling the pages, and Toll responded: "It is what it is."

In many cases, "it is what it is" was the only thing that could be said about batched[6] living in jail. Aside from the complicated concerns of *using* a *Smooth Girl Magazine*, batched living led many residents to fight their bodies to avoid shameful situations. Byron was my last celly before I left Golden County jails for the final time. Two days after he arrived, I noted that he had not used the toilet in the cell, which meant that he wasn't relieving himself at all. He slept—a lot—so I figured his body was on a different schedule than mine. I worried that he thought he wasn't permitted to use the toilet, so I made sure to remind him that he could. He said he would go during dayroom time if he needed to. I thought that was extreme because dayroom time was so precious, and if a deputy let him in our cell to use the toilet, there was no guarantee a deputy would let him back out.

Another day passed, and it was top tier dayroom time. A few minutes in, Byron went to the sally port to get the pod's attention. Then he quickstepped toward our cell. We joked that he was going to masturbate and that, apparently, it was urgent. Dayroom time ended a half hour or so later, and when I neared the cell, I realized that he had been evacuating over a week's worth of digested food that he could no longer hold. The cell's air was putrid, and there was no place else for me to go. So, I entered that tiny rectangle of awful and shut the door.

Byron's strategy was a common one, and, of course, it always failed. A toilet in a small room means you *can* go, but there remains the pressing awkwardness of relieving oneself in the presence of strangers. Urination and bowel movements were always shared experiences in jail. Some residents put themselves through terrible aches to avoid that situation only to be forced to create an endurance strategy for it.

In open units, residents created curtains using sheets and the drawstrings from uniform bottoms. In closed units, some residents, like Ken and D-Double, created elaborate closures with sheets. Others had no coverings, but they came to an agreement about how to use the toilet. In my cell, the top bunk guy draped his sheet at the foot of the bunks because that's where the toilet-sink was—just inches away. Without that sheet, I could lay on my bunk and look up to make eye contact with my celly while he relieved himself.

About a month into our time as cellies, Scott revealed that he had been "holding it" during his first week in Sunland. I told him I understood. After completing two months in jail, I still had a hard time using a toilet in front of anyone. Often, I had to flush two or three times to stimulate urine despite the pressure I had built up all day. I knew I had to go; I wanted to; I tried, but I just couldn't urinate—not immediately. During my entire time in jail, I tried to relieve my bowels only when I was alone or during sleeping hours. When I couldn't avoid going in the presence of others, I found myself fake coughing or fake sneezing just to break the uncomfortable silence between flushes.

Sometimes, to prepare Scott, I announced that I was about to go in a little while. "I will never get used to doing this in front of everyone," I once commented while laying toilet tissue over the seat.

"Don't get used to it!" Scott said. "That's the point. Why would you wanna get used to this?"

I never did. Even as our stinks started to become more alike—a hindsight-obvious consequence of cloistered living and eating the same foods—I never got used to the biology of jail time. We all started to smell the same. Holding cells tended to have a metallic mildew and milk smell. Resident bowel movements had a more or less faint odor of old beef—not rotten but browned by age. The smells secreted through the skin and gave shared spaces a sour malodor. God forbid a resident had an upset stomach because there was no keeping that to himself. Toilet air communicated freely with everyone via the ventilation system.[7]

Biological assaults were fundamental features of jail punishment. Community showers and phones were microbial cultures. We all wore clothes worn by the legions of humans processed through the jail system. We slept on bedrolls that were damaged and dingy through wear, and no one was guaranteed a daily shower. Jail destroyed the barrier between the personal and the public, and where that barrier was not destroyed, it was ruined by its own permeability.

These were the structural problems of being batched with strangers. Our constant close contact chafed at us, and without a system of rules to reduce the displeasures of each other's company, there would surely be conflict. In response, we used what I call the *politics of politeness—a set of flexible norms for moderating the social friction endemic to jail life.* By *social friction,* I mean the *charged-up frustration and irritation that potentially roughen the flow of social interaction.*[8]

Like so many other annoyances, social friction was worse in jail, but many of the norms constituting the politics of politeness directly addressed problematic situations involving biological processes. A resident plainly told you how to do a thing when you started to do it wrong; you may have mimicked others; and in closed units, your celly covered the politics of politeness as an extension of the orientation. Whatever the means by which a resident learned the norms, their value was universally understood. Unless someone was waiting for their immediate turn, you had to wipe the shower down with your racial group's "wipe down towel," and basic daily hygiene was mandatory. Spitting in the sink was a violation; only spit in the toilet and then flush immediately. In Chapter 1, I noted that experienced residents knew toilet etiquette: "float one; soak one"; flush continually while urinating; sit down and flush to pass gas. However, flushing the toilet while someone ate was a violation. Your rep told you that rule explicitly, and residents were careful to not violate it. However, once in Providence 20D1, I was the last one eating lunch. I suppose I was too quiet for everyone to notice, so a southsider used and flushed the toilet while I was finishing my meal. "Ugh," I responded in disgust.

Joker, the southsider rep, immediately looked my way, surrendered his palms in the air, and started repeating "Hey," as if he couldn't think of anything else to say. He was afraid—not exactly of me—but of the potential for interracial conflict. I looked down and away. To be honest, I wasn't going to do anything more than show the disgust I'd registered. "Eh, Lucky," Joker said to the southsider who flushed the toilet. "You're on sweeping duty."

"Whaaaaat?" he looked around. "Who was eating?"

"Walker," Joker said while pointing his head in my direction.

I could see that Lucky wanted to say something. Perhaps I'd been at the tables unreasonably long. I could see that he wanted to make a case for himself, but he held his tongue. It wasn't worth it. He violated decorum, and his punishment was sweeping the southsider side of the dayroom.

Beyond avoiding biological offenses, the politics of politeness encompassed more general social situations. For example, sitting on the tables was a violation, as was searching through food trays for more favorable portions. And, if your celly decided to stay in the cell during a mealtime, you were given the right of first refusal to get his tray.

These ethical codes reduced but didn't neutralize social friction, and as a result, it was quite easy to irritate someone. The inescapable other—scratching, mouth breathing, snoring, chewing with his mouth open, blinking, giving the same old talking points in recycled conversations—it could be infuriating. "You can just swap most niggas in for other niggas, and ain't shit changed," LK once observed in a low rather desperate tone. He later told me in serious jest: "Niggas lucky I ain't got tired of the people in here yet—'cause I would do something to change the scenery." To be clear, LK was referring to beating someone up and having that victim or himself removed from that housing unit.

The more common strategy to avoid all the resident bodies was just to stay in the cell during dayroom time—if your racial group's politics permitted it. On a few occasions, after hurrying from my cell for dayroom time, I saw D-Double get to his cell door, peek out, wrinkle his face, and close himself in the cell. He once grumbled, "Ain't shit to do out here" before shutting himself inside.

Ken explained that he sometimes stayed in the cell during dayroom time because he "was in the middle of a workout" and "Besides, there's nothing to do out there."

Toll echoed that sentiment: "Dayroom is boring." He went on to say that we had to go out of our way to laugh or get on the phone; otherwise, we would be bored. He said that's why he found himself trying to "make fun" in the dayroom. I certainly understood how they felt. There was an unchanging background to jail life—countless faceless residents—just orange jumpsuits coming and going but only rarely coming to the fore. They mostly remained fixed in the background of dayroom activities, and the sameness made it hard to find the energy to leave one's cell.

Residents in open units didn't have it any easier. Whereas a cell could provide some sense of being backstage, residents in open units had no place to be alone to prepare themselves for social interaction. One of the more unexpected annoyances of this kind had to do with the bunks. Every time the top or middle-bunk resident climbed up or down, they briefly encroached upon the space of the resident on the bottom bunk. It was irksome to have a resident constantly putting a foot near you as he climbed up or down the bunks. To combat that, residents adopted an attitude that I recognized from my childhood. My mother would say, "Stop going in and out of the house! If you're in, you're in!" No one had to say that; you would be shot an annoyed look, and you learned that it was best to stay on or off your bunk for as long as possible.

Indignities and Intrusions

Batched living subjected residents to each other's bodies, and healthcare staff leaned away from the dignities normally afforded patients and into the mortifications common to penal residency.[9] Flip had been coughing in our cell, and he said each cough gave him a sharp pain in his chest and the center of his back. When he saw a nurse about it, she didn't take his temperature, she didn't listen to his lungs or heart, and although he was taking medication for it, she didn't check his blood pressure. Instead, she cut him off mid-description of his symptoms and told him he had a cold. She sent him back to the housing unit with a prescription for a "cold pill." A week and a half later, he was still coughing, sneezing, and pain ruined the little bit of sleep he had been getting.

He went back, and someone in a white coat (he said "doctor," but it may have been a nurse or physician's assistant) said she would order X-rays in two weeks, but he would be out in two weeks, he told her. "Oh! That sounds good," she said. He said she seemed relieved that he would be gone before she could treat him again. He added that his shoulder pain was worsening. She checked the range of motion in his shoulder to ensure nothing was broken, told him not to "move around so much," and then prescribed ibuprofen. Again, no one checked his blood pressure or temperature, and I worried about being in the cell with him while he hacked all day and night.

He said he was afraid to complain about the medical staff or how he was feeling; he had complained before to no avail. Plus, he figured the medical staff saw patients on a first-come, first-served basis and he worried that the staff would purposely misplace his request sheets and he would be skipped in line. It was a valid concern, as nearly all of Flip's interactions with medical staff were negative, and it was often that the pill call nurse skipped some or all his daily medications. Then he would have to plead his case through the cell's intercom. Sometimes a deputy let him out; sometimes they told him to wait until the next pill call. One poignant example came when we were on lockdown, and the runner entered the dayroom with a nurse to pass out medication instead of holding a line at the sally port for pill call. They bypassed us while Flip was at the cell door. "What about Maxwell?" he yelled his last name to get the deputy's attention. The deputy told him to wait until the night pill call.

Flip explained—from behind the cell door—that he took pain pills. The deputy said "only important medicine" was being delivered at that time.

"Those pills are important for my pain! They help with the pain."

The deputy and nurse continued on. We remained on lockdown through the nightly pill call. A different nurse and runner entered the dayroom and stopped at our cell. Flip was at the door complaining that he hadn't gotten his day's medication, and I laid on my bunk wondering whether my medication would, again, be forgotten by the nursing staff.

Flip kept up his demand for an explanation as to why he wasn't getting his medicine regularly. The nurse, a cool-tempered Black man, pointed passed Flip to me on my bunk and said, "Well, you're holding me up, and I have to check on him." I nodded but didn't get off my bunk. Flip got his medication but no answers. As for me, the nurse and deputy forgot about me after the interaction with Flip. I had to hit my cell intercom button and be called down to the sally port just before the nurse left.

It wasn't just the daily negligence of forgetting medication that was so troubling. Flip's description of scant to absent physical examinations by medical staff was typical. Toll described a rash he had near an armpit that itched or hurt when it got dry. He said the nurse made it clear she didn't want to touch him. She never asked to see the rash and told Toll to put baby powder on it. He was shocked because, as he told her, it *sometimes hurt when it was dry*!

During recreation time, we often kicked off our slippers and played basketball barefoot because the slippers were likely to fall apart if you planted and turned too hard in them. Then you would have to go hours, or potentially days, before deputies ensured you got a replacement pair. While playing, I rubbed loose a quarter-sized flap of skin from the ball of my right foot, and it bled in puddles. There was a toilet outside in the rec' area, and someone got me the roll of toilet tissue. I paused before using it thinking about all the living things that might be on a roll of toilet paper by the outside toilet in the rec yard of a jail. I couldn't stop the bleeding, though, so I hobbled to the side, and there was some discussion between D-Double and Ken (as if I weren't there) about whether I should be allowed to alert the deputies. We had only been outside a short while, and deputies were likely to shut rec time down for everyone. Meanwhile, it was stinging a little but I was careful not to wince. I waited until the end.

When I showed the deputy my foot and told him that I needed to see someone about it, he was immediately embittered: "Damn! Now I have to write that up!" I was shocked. Just a few minutes later, a nurse met me at the door to the yard. The deputy was still steaming over having work to do. She didn't touch my foot—not once. She squirted sterilized water at it and half-ass poured hydrogen peroxide onto it. Then she gave me a small amount of Neosporin in a paper cup, some gauze, and a wrap. I put those materials together on my foot.

"No more basketball," the nurse told me.

I couldn't stand to put pressure on the foot, so not playing basketball wasn't a problem. However, walking around was hard. I requested crutches but wasn't given any. Two days later, I was called to the nursing station to have my wound redressed. A different nurse removed my bandages, looked surprised at my foot, and asked whether the previous nurse had put any hydrogen peroxide on the wound. "A little," I said. He poured some on my foot, put more Neosporin on it, and rewrapped it for me. He appeared aware that I'd wrapped my own wound, and I imagined that he knew why, though we never discussed it openly. It was just in the way he seemed annoyed at having to do something right that was so obviously wrong and the look on his face when I told him the previous nurse had put "a little" sterilizing solution on my foot. He had only done his job, and I accorded him a level kindness that must be contextualized within the normal responses of deputies and medical staff to residents as patients. Poor patient care was par for the course.

I had a wisdom tooth extracted while in Sunland. When I arrived in the makeshift dental office, the dentist asked me about my medical history while the deputy escort applied a set of shackles: cuffs at my ankles connected by a short chain and a waist chain connected to the cuffs on my wrists.[10] The setting's contrast could not be sharper. I followed the deputy's instructions to lay in the dental chair, keeping my thumbs tucked in my waist chain at all times. Meanwhile, the dentist wanted to know when I last had my blood pressure checked. I told him it had been months—maybe more than a year. "It should be fine," he said. Then he got started.

During the procedure, the deputy was never more than three-and-a-half feet away, and I felt extreme levels of vulnerability. My mouth was forced agape, I was shackled, a deputy stood watching, and the dentist chastised me throughout the procedure because he was having a hard time with the tooth. As my tooth crunched under the pressure of the dentist's tools, he told me, "Look at that! Look how easily it just breaks." I wondered whether he was talking to me, his assistant, or the deputy. The tooth kept breaking, and he kept berating me about sugar, poor health, and poor hygiene. He was very comfortable lobbing assumptions at me.

When it was over, I was hungry and I asked whether I could eat on the other side of my mouth. The nurse said I couldn't but the dentist said I could, and neither cleared up which was true, so I didn't eat for fear that I'd get a dry socket in my jaw. Unlike my free society experiences with having wisdom teeth extracted, I wasn't given a water syringe with which to wash food from the hole in my gums. Nor was I prescribed a narcotic for the pain, and what I was given was to last only a day and a half. I'd have to submit a kite for more, but I didn't bother.

Submitting a medical request "blue slip" (a kind of kite) wasn't a straight-forward process. Like every kite, you needed to give your rep the blue slip before you could try to turn it in to a deputy. More personal information for reps to learn about you. The small form asked for your "name," "booking number," "date," "location," "signature," and there was a place to check whether you wanted to make a complaint about the medical attention you had received. However, there was no obvious area in which to describe the reason for your visit, so you might assume that you would tell the nurse once you got there. You would be wrong. There was undesignated space outside the area where you wrote your name, date, and so forth, and that's where residents were sup-posed to scribble their medical issue. If you didn't write your issue there, if you didn't fill in any part of the form, if you got something wrong, or even if your slip was dirty or soiled—your blue slip would be ignored.

Sisqo had put in several slips regarding hemorrhoids, and none were answered. He said he was seeing blood. I told him to write "I'm bleeding constantly!" because I figured that couldn't be ignored. Well, after about five more blue slips and talks of suing the county, he finally saw the nurse who, oddly enough, gave him a tuberculosis test and the suppositories he actually went for. He said he was happy to have gotten what he got, but he really did need something to "soak up the blood."

The blue slip itself, and the ways that deputies and medical staff handled them, were barriers to asking for help. That's why I didn't bother submitting for more pain medication. It was easier to fight through the pain. Havocc explained to me that there was a time that he couldn't ignore a medical issue. He told me that he started an earlier stint with signs of a sexually transmitted infection. He decided to put in a blue slip, and days later he was called to the nurse's office. After explaining his symptoms, the nurse had him drop his boxers, and she approached him with a long Q-Tip. "When I saw that, I was like, 'Hold on. Hold on.'" He was exposed with a deputy there, overseeing the nurse with a Q-Tip in her hand. "I kept saying, 'Hold on' because I was nervous, and [the deputy] kept saying, 'Just do it!' Man. Shit was crazy."

And what do you tell yourself when you are criminally objectified but you are also a patient who is yet denied the normal rights or dignities we accord patients? Sometimes we complained to one another about an interaction with a nurse. Sometimes we laughed about how poorly treated someone was. Whatever the tenor of those conversations, they always ended with some version of "That sucks" or "This is that bullshit" or, more broadly, "It is what it is." You noted that biological violations were endemic to jail time, and there was little use in talking about the issue further.

Not every intrusion by deputies was biological; most were built into each jail's physical plant and management practices. Closed circuit cameras were everywhere, and in open dayrooms deputies sometimes appeared at the gate or door just to see the goings on in person. There weren't cameras in the cells, but deputies had another option available to them. Flip and I were nearly out of toilet paper, so I hit our intercom button to request a roll. "I'll see what I can do," the deputy responded.

"Don't see what you can do," Flip said under his breath to me from his bunk. "We need some toilet paper." I turned to him and said we wouldn't be getting anything any time soon.

"Well, if you think it's a lie, it will be," the deputy chimed in. Flip and I stared at the intercom and then one another. Until that moment, it had not occurred to us that deputies could simply turn on the intercom from the pod to listen to any cell of their choice, and we wondered how often they did that.

That moment revealed that the panoptic reach of deputies was greater than we thought, but sometimes deputies went out of their way to assert their presence in our lives. An outrageous example came when the runner entered the dayroom differently than most did. Gray hair stood erect atop his generous head with the sides faded to the skin. He was about 6'2", 220 lbs, with an unbothered face, and he promenaded through the dayroom instead of quick-stepping through the security check. Whereas runners often glanced into cells during security checks, this runner stood and stared into a cell before moseying on to the next. Initially, his security checks were uneventful though strange, but then he entered the dayroom with mail. "Mail!" a resident on the bottom tier yelled out. The announcement stopped the runner in his tracks, and with a hand on a hip and disgusted look on his face, he scanned us in our cells. Then he plodded slower than he had before.

When he reached LK's cell—next to my own—he leaned his back against the railing, crossed his legs, and called out LK's last name. After getting an affirmative response and checking that LK had his wristband—in his cell, which was strange—the runner opened LK's letter, pulled out the pictures, and slowly sifted through each one: LK's wife, kids, and sisters. It was one of the meanest things I'd seen a deputy do, and I felt as much anger as I did sadness for LK who stood in his cell while the runner violated him. After looking at each picture, the runner slowly stuffed them back into the envelope with care before sliding the letter under the cell door and moving on.

Everyone knew deputies listened in on phone calls and read, or at least skimmed, our mail—our letters arrived opened—but I'd never known a deputy to do it like that with such obvious disrespect. Unfortunately, there was no endurance strategy for something like that. We could put it out our minds that deputies opened and viewed our mail before we got it, but how should one prepare for a violation of that degree? It was a reminder that residents could not construct walls around the personal to keep out the public. Jail wouldn't allow for that.

Visitation hours produced a similar kind of indignity. A standing booth visitation area in Providence gave residents very little space with which to hold private conversations with their visitors.[11] Z-Pod's visiting room was worse. The space was just to the side of the command pod and up two small flights of stairs. Brightly lit, it featured sitting booths outfitted with safety glass and a black phone (that I'm sure was never cleaned) with which to communicate with one's visitor. When you sat at the booths, there was about four feet of distance from your back to the wall. Straight to the back of the room was a smaller room in which residents could meet with lawyers. That space was supposed to provide a higher level of privacy than the booths; however, the little room was separated by a sound-permeable door and clear windows, so everyone nearby could see and hear what was being said in that little room. Hell, *visitors* probably heard some of those meetings from time to time.

During one visit, I could not help but overhear a young black resident stumbling through "what happened" while his public defender, a creature rare to jail visiting hours, took notes. The lawyer listened to the young resident's story and then told him he was facing charges of armed robbery, burglary, possession of stolen property, and false imprisonment. She added that he could "pray to god" but that "12 years is a good offer" from the assistant district attorney and that he should sign the deal quickly.

He responded that he needed time before he could just "sign away 10 years," adding that he wasn't 20 years old and that he wouldn't get out until he was 30.

"How much time do you need?"

He said he needed a month, and she said he had two weeks at best, warning him: "You know, [Golden County is] a bitch of a county." She said another guy with similar charges "got 36 years."

I listened to that very personal exchange without craning my neck or straining obviously to catch what was said. If I was privy to the content, so was everyone else in the visitation room.

Meanwhile, we sat at booths—the four or five of us of varying ethnic backgrounds and differing racial classifications—inches apart as we tried to hold personal conversations with our visitors. Even when I couldn't hear exactly what was being said, I couldn't help but to read the emotions on the faces of my fellow residents and their visitors. Other than the occasional smile, I decided not to show much of any emotion during visits. I didn't want to share my visitor with others in that way. Following one visit, Ken apologized to the rest of us in the room. His mother had cried uncontrollably throughout the whole visit. Ken described her cries as "ruining everyone's visits." Everyone there surely heard her crying, but no one said they felt bothered because of Ken's mother.

In fact, during that same visit, a southsider had spent most of his time yelling at his distressed mother: "They're tryna give me life!" Later, as we headed back to our housing unit, he explained that he was just trying to keep his mother from being sad. I thought that a funny way of accomplishing that goal.

In sum, privacy was only in the mind—especially in open units, but in either unit type, a deputy might be listening to your conversation, and another resident was nearly always within earshot. Still, residents had devised a way to gain a modicum of privacy using what I call *penal sign language* (PSL). It was a remarkable endurance strategy—adopted from American Sign Language (ASL). Residents used hand gestures and finger positions like logograms to indicate words or phrases. For instance, the letter "g" was made by fixing one's hand into the shape of a gun. Or, making a gun with one's hands could mean "shooting something" over—that is, passing it—and it could just mean to shoot or that someone was shot. Context matters. Most words, however, needed to be spelled out using an adapted version the ASL alphabet. At the end of each word, the signer waved the signing hand downward as if wiping away what was written in the air. Fluent signers were exceptionally fast, conveying a lot of information in a few seconds, and the best signers could look away while signing once it was clear the other person was reading the message. When, for instance, Toll returned from a court appearance, he was withdrawn, as residents usually were after court, but when Herc signed something to him, he signed a reply in a flurry of finger and hand gestures while looking away.

The PSL system was a way of sharing private information, and I thought it was a cool way of communicating. It just looked fresh, seeing someone signing a message with the most unbothered disposition to someone across the dayroom or through the sally port glass in an adjoining dayroom. After Henry, the white power comrade and rep for Z-Pod, DP'ed the wood who refused to go to dayroom time, Henry signed a confirmation message to a wood passing through the sally port about the discipline session. The two shared a laugh, and it happened in under 15 seconds.

I didn't enter jail knowing PSL. Toll, LK, and Herc told me they learned it in "YA"—California's juvenile justice system. I started off trying to see if I could just pick up PSL by watching. That was a no go. Fluent PSLers were too fast, and they signed too infrequently for me to learn by watching. Plan B: I asked D-Double to teach me, and while he agreed initially, he wasn't motivated to follow through. I had to keep asking him about it.

Finally, he cocked his head to one side, raised an eyebrow, and asked: "Why you wanna learn this?" The question had a tone of suspicion. It wasn't a good idea to develop a reputation for asking residents a bunch of questions—especially about how or why something was done. The questions could be interpreted as investigatory instead of inquisitive.[12] I hadn't prepared for that question, and I could tell the tenor of our interactions would sour based upon how I responded. I stumbled through some nonsense about the need to be able to talk without talking. D-Double didn't say anything, so I added that I might as well learn it since I wasn't going anywhere.

"Aight, nigga," he said and turned and walked away without indicating whether he believed me. In any case, I ended up asking Ken to teach me, and he was immediate with his help. I practiced in my cell, signing book titles and sentences. Seeing that I was serious, D-Double suggested that I first try to learn to read fast. That way, someone could sign a quick message to me, and I was happy to try that, but Scott was my celly at the time, and he didn't know PSL at all. He didn't even want to know. With practice, however, I got good enough to sign a message to D-Double that I wanted hot water or the checkers or chess board or a book. But I never got up the signing or reading speed necessary to chat in PSL.

For a long while, I thought deputies didn't know PSL, and some definitely didn't: "There will be no signing [or] there will be no dayroom," a deputy announced at the start of dayroom time. No one who could sign complied with that threat. I'd see residents sign to each other while being escorted here and there—always in the presence of deputies. However, while in the Barracks Jail, long before I learned PSL, a deputy made eye contact with me and signed something with a smirk. I had no idea what he had communicated, but I surmised that he must have thought it was clever or funny because he seemed mighty pleased with himself. He read my nonresponse and asked if I knew how to sign.

"Nope," I replied.

He seemed disappointed and immediately uninterested in conversing with me. Months later in Sunland, I saw D-Double exchange a few signed messages with a deputy. From then on, I assumed every deputy knew PSL and I knew that strategy wouldn't always work if I had something sensitive to communicate to another resident.

Ultimately, learning PSL was a minor victory. Anyone who knew it could *read* your conversation. Likewise, a "pizza"—while delicious—was temporary. A cleaned cell got dirty again if you didn't keep up your efforts. Eventually deputies confiscated the dice and dominos you made. Your projects did not immunize against the vacuity of jail time. The politics of politeness addressed, but didn't solve, the problems of batched living. Endurance strategies failed not just because they were inadequate but because the circumstances of jail living were relentless in outpacing your ability to keep up the fight. There were vagaries that shocked you off your game and there was always time—palpable and looming.

Alone Time

Scott was released about three hours ago, and the thing that I keep noticing is the echo in this cell. I'm trying to enjoy this alone time, but I'm worried that I'm going to be transferred to a different housing unit or jail. I don't want to pack up and start all over, learning the idiosyncrasies of the residents in a new dayroom—I don't want to do that.

Thirty or so hours later in the middle of the night, Byron entered our cell. I was asleep. I looked to see who it was, but I didn't get up to greet him. I figured I would rundown the cell rules and the politics at breakfast. Breakfast came and he didn't get up. We'll see how this goes.

7

Time

Our relationship to time in free society is radically different from that in jail. Normally, we go to work, to bed, and to leisure activities according to the time[1] and, in so doing, we move through different identities and roles: parent, employee, churchgoer, coach. Each is roughly compartmentalized by time. In this way, time structures and gives meaning to social life. We use time to mark milestones that inform how we understand ourselves and others. Time gives us a sense of progression through life. But time in free society is conceived in terms of scarcity, so we are careful about exchanging our time, saving it, or wasting it on things we don't really want to do. We control time, and the wealthy[2] are so, in part, because they control more time than others.

Jail time is nearly diametric. You do not control time in jail. It is thrust upon you and you "serve" it. Rather than scarcity, you confront the agonizing awareness of the boundless excesses of time, and that comes with a paradox in which you must live: boundless time that is as routinized as it is unreliable. There can be no grasp on the "future," so you live in the constraining immediacy of every present moment. Less obvious at first, but no less problematic, is the destruction of the relationship between time and identities—time and a sense of progression through life. There is only the all-encompassing status of the criminal, and it imbues you with a sense of animated suspension in a world that is impossibly far away from the free world you once knew. Kids grow older. Romantic relationships starve for nourishment. Time-based milestones happen without you, and you cannot say when any of that will change. And so, a fight develops. You fight time itself, so you think, to remain tethered to purpose and movement in the exact ways that time in free society would normally do for you. You "do" indefinite time, and in all your doing, nothing is ever built, improved upon, or solved. But the worst of it— the thing that everyone in jail understands in spirit and flesh—is that your time is yours alone. You are surrounded by others, linked by the time you all do, and you may have a mother, an aunt, a wife, or girlfriend who supports you,[3] but none of that changes the essential fact that you do time in isolation. In jail, it is always just you and time.

Timetables

Most dayrooms had at least one newspaper, but it had to be shared. You could put in a bid to get it, but days might go by before you did. Most dayrooms had a television, and a lot of the time, it worked; however, we rarely watched the news to get the date and time. Dayrooms usually had a clock—sometimes one that told the time—but you could easily go months without ever seeing the sun. Weeks into constant cell light and no access to natural light in Sunland, I noted that the clock read 7:26, and I felt no particular way about whether it was a.m. or p.m.[4] Except for my time in the Providence trustee pod and Providence's 31C3 tank, I always went days or longer without seeing natural light. As a result, I could not track time by clocks or days the way we do in free society. The jail's schedule made sure of that, but I soon discovered that I wasn't alone in finding it hard to keep track of the passage of time. Others had faced that issue and devised a plan.

I blurted to Flip that I couldn't keep track of what day it was and that I worried that my release date would come and go without me knowing. Flip shuffled in our cell the way he often did. Five shuffles from the table to the door and then he suggested the obvious—that I keep track of time. "Like, you know they gotta feed us no matter what—breakfast, lunch, and dinner," he said while pointing to a different finger for each meal. "So, that's a day. That's how I do it." It was an elegant solution to a difficult problem: locating the self in *when*. It didn't occur to me at the time, but I'd met a southsider in intake who told me he had been there for three days. The Providence intake area had no access to natural light or clocks, so it may have been that he counted meals—nine of them. But if it had not occurred to me to construct a timetable around meals, I figured maybe others were doing it, yet differently, so I made it a point to find out.

As it turned out, residents often created multiple timetables,[5] using events,[6] not clocks, to organize life and to create a sense of progression through time in jail. There was "dayroom time," "lights out" time, "visitation time," "feed time," mental health time, time for pill call, recreation time, mail time, "face card" time, "court bodies" time, time for prison transfers, time for commissary orders and deliveries, and time for clothing exchanges.[7] Though some of these events tended to occur around a particular clock time, none were beholden to the clock. They occurred whenever they did—as it was convenient to deputies, so there was little point in focusing on *when* they happened as opposed to *that* they happened at all. That is the principal difference between clock and event time: the focus on measures of time (clocks) versus occurrence (events). (Part of what made intake processing so disorienting was the dramatic shift in temporal organization from clock time to event time.)[8]

In addition to meals, Flip counted the pill calls: "That's one," he would say after the morning pill call. Paul-Bunyan scheduled his time around routine trips to mental health.

Deputies didn't deliver mail on Sundays, and Scott's girlfriend wrote him every day—sometimes twice a day. When he didn't hear from her, he would remark: "It must be Sunday . . . I didn't get a letter."

LK had a similar timetable in that his wife visited him twice a week without fail. He relied on those visits for his emotional wellbeing as well to track time. I sparked a conversation with Ken about how he tracked his time: "After a while, you stop thinking about it," he said. "You just go to court and two weeks later, you go to court again—like that."

Beast caught the end of the comment but added: "Yeah. You go from court date to court date, and for me that's every three months."

Ken kept other timetables, too. "Hot links come every other Friday," he told me. I hadn't noticed that pattern at all. "Shit. I can even tell you the deputies' schedules—like who will be here."

The bases for which residents created timetables showed a lot of diversity. In the end, I learned the following. First, our timetables reflected how events gained significance over clocks. In free society, life is profoundly structured by clock time, but in jail, events dominate social life, and the transition wasn't a smooth one. It's why some men in intake found themselves desperate to know the time even though that information wouldn't change anything. It was the same for residents in court holding cells.

Second, timetables were idiosyncratic to those events that mattered most to the resident constructing the timetables. I didn't have regular visits, but I hated the Sunday clothing exchange, and in trying to learn how others tracked time, I realized that I'd created a timetable from Sunday to Sunday. Flip relied upon his medication. He generally had no commissary money, so tracking meals and pill calls made sense. LK and Scott depended upon the support of women in their lives, so they tracked time by that support. Ken explained that he kept a bunch of timetables just to keep his mind busy—thus creating a sense of temporal movement and an endurance strategy against the tedium of jail routines.

Whether constructed purposefully or organically, resident timetables were important for locating oneself in the cross section of place-time. You could never be confused about where you were. Your position in "place" was sure, but it wasn't so easy with time. Timetables helped to keep us from living what could feel like an unstructured life where the past collides with the present, and the future is so unknowable as not to be worthy of heavy thinking.

"Hard-Timing-It"

I told you a fight ensues in the doing of jail time. Of course, you cannot fight time, but you nonetheless try because "fighting time" is in your knowledge base as a thing that is possible and that you should do in this kind of situation. No one tells you how to do it precisely because it cannot be done. The actual fight is turned inward,[9] and this is a fight that is far more common to the human condition—especially for those who have been denigrated and demoralized without ways to reestablish their dignity. You fight to repress the thick fog of negative emotions weighing upon you from the inside out. This is the most important endurance strategy you can have, but it cannot be passed from one person to the next like learning to make dominoes. Jail time is a solitary experience, and you are on your own with figuring out how to repress the anger, the fear, the frustration, the shame, the guilt, and the resentment that you feel about the whole of your circumstances. Whatever the means that you choose, no endurance strategy is a permanent solution. Sometimes you don't get to exchange your boxers; sometimes deputies put you in a day-room with residents who hate you. And the jail is always cold. Your friend doesn't put that money on your books. The stink doesn't go away and neither do your sleep problems. Eventually, there will be a trigger—something vicious or ostensibly small in consequence, and you may only observe and not even experience it in your own body, but it will send you beyond the bounds of what you can repress, and then you will be *hard-timing-it*.

Hard-timing is a period of emotional breakdown—when your endurance strategies have failed you, and you feel an overwhelming mixture of diffuse anger[10] and diffuse sadness. When hard-timing-it, your senses sharpen to the jail's environment and your vulnerability and your lack of efficacy. You become more aware than you want to be of just how awful your circumstances are, and the jail's preservative-packed food from which a mad chemist stripped nearly all the natural flavors is so much worse. Your celly feels like a throng of people. The cheap, industrial detergent in your oranges is nauseating. The air conditioning system is extra loud in the silence, and the stupid conversations others are having are sharply irksome. When hard-timing-it, expect a combination of two reactions: a riot of repressed frustrations will express themselves through you, or you may suffer an acute withdrawal into the deepest blues within yourself. The latter was more common in my experience, but I saw the former's potential—especially in LK.

More than others, LK had a fight at the ready. He once confided that he had been fighting his whole life because it seemed that there was always someone who wanted a fight. As a reminder, he and his brother were in jail because of a fight. Having a fight at the ready is rational if you perceive yourself to be under constant threat. To one degree or another, we were all bracing in Golden County jails. Five days into Scott's time in Z-4, my own worries led me to ask him if he had concerns about getting out. He had a release date, but he said, "Yes. Like they'll put another case on me." Flip and Lee also expressed the concern that *something* would keep them from being released according to schedule.

But having a fight at the ready made LK a bit of a live wire. His mother knew Scott's mother. They had been through the same drug treatment program—something they discovered while in jail. After that discovery, Scott and LK regarded each other as cousins, so when Scott got into a fight in the dayroom over phone time, LK felt obliged to insert himself.

Scott was a skinny guy—about 5'9". No one would be threatened by his presence. His opponent, Brian, was a black resident who had only been in our dayroom for about a week. He was slightly taller but no less slim than Scott, and he had spent most of his first week rubbing people wrongly: complaining and making snide remarks. An interesting point of information: When Brian first joined us in Z-4, he had fresh bruises. LK learned and shared with us that Brian had been in G-2 with LK's brother, who put a whooping on Brian for one reason or another. We filed that in back of our minds whenever Brian became annoying, but I don't think Brian knew who LK was.

On this particular day, Scott was on the phone with his mother. He had made his bid earlier, and while the rest of us were honoring Scott's phone time, Brian—for reasons that only he knows—approached Scott mid-conversation and hung up the phone. Before Scott could fully register his shock and anger, Brian took a swing at him. Scott dodged and slammed Brian on the ground. The fight was over in an instant. LK hadn't seen what happened, but he listened with growing anger to Scott explain the fight. Brian's celly, Dago, passed by in that same moment, and LK socked him in his face under the dubious claim that Dago somehow had something to do with what Brian had done. That made no sense, and hours later, we watched from our cells as Brian headed to the sally port with his bedroll and property box. D-Double hadn't arranged that transfer, so Brian must have told the deputies that he didn't feel safe in the unit. That would follow him for sure. Dago headed to the sally port soon after, but he wasn't carrying anything. He returned to his cell, and during the next dayroom time for top tier residents, Dago explained that deputies had asked him if he felt unsafe to which he said "no one is threatening" him.

In any case, that event encapsulates who LK was to me, so when news spread that my official release date was just over a week away, I felt uneasy because the friendly banter I'd once shared with LK became noticeably contentious. It wasn't outright conflict; he was just being short with me. Simultaneously, I was emptying my commissary account to buy food and phone time for him, Herc, and Toll. Orders were capped at $30, presumably to reduce the likelihood that a resident would be extorted for everything in his account, so it took two cycles before I was done. But while my generosity hit its mark with Toll and Herc, LK was unmoved. We didn't laugh or joke with each other anymore. Finally, he looked at me with envy and confessed: "I just don't want you to leave . . . I should be getting out." After that, I stayed away from him, which he made easy because he started spending all his dayroom time on the phone. Then he stopped coming out for dayroom time altogether. He stopped interacting with us, and I was no less worried. I wondered whether he would hurt himself or explode in anger and attack me as I headed to the sally port to leave. A fight could lead to a new charge, and that would mean more time. I really couldn't do more time—not while being so close to getting out.

I understood how he felt. It made me queasy to see others being released, and you could always tell when it was a release and not a transfer. It was the uncontrollable smile and pep in their step that signaled freedom on the horizon. I saw Flip leave, and eventually I would see Scott leave, too. Both times, I felt a kind terrible desperation and painful envy in my body mixed with something like happiness for them. That feeling is why residents didn't broadcast their release dates or give updates as that magical day approached.

While at court, Scott said he met a guy who was complaining about his chains and how he didn't want to hear about anyone being released. Scott said he interjected that he wasn't going anywhere. *That must have been awkward.* But that's exactly the point: you meet a resident in a moment of hard-timing-it; you don't know how long that moment will last or to what consequences, but you know that talking about how soon you'll be free is definitely not the right move.

No one liked to see others leave. Scott openly described the experience as "hard time," but even if he hadn't, I was in the cell with him when he would retreat to his bunk after we watched someone walk to the sally port to be released. I watched him rock slightly and silently until he fell asleep. I understood why we sometimes wouldn't talk for a day or so afterward. Lee said he felt the same way. On one occasion, three residents left at once—one of whom, David, had been with us for a few days. It was top tier dayroom time, so David walked past us on his way out. He and D-Double dapped each other. Herc more so pushed David's hand away than offered a friendly handshake. LK didn't say good-bye or offer dap. He just stared with his fuzzy cornrows and muscular shoulders drooping forward.

Part of why someone else's freedom was so painful was that it was an unwelcome reminder that you weren't going anywhere and that you couldn't say when that would change. There was always this lingering, mostly latent, feeling that maybe, you would never get out. You rode the Hope Rollercoaster, but you were still in jail. Then someone else left, and you couldn't do a thing about being there. You knew it wasn't true, but it was hard not to feel as though someone was flaunting their freedom in your face.

I always forced that pain upon myself. For me, someone else's freedom was just part of the scenery, and there would just be someone new anyhow. Besides, I'd been on the opposite end—the giddy guy getting released while others milled about, pretending to be unaffected by my excitement. And I'd seen others do "easy time"—*the feeling of emotional impregnability despite the difficulties in one's situation.* Nothing in the baseline circumstances of your jail time change, but you feel shielded from the negative emotional effects of it all. You got confirmation of your impending release, and nothing could spoil your mood because you would soon be free. You got a letter from the right woman saying she would put money on your books and pay you a visit, and nothing else mattered—not the deputies, not the guy on the middle bunk who snores, not nothing—at least, for a little while.[11]

Still, for LK, seeing others leave was a trigger for hard time, but that wasn't the only trigger. One of the first times I knew LK to do hard time came when he returned to the tables after a phone call. He had a troubled look and clenched fists.

"You good?" I asked.

He had just learned that one of his three daughters was sick. It was just a cold, but it came on the heels of the previous week's news that his sister, a few cousins, and some of their friends got into a fight in a club. Afterward, his sister "went into the bathroom to fix her hair; two girls came in after her and started slicing her up . . . You could see her teeth" through her cheek, LK said. His sister was in the hospital, and he blamed himself for not being there. He couldn't shake his guilt. "Niggas betta stay the fuck outta my way. I just don't give a fuck 'bout no one and nothin' right now." His eyes were deadly serious. Over the next week, he became a recluse. "I'mma just stay in my fuckin' cell cuz if not, yo, Egypt, I'm just gonna hurt one of these niggas, ya know? I just got a lot of hate right now . . . 'Don't wanna be here. 'Can't do shit . . . "

His daughter got over her cold, his sister recovered, and LK overcame that period of hard-timing-it only to face another. It was about six or seven weeks before I was to leave—before our interactions turned sour. He returned from an "attorney visit" to the dayroom with moderate excitement. His lawyer had told him that he might be released just a few days later—on a Friday. We started congratulating him—mixed with a bit of reflection on our respective situations. Toll said he wished it was him getting good news, but he nonetheless said he was glad someone was getting out.

D-Double, however, bitterly sucked his teeth: "Nigga ain't goin' nowhere." The comment was so arresting that it paused our conversation before any of us said how foul it was to say that. Well, that Friday came and went—and so did several others. *Something*—I never learned what—had happened in his case, and LK became despondent and withdrawn. In the end, I left before him—without incident.

Though some events and circumstances increased the likelihood of hard-timing-it (court outcomes, for instance), there was no predicting hard time. Breakdowns in one's emotional fortitude came when they came. Herc described the anger and "depression" he felt at having to convince his family to put money on his books. "It don't gotta be a lot," he said to which I added that just $5 would help because that bought a lot of $0.31 soups. "I told them that!" Herc shook his head and hung it low. Without free society support, hunger was constant. We weren't fed enough to be satisfied, and most of us came from poor families[12] who could not easily let go of $20. Plus, at that time, if say, your mother wanted to put money on your books, she would have to drive to the jail you were in and physically make the deposit. A two-hour round trip could be a major barrier—especially to drop off $20[13].

Herc was the youngest of seven boys, and he had four sisters, so he understood that it wasn't easy for his parents to help him, " . . . but I'm fucking hungry!" He said he hated begging them, and he hated accepting the little bit of help that I gave him from time to time. Like Lee once told me, Herc said he didn't want to feel like he owed anyone, but also it was demoralizing. He said he would be "staring at other niggas soups like—." He didn't finish his thought, but I suspected he found himself contemplating how to take someone else's food. I told him I understood. His family kept telling him that they would send something in a few days—presumably when it was convenient for them. "Shit. Nigga! I'm hungry now!" Herc said with a sad chuckle. His near constant hunger robbed him of his ability to laugh and joke on more than one occasion. It disrupted his sleep, and sometimes, hunger made him "not even wanna hear what niggas be talkin' about at all."

I empathized with him. I'd been too hungry to listen to Flip or Scott talk. In my opinion, hunger-induced hard time was more deleterious than other triggers. It was hard to manage the politics, to gird your emotional self for an in-custody court appearance, or to play a game with your celly when you were hungry. It seemed hunger permitted hard-timing-it to sneak upon you like whisper in your ear, telling you how much you hated it in jail, and soon, that's all you could hear and feel. But hypersensitivity to how despicable jail living was only made your time harder to endure. If you were LK, you lashed out. If you were Herc, you withdrew into yourself. It had not occurred to me at the time, but they were cellies, and thinking back, I have to wonder how those opposing styles of hard-timing-it coexisted in one cell.

With time, I learned subtle clues that hard time was not far. Of course, your endurance could be torn asunder in a single event. It didn't have to be a slow-moving blow that got you. The night that Scott received five letters was too much for me. Before I'd surrendered myself, I practically begged my girlfriend at the time to abandon me because I suspected that it would be too hard for me to *do* jail time while wondering about one infidelity or another. She refused and promised to be there, but two months in, I'd not heard from her. Meanwhile Scott's girlfriend wrote him daily. I'd been handling my envy stoically, but five letters in one night made me feel more abandoned than I could, at the time, endure. I stopped talking to Scott for a few days. It took that long to rebuild my emotional reserves.

Less dramatic but more common, I noted that a resident was at an increased risk for hard-timing-it when he started to focus on the unchanging character of jail time. Scott stared out our cell door window and observed: "Same games; same crimes." Then he threw himself on the top bunk. A few meals later, he complained about everybody being "basically the same." He opted to stay in during dayroom time. Soon, he became withdrawn—only speaking to nitpick about the details of the housing unit.

Toll had a similar pattern. When he wasn't aggrieved about a court appearance, hard-timing-it for him often started with an observation about a structural detail that particularly bothered him. We were in the dayroom not talking when he explained that he "could write a write a whole book on just the paint on the walls—how it makes you crazy." The relentless sameness of the character of jail had a dulling effect on one's emotional wellbeing. I remember feeling *blah*—listless—and eventually I had to fight to leave my bunk.

Indeed, it's that fight—your renewal of your energy to endure—that was the slower path to breaking free of hard time. Good news could be a shortcut, but good news was a rarity. Paul-Bunyan told me he felt "hopeless, like my body was heavier than normal" after a series of bad news events regarding his family. "I was hard-timing-it big time then." He said it took him some time to "snap outta that."

That was my usual path, too. My mother wrote me while I was in Sunland to tell me that Micah hadn't been taking his homework seriously. Normally, he was endlessly excited to fill his brain with information for later regurgitation to anyone who would listen. I felt stabbed by the news that he seemed to be losing that spark. *If I wasn't in jail*, I kept thinking. The thought was affixed to my mind for quite some time during which, every tiny detail of jail felt magnified. Until that point, I'd been treading water, but with that news, I let myself sink for a few days before kicking to the surface again. In any case, you couldn't know when you would be hard-timing-it; only that you would be.

Byron

My new celly, Byron, put me in a difficult situation. I was like a frustrated parent, nagging him to stop walking in the cell with his slippers on. The boy wouldn't listen! Yesterday we played basketball during rec, and while the rest of us showered at the next opportunity, I had to tell Byron to shower. Of course, he didn't have soap, so I had to give him some, and instead of standing inside the shower first and removing his boxers like every other man in this dayroom, he got stark naked and *then* got into the shower. Then, because he was the last to shower before the end of dayroom time, he ran to our cell and stood naked, drying himself off while trying to talk to me about his former girlfriend. I suppose I should be thankful because he mostly sleeps—in his oranges, mind you—and good grief does that man stink: onions and sour milk.

Toll and D-Double were sure that Byron is detoxing: "That stuff is coming out of this skin," D-Double explained. "I've had a few cellies detox. It is what it is. He can't help it. He's gonna stink no matter how many showers he takes."

I wanted test that theory, though. Byron hadn't taken enough showers for us to be sure. Herc told me to whoop his ass, but I didn't wanna fight a grown man because he wouldn't shower. LK said he can't stand the way Byron smells, and that it's my responsibility to do something about it. "Huh?" I asked with confusion.

"Yeah, nigga. That's your celly. Your responsibility," LK doubled down.

I threw my hands up. I wasn't sure whether LK was serious. My release date was just over a week away. *I'm supposed to beat this man up and jeopardize my release? Naw.*

Herc said he would help me. The pod popped the cells for dayroom time, and Herc appeared in our doorway with noticeably affected anger and bluster. "This fuckin' cell stank!" he said with a curled lip. I had to hide my smile. He directed his attention to Byron: "Nigga, you need to wash yo' ass and clean this fuckin' cell. We don't play this stinky bullshit you're playin.'"

I joined in, "He want someone to get on his head so he can learn is all."

Byron looked concerned. "Naw. I'm gonna clean it up, and I can get an indigent kit from the deputies, right?" This was not his first time in jail, and I'd already told him to how to get basic supplies, so his question was meant to pacify us with the idea that he had a plan to do better with his hygiene. He followed through, though—not up to my standards but enough to keep the pressure off me to do something about him stinking before my release.

8

Nightmares and Respite

Scott's snores were interspersed with whimpers throughout the night. I laid awake. Breakfast was just over an hour away, so I didn't see any sense in trying to get sleep. When Scott woke, he was sweaty and disoriented in our cold cell. "I was going through it last night," he said as he got ready for breakfast. I nodded. "Make me don't e'en wanna sleep."

Early into my longest stretch in Sunland, I started recording my dreams. I can't say that I was looking for anything in particular. I'm not the kind of person to interpret dreams as anything more than a congeries of emotions, lingering thoughts, and circumstances, but hearing about the kinds of dreams other residents were having, I began to understand just how consequential jail[1] could be for setting the themes for resident dreams.

One night I dreamed that I was my teenage self but in the present day. I was standing with my son, Micah—nearly eight-years-old—in one of my childhood living rooms. My mother was walking in and out of the living room, gathering supplies for bingo night, and I was trying to convince her to stay because I was sure something awful was about to happen. She was unmoved, and suddenly I was discovering my son, dead, floating in water. Was it a pool? The tub? I have no idea, but I knew in that instant that it was my fault—that I'd been neglectful. I grabbed up his lifeless body and ran into the night air. Standing in the street, holding him, I bawled until I awoke, sobbing.

More often than I care to admit, in fact, the tickle of tears tracing the contours between my nose and cheeks woke me from a painful dream. On another occasion, I entered a dream running. I don't know to where or from whom, but I felt I was running away. I ended up at the now-gone K-Mart on King Hwy and Lightning Ave where I once worked after graduating high school. I had the sense that I'd been there before, in that store, under the same conditions (whatever they were). I ran by the bedding area, saw an amorphous woman that I nonetheless recognized as a coworker. After a kiss and agreement to meet after her shift, I continued my escape. I came upon a favorite movie theater. There I saw my coworker again—this time on a moving walkway. She was chatting with a friend who warned her that I was a deadbeat father. I appeared next to the two women, and we took an escalator down. At the bottom was Micah, in his late teens or early 20s, holding a gun and urging me to turn myself in. I ran. He chased. We came upon a narrow tunnel to trains, and police were everywhere. Suddenly, Micah was attacking me while the police tried to stop him. I yelled that Micah had a gun, and the police wrestled harder against him. He shouted, over and over again, that I must be stopped. A shot rang out, and I clutched my side. A gash opened on the side of my head, and I slumped to the ground. *Had someone hit me, too?* Dying and gripped with sadness and regret, I yelled to Micah, trying to assure him that I forgave him for shooting me. My yells became indistinct groans, then shallow breaths. I gathered myself for one last shout, and that's what woke me: the sound of my voice calling for my son. I guess "I was going through it" that night.

"Everyone Does"

If I might inject some retrospective self-psychoanalysis here: Each time I was arrested and jailed, I felt all the more guilty for being an awful father—a single father who wasn't living up to his responsibilities. Reaching back with the strengths I currently have, I'm ashamed of my weaknesses then. I cannot shake the guilt of my failures: how I mishandled depression, falling down when I needed to remain standing, resisting the help of others because I'm a big Black man. I find myself scrutinizing the smallest misstep my children take. *Is this because I was an awful father so many years ago?* It's magical thinking and a terrible existence, questioning yourself and whether the fruit you're tasting comes from the tree planted in your own deeds. When I was locked up, it seemed the weight of that guilt pulled on my dreams, causing movie-esque scenes in which I was chased by the police or deputies or mental health staff; sometimes I was wounded while defending my child, or I was in some strange revenge mission to kill someone who had sexually assaulted my son or an ex-girlfriend's youngest daughter. Never was I there to stop the initial harm, and my sense was always that I had been neglectful. Whatever I was doing was too little, too late. And so, when I slept, nightmarish distillations of my emotional self dripped and sizzled like acid on my consciousness, etching into my psyche themes of loss, rejection, fear, violence, captivity, and regret.

But Scott and I weren't the only ones going through it in our dreams. During church in Z-Pod's program room, a normally stoic southsider who regularly led prayer described a recurring dream in which he was pinned with dogs barking angrily at him but always just out of reach. He said there were "serpents striking" at him. He figured it must have been god that kept the serpents and dogs at a safe distance. It was a surreal thing to listen to a man tell of being trapped in his dreams with angry animals trying to harm him.

After that, though, others in our "prayer circle" slowly began sharing. In each case, the rest of us nodded, as if to say, "Yeah. I had that one, too." Each person's dreams were as intrusive and traumatic as the previous.

It's clearer to me now than it was then that dream content can be profoundly sociological. The kinds of dreams we have, and the intensities therein, are partly shaped by social circumstances.[2] In this sense, dreams are not just individual but social experiences, and they are likely patterned thematically in conjunction with the types of roles and encounters we have across the life course. Your dreams are not wholly your own, and the effect is amplified in cloistered organizations like jails.

For some residents, that meant an increase in certain kinds of dreams and a decrease in the likelihood of others. I had more than my fair share of traumatic dreams, but none of the dreams I recorded were erotic[3]—even as I pined for my girlfriend at the time. And I count myself lucky on this matter because such dreams would have made the loss of a woman's touch all the more painful.[4] Neither did I have what I call *productive sleep* wherein the *mind tinkers with an idea and solves a next step in the middle of the night or just as you wake.* In jail, that creative machinery was on the fritz. Some days, I had clearer purpose of thought than others but, on the whole, I was not operating at capacity.[5]

Still, my response to my nightmares and poor sleep was simple: *It is what it is.* That's what I told myself, but Scott reached his breaking point with troubled sleep. He had had a run of days with very little sleep, and while awake, he worried about what might come up in his dreams. I thought it was a little like setting a drink near the edge of a coffee table, then telling someone not to knock it over. You can't really imagine *not* doing something, and Scott couldn't imagine *not* having a bad dream. Ignoring that my own dreams scared me, I couldn't help but wonder whether his constant fretting about bad dreams increased their frequency—maybe his anxiety forced the content to the fore of his mind. "I just wanna sleep," Scott said desperately. Then, he announced that he was going to mental health for help.

Flip, my first celly before Scott, had problems sleeping, too. He had regular visits with mental health staff, and he was given a sleep aid in the form of a pill. Whatever he was given, it didn't help him sleep. Initially, Scott's experience was different. He returned from that first trip to mental health with a prescription for a sleep aid that seemed to work. Thirty minutes after taking the pill, he was knocked out for four or more hours, which was great, but then he experienced a new sleep problem: Scott stopped remembering his dreams. "When you don't dream, it's like you didn't sleep," he declared.

"That makes no sense," I retorted. "Your body rests from sleep—even if you don't remember the dream." I wasn't sure of that, but I thought I saw it on the Internet somewhere, so I said it with confidence.

"No," he said, explaining that it wasn't that he couldn't remember his dreams. "I ain't havin' no dreams at all—like nothing."

"They say you dream even if you don't remember it," I said—again, the Internet.

"I ain't been dreamin' at all."

We continued the debate for a few minutes more, and then it was day-room time. We involved Toll in our discussion: "I don't know about dreamin' cuz I hardly have time to. I barely sleep," he said. We laughed and agreed. "Nigga, I'm just so rested, I don't need sleep anymore," he continued with half a chuckle. Then Toll asked something that still sticks in my mind. He described "getting comfortable" sometimes on his bunk, and he asked, "Y'all don't get comfortable sometimes?" He rolled his shoulders as if pulling up an imaginary comforter.

Scott and I replied with different versions of, "Hell no!" and there was a brief pause as the three of us took that in. Scott broke the silence by again asserting that without dreams, it was impossible to feel rested. Toll responded that even with the little sleep he was getting, he didn't remember most of his dreams. I said I looked forward to my dreams—good or bad—because they were a natural check that my mind was still working.

Toll replied that he daydreamed far more often than he dreamed at night, adding that "lately . . . even" his daydreams were repeating themselves. He said he would be in bed thinking so much that his thoughts started repeating until he "ran outta shit" to think about. Then his celly, Lee, approached, and Toll launched into a familiar complaint. During our frequent periods of lock-down, Toll said he would be wide awake, but Lee slept "like 20 hours a day," and when he was awake, Toll said of Lee, they didn't talk or directly interact much. "Nigga don't play no games or none of that shit cellies play."

Lee didn't dispute the characterization. He merely shrugged and added: "Just the same old shit," as if to say there was almost no point in being awake at all. Toll took that as confirmation. He said celling with Lee was like being in solitary confinement.[6] But, Lee's sleep behaviors weren't uncommon. In open dayrooms, residents laid silently and nearly motionless on their bunks for most of the day. There weren't activities available that motivated residents to leave their bunks, so while some of us couldn't get to sleep or stay or asleep, others slept or laid on their bunks for excessive periods.

Regarding the repeating dreams and daydreams Toll described, he may have been experiencing some form of ruminating, or just as likely, his mind might have been looping whatever sensory information it had on hand—a kind of *deprivation dream*, if you will. Indeed, sensory deprivation may explain, in part, why residents kept having the same conversations with the same statements and the same points of view. We looped topics during waking hours, and that looping apparently bled into Toll's dreams.

That resonated with me. I'd recorded a dream in which I was approaching a group of 20-something-year-old Black men outside of a park or schoolyard or a stoop—the scene was a moving target. Each of the men had on Timberland boots, and in my dream, I figured I was in New York. I watched the group—the eight or nine of them—talking as if on mute: their lips moved and hands gesticulated, but the scene was silent. Then I heard the opening keyboard chords to the remix version of Jodeci's "Come and Talk to Me." I hadn't heard that song in years. As the music progressed, the guys fell in line and performed a choreographed dance routine. For some reason, I felt ashamed that I didn't know the steps. The anxiety about not knowing the dance lingered after I woke and mixed with confusion. I wondered why my mind had called that song up and set it in that scene.

Intermittently, I had other deprivation dreams. Almost without exception, they involved a song I hadn't heard in years, a film or scene from a television program that I'd long forgotten, or a place I hadn't seen in over a decade. Sensory deprivation could be a tricky matter. Toll's thoughts and dreams became reruns while my mind fished around for bits and pieces of nostalgia and stitched together motley dreams. Of course, I couldn't recall every dream. Sometimes I couldn't remember a dream with any detail, and the harder I tried to write what I'd experienced, the foggier the dream became until I was left with nothing but emotional residue. I *felt* the dream content.

Scott was describing something different, though. His sleep had become a void, but he stuck with his trips to mental health, he kept getting a few hours of sleep, and I started to wonder whether I should do the same. It wasn't until I had a brief conversation with Beast that I committed to a mental health trip. "What's up, Egypt," Beast said to me. As mentioned previously, residents sometimes called me "Mike" and sometimes called me "Egypt." I told him I was doing OK, but because the issue was fresh on my mind, I told him that I was having problems sleeping. "Everyone does," he said. Then he explained that everyone goes to mental health "eventually." Three years prior, when he was just starting out in jail, he had gone to mental health for sleep-related problems. His candor spurred me to seek help. I figured if he, as the southsider rep, wasn't embarrassed to admit that he had taken a mental health visit to improve his sleep, I could do the same. I put in a kite.

Nurse Bee

My first mental health visit was with Nurse Bee. I sat in the little booth with my back to the hallway, and she sat behind the glass partition with her back to a busy office area. There were always people crisscrossing behind her, and I worried about my privacy, but I didn't feel that I could press the issue. She opened the session with a kind smile and greeting. It was disarming. I had taken my seat with all my defenses up, ready to completely disengage from the conversation if I sensed she was saying or doing the wrong thing—whatever that might have been. I hadn't had the best experiences with mental health staff in Golden County jails, after all.

She flipped through some papers in front of her, pulling from the bottom of each page because they were affixed at the top. She mentioned something about my release date and asked me whether I knew it. Before then, I'd tried and failed to calculate it on my own, and I was starting to feel as though I didn't really have one. *Maybe they tricked me with signing that deal, and I'll just be here in until . . .* She read the date to me with a smile, and I immediately felt relieved. I had been officially scheduled for release, and I just needed to endure until then. My appointment ended soon after that. We were only meeting each other—not discussing my problems. Yet, she left quite an impression upon me. She asked me if I'd like to see her again, and it felt like a genuine ask—not a command disguised in question form. She didn't make me feel like it was my agency against the structure she represented; she wasn't pushing herself on me the way the jail environment intruded upon every other corner of resident life. She told me, "Some people like to come down here because they say it's a nice environment . . . Others don't want to get stuck down here . . . It's cold." All of that was true.

I scheduled my next visit, we said our good-byes, and I listened as she entered the neighboring booths to talk to patients on either side of me. The partitions were thin corkboard, so there was even less privacy than I thought. I came to hate hearing patients in neighboring booths describe nightmares about blood and family members crying. Paul-Bunyan, the burly wood with whom I regularly conversed, told me he wanted to tell the psychiatrist about the uncontrollable anxieties he had been having about his impending trial and the terrible daydreams those anxieties caused, but "there ain't enough privacy" and "it was bad stuff."

On that day, however, still my first day, her next patient described the sleep problems he was having. She told him she was going to give him a "skill" to help. He might not have noticed the tension in his own body, she explained, but residents walked around with a lot of tension and then laid down with that same tension in the form of contracted muscles. I instantly thought of how bracing might be contorting my body. Then she described a "body scan" technique that might help. She said to lay on your bunk and focus on conscientiously relaxing the muscles in one leg from the hip to the toes. Then do the other leg, the pelvis, stomach, body, arms, hands, face, jaw, and the top of the head. The goal, she explained, was to release tension so that when or if sleep came, the body would be relaxed and ready to be refreshed. I still do this sometimes. That patient's session ended as quickly as mine had, and she entered the booth on the other side of me with a patient who dominated the conversation, pouring his mind out onto her. Though Nurse Bee noted that he was going over his allotted time, she nonetheless stayed with him. She didn't rush. She didn't interrupt. She listened.

The Master's Tools

I reentered Z-4 in the same state in which I began my appointment with Nurse Bee. I'd ear hustled the "body scan" technique, but my trip to mental health didn't improve my sleep problems. In fact, every time I went, I was reminded that nightmares and interrupted sleep were germane to being jailed and sleep health was directly impacting our physical and emotional health. In hindsight, it was absurd to think sleep-related problems in jail could be solved by mental health experts—in jail. Audre Lorde was right about the master's tools not dismantling the master's house.[7] I suppose none of us could be blamed for trying. As residents, what other choices did we have? What other choices could we even imagine? Sociologist Pat Carlen[8] made a similar point about women's prisons that applies here: Penal organizations can't be used to fix anything in the lives of their residents because penal organizations just break shit and are governed by logics that necessarily thwart attempts at reform. The notion that rehabilitation of any kind could occur in a place designed to cause pain and destroy human potential is misguided at best. Any successful attempts at rehabilitation should begin with questions that reimagine penal goals—questions that lean into care instead of punishment. There is an inherent foolishness—a purposeful ignoring of basic realities—in penal reform initiatives for residents who are hungry, cold, and sleep deprived.

Scott tossed on his bunk above me every night before he could find a sleep-worthy position. "I just can't get comfortable," he would say. Flip used to wake up with shoulder and back pain all the time. I knew their pains in my own body. When you laid on the bedroll, the sponge mattress flattened to the metal slab under it. As you planted your weight on an arm to turn over, that was your elbow—bone—on metal. I used to toss and turn all night, switching the position of my head from one numbed and tingly arm to start fresh on the other. Laying on my side, a hip pressed against the bedroll—that is, the metal frame—shunting blood from that leg. I toughed through more than one pinched nerved that fired up my nape and through a shoulder when I turned wrong.

During breakfast, we mostly ate in silence while rubbing our knees, pressing our backs, twisting to feel a couple of pops, stretching, and rolling our shoulders and necks. Sleep was physically and mentally painful, and it tended to make residents especially grumpy. With few exceptions, eyes scythed through the resident who tried to spark up unnecessary morning conversation. It usually wasn't until closer to lunch that residents felt recovered from the night enough to converse.

The fact is our sleep was so immiserating because poor sleep health was built into the physical plant and daily operations of the jails. Aside from the wholly inadequate foam mattresses we were given, it was always cold. Part of that had to do with the too-little blankets, but there was cold air constantly blowing. Inexperienced residents quickly learned that wearing their oranges all day and sleeping in them to stay warm was considered "dirt bag" behavior. After all, clothing exchange was only twice a week, and that didn't mean you would find clothes that fit or that the jail wouldn't run out of something before it was your dayroom's turn. Residents sometimes wound up wearing some clothing items for over a week. But no matter what, sleeping in county oranges because you were cold was unacceptable.

In open dayrooms, there were no good endurance strategies for the cold. You just had to deal. In closed dayrooms, however, residents had one useful strategy. Each cell had two vents: one sucked air from the neighboring cell; the other pushed air into the cell on the opposite side. Covering the vents with paper created stagnated air, but it also warmed the cell a bit with body heat and breath: another common tension between what the body needs and jail conditions.

And then there was the mealtime schedule and the lights. Deputies worked from 6:00 a.m. to 6:00 p.m., and they served breakfast around 4:30 a.m., lunch around 10:30 a.m., and dinner around 4:30 p.m. It is a massive understatement to say the schedule was disorienting. You may have been free just six hours earlier, and if you were a first-timer, your sleep was likely poisoned with thoughts racing uncontrollably, but at about 4:25 a.m., deputies cut on the dayroom lights, signaled the reps to the door or sally port, and you had five minutes to sit at your race's table for breakfast. But it was often hard to leave one's bunk or cell that early in the morning. The inertia to stay put—even if you were awake—was strong. The body aches, nightmares, disruptions throughout the night—it was a lot. Then the decision was this: Do I find the energy to get up now, or do I lay here until lunch? The latter was easier to choose if you had commissary food stores to bridge the gap between breakfast and lunch, but you needed to be careful about that because the 12-hour, forced fasting period between dinner and breakfast required snacks to stave off hunger headaches. You didn't want to run out of food and exacerbate poor sleep with hunger pangs.

In most cases, it just made sense to get up for breakfast—even if just to try to save whatever was served for later—because you could never bet on the schedule being kept. It's one of the many paradoxes in jail that life was as unpredictable as it was routinized, and one of the more infuriating examples of this came whenever there was a scheduling snafu. If something happened that put deputies behind in their plans, residents paid for it. Perhaps court let out later than expected or there was an issue in the kitchen, a fight somewhere in the jail, or a deputy momentarily lost her keys or needed to use the restroom. Whatever it was, deputies passed the disruption on to residents. For instance, on the day of my final clothing exchange, deputies got a late start tossing cells and didn't finish until 2:00 p.m. They gave us lunch at 2:30 p.m.

Then, because why not, they served us dinner at 4:15 p.m., and most of us forced ourselves to eat or squirrel away what we could in preparation for the gap between dinner and breakfast.

That schedule may or may not have solved some administrative issue, but it took a physiological toll on our bodies. It's safe to say that most residents didn't enter jail with a circadian system tuned to the jail's timetable. Hence, residents experienced a disruption in those biological clocks that regulate physiological processes in accordance with the daylight schedule.[9] With good sleep health, smaller deviations from the day's rhythm might not matter, but chronic and dramatic disruptions—like those created by the jail schedule— are associated with reproductive problems, sleep disorders, inflammatory diseases, and mood disorders like major depression.[10]

The problems we confronted in the jail's routines were exacerbated by the lights. Once deputies cut on the dayroom lights for breakfast, the lights stayed on until 10:00 p.m. In open dayrooms, residents could throw their oranges over their faces or curl in a fetal position to pull their blankets over their heads in a losing battle against the bright lights. In closed dayrooms, the lights combined with the clangs of the rep's cell doors popping open and then slamming shut.[11] In the trustee pod, there were two interruptions for breakfast. Deputies cut the lights on and off around 2:30 a.m. when my cellies were summoned to the jail's kitchen. They cut them on again two hours later when we were summoned to the dayroom to eat, but then trustee pod deputies usually cut the lights off after breakfast until a more respectable morning hour—a privilege not afforded to GENPOP residents.

Indeed, the lights in GENPOP housing units weren't just "on"; it's more accurate to say residents were subjected to constant, artificial light. Whatever the logic by which deputies determined when to cut on or off the dayroom lights, it wasn't applied in any coherent way. In open dayrooms, deputies apparently cut the lights off to signal that it was time for residents to sleep or reduce our activity. However, we weren't relegated to our bunks, and many residents laid on their bunks throughout the day only to come alive, so to speak, after lights out. If deputies thought it a security issue to allow residents to interact in relative darkness, they didn't show it.

Nearly every night in closed dayrooms, however, deputies launched a campaign against covering the lights. The problem was that deputies cut the dayroom lights off around 10:00 p.m., but they never cut off the cell lights—ever. Being subjected to uninterrupted light could, among other consequences, suppress production of melatonin, making it physiologically harder to fall asleep, weakening the immune system, and negatively impacting "circadian rhythms in locomotor activities."[12] For the resident sleeping on the top bunk, the cell lights were especially problematic because they were about three-and-a-half feet away from his eyes. Closing your eyes didn't block the light out. Tying your T-shirt over your eyes was no solution: tie it too loosely, and it came off easily; tie it too tightly, and it pressed your eyes against your eyelids, and you watched bright phosphenes and risked a headache. The better option was to find a way to cover the lights.

In Sunland, a tall resident could stand on the tips of his toes and reach the lighting fixture from the floor. Shorter residents could stand on the bottom bunk, the stool, or the table to reach the lighting fixture. The best way to dim the lights was with empty potato chip bags purchased from the commissary. Save the bags! Spread open six or more bags and then, using toothpaste as an adhesive, affix the potato chip bags over the light fixture. Newspaper worked in lieu of potato chip bags, though not as well. When done right, the cell went from a brightly lit space to about as dark as a massage room. And, if you were on the bottom bunk, you could tie a sheet to the handgrips on the top bunk to create a tent. That meant losing a layer of warmth, but it blocked more light. Either way, covering the lights was a significant boon to sleep.

A pair of southsiders on the bottom tier of Z-4 had figured out how to blacken their cell, so you couldn't see inside from a distance. "Them niggas cracked the code," Herc said of their cell. Top tier residents used to walk by their cell and ask them how they did it, but the pair just smiled proudly.

Most nights, deputies tied the privilege of dayroom time to our willingness to sleep with the cell lights uncovered. "Get all that shit off my lights," a deputy commanded, "or there's no dayroom time for this pod." The use of possessive pronouns was telling. Deputies using possessive pronouns about jail facilities tended to experience our efforts to create creature comforts as personal attacks. When they ran the pod, they were noticeably more heavy-handed in their commands and punishments. As the runner, they often kicked the cell doors loudly to startle residents with demands to uncover the lights, to respond to their last names being called, and to show their faces for the "face card" check. They would stand there, jeering into the cell at you, apparently hoping you would make a wrong decision.

One night, around 2:00 a.m., the runner entered our dayroom to do a security check while dribbling a basketball. He dribbled and walked along the bottom tier, paused to walk up the stairs, dribbled casually along the top tier, paused again to walk down the opposite stairs, and then dribbled his way through the sally port back to the pod.

On a different occasion, a less emotionally invested deputy—young, new to us, and slightly built—chose a random security check to tap on the cell door window and tell LK and Herc to uncover the lights. I heard the deputy, but it wasn't until breakfast that I learned how Herc responded. LK said he hadn't heard a thing. Herc said he looked over his shoulder at the deputy outside his cell door: "I turned over, mad as fuck, like huh?" Herc said he looked the deputy over and then, "I just turned over on my bunk. Ha! Ha!"

"Right. Nigga, I been here longer than you," Toll said as if talking to the deputy.

Other deputies apparently cared about the lights only as much as their superiors did: "Take all that shit off the lights," a deputy announced. "I don't want to get yelled at again." She added that we would be denied dayroom time if we didn't comply. I always thought it striking whenever deputies asked us to suffer for their sake—as if residents should at all be invested in what made life easier for deputies.

In sum: sleeping in jail is detrimental to your physical and emotional health. You may suffer nonrestorative sleep, fatigue, nightmares, day-mares, and short sleep durations,[13] and each may be a symptom of poor sleep hygiene or an independent factor contributing to it.[14] Proper sleep hygiene is important for healthy cognitive functioning and memory consolidation,[15] and deficient sleep is associated with a decreased ability to process one's own emotions and to accurately recognize emotions in others.[16] You may also increase your risk for obesity, hypertension, stroke, heart disease (the second leading cause of death in American jails), diabetes, and mortality by cardiovascular event.[17] We should think of these comorbidities in light of Beast's aphorism about residents taking mental health appointments for help with sleep: "Everyone does." American jails are filled with our nation's poor, and like every other resource in American society, good sleep hygiene is stratified such that the poorer you are, the worse your sleep health—a reality that can only be worsened by jail time. You may not enter jail with a sleep disorder, but you are likely to develop one while there.

Empathy

The jail's mental health staff could not address any of the factors that contributed to our bad sleep hygiene, and I knew that, so why I did I make a habit of going? At first, I continued going just to see Nurse Bee. It was her empathy. She seemed to understand that she couldn't fix our problems. She couldn't prescribe medicine. But she could listen and offer positive reinforcement. There was another nurse whose name I never learned, and there was the psychiatrist, Dr. Cross, but Nurse Bee was everyone's favorite because she created a safe space for patients to be vulnerable and uncertain and angry and sad and happy—to express a fuller range of emotions without rebuke.

There were so few places like that in jail. Just her kind ear and the softness with which she handled our troubles—she was an emotional salve. Sometimes, she defended patients against themselves, offering encouragement to not give up hope and to remember a life beyond jail walls. Other times she gave us simple remedies like the "body scan" and folksy advice for breaking habits: "If something is bad for you, it's bad for you," she once told me. That might have come off especially vacuous and even offensive if the other nurse or Dr. Cross had said it, but Nurse Bee came across genuine—even if unhelpful.

Her attitude toward us contrasted sharply with that of Dr. Cross. He always seemed preoccupied, like I was keeping him from something more important. Paul-Bunyan echoed that sentiment. He said he felt that Dr. Cross was "rushing" him out of their sessions. Additionally, Dr. Cross apparently had little understanding of jail time and even less interest in learning about it.

After one of my sessions with him, I listened in as a paisa from Z-1 described the troubles he was having. Paisas were frequent victims of southsider violence, but this particular paisa had been named the southsider "phone monitor." Blacks handled phone time by "calling it" during mealtime. We noted the order of the claims, we proceeded accordingly, and if someone was waiting behind you, your phone time ended after the first prerecorded message that told the person you called that you're an inmate in a correctional facility. Woods handled things much the same way. In Z-Pod, however, there were so many southsiders that they created a role to manage how long someone could be on the phone, and they rotated who performed the unwanted duty of telling someone their phone time was up. It was that paisa's turn. He said others sometimes ignored him, and instead of becoming upset with the southsider who refused to get off the phone, those waiting their turn directed their anger toward the phone monitor. Dr. Cross told his beleaguered patient to put a kite in with a deputy to which the patient explained that he was not permitted to do that by his rep—that doing so could earn him a DP. Dr. Cross's response was to "take the lesser of the two evils," but he didn't say which option he thought that was.

Hearing that, his patient changed subjects to his hair loss. He said the medical staff had been ignoring him. "I told you," Dr. Cross said without the slightest hint of empathy, "that's a simple fungus." He continued by saying that the medical staff would give him "ointment to treat it." Whether Dr. Cross's diagnosis was right was beside the point. The medical staff had accused the patient of pulling out his own hair. Dr. Cross countered that when people pull their hair out, they typically pull it all out—not just hair from one spot.

"Exactly!" the patient exclaimed, but it didn't matter.

Dr. Cross said he could verify that the hair loss was not psychiatric. Then he told his patient to ask to speak with a supervisor, adding that "There's a chain of command" and that he should go to the next step.

The paisa pressed on, saying that a nurse had twice told him that it would cost $2,000 for him to see a dermatologist and it wasn't worth it. The nurses, he said, would just glance at his head, say "OK," and send him back to his cell. Again, Dr. Cross suggested escalating the complaint up the chain of command that he apparently thought existed to help us with these kinds of grievances. His patient grunted a scoff, and Dr. Cross seemed fed up. He said he didn't have any authority to tell nurses or anyone on the medical staff what to do—that one of their superiors would have to intervene. My mind went to men who were skipped during mealtime in the Providence intake area and how deputies blamed the lapse in care on a phantom deputy who would have to right the wrong.

At this point, the paisa's energy changed noticeably, as he resigned to saying, "OK" to whatever Dr. Cross said. He chuckled with frustration and said that he really just needed to vent.

Not one to let us have the last word, Dr. Cross told his patient to find the right people to vent to. I wondered how he could ever hope to do his job with any measure of success if he was so obviously uninformed and so terribly inept in his position.

"I Wish You Were My Therapist"

I mostly tolerated the appointments with the other nurse and Dr. Cross. But even when I got to see Nurse Bee, she wasn't always the highlight of the trip.

I developed a rapport with the other patients. In fact, Paul-Bunyan and I grew a friendship, and I started looking forward to chatting with him.

Paul was a mountain of a man—a 6'7" kind-faced version of the World Wrestling Entertainment star known as the Undertaker. Paul had an amazing knack for keeping track of time. He spoke in terms of weeks and months and always with some event tied to another, so he was sure what happened and when. He took 13 pills a day; in fact, he told me he had "gotten it down to 13." That sounded like a lot of medication, and I thought I should be able to notice a deficit in him, but I couldn't. In hindsight, it never occurred to me that some of the medication might have been for physical and not mental ailments. When he spoke, he seemed smaller than his physical stature—more like a wounded dog than an intimidating man. I never learned the charges he faced; nor did I ever try. I knew that he had been in jail long enough to have seen D-Double when he arrived years before. I didn't ask Paul how he knew of D-Double, but they had both been in Golden County jails for years, and there were a half-dozen ways they could have met. Paul said he knew D-Double by a different name, which I found interesting: "I call him 'Perch,'" he said. "The rest of us call him 'Perch,'" in reference to a gang tattoo on D-Double's arm.

My friendship with Paul was based upon a simple exchange:[18] we listened to one another and offered reflective thoughts. It's hard to overstate how impactful that simple action really was. One of the consequences of being batched with strangers is an overwhelming feeling of anonymity that generates a gnawing desire for recognition of individuality, and it didn't take much to momentarily abate that feeling.

Resident relationships tended to be mechanical. They certainly didn't start in an organic way. We were forced together, and in many cases, those mechanical relationships would never have happened if two residents had met in free society. This was abundantly clear whenever a "friend" left jail. I met Flip during his second time being in Z-4. Before his previous release, he told Curtis that he would write him and put money on his books. Well, Flip immediately forgot about Curtis when he was released. As his newest release date approached, Flip promised again that he would write and support Curtis. Well, Flip got out again and Curtis never heard from him: mechanical friendships. My departure was hardly different. I promised four or five residents that I'd write. No one believed me. Herc was particularly dismissive: "Whatever, nigga."

When I got home, I did write—four letters—and even though it took me four months to write those letters, the guys I wrote were very appreciative. Herc wrote back that he was shocked to receive my letter, and he asked for pictures of women. Toll wrote: "What's up with you, man how are you doing? Its [sic] good to hear from you. I wasn't expecting [to] hear from you, honestly, I thought you forgot. But that's good to know your [a] man of your word."

LK was more demonstrably emotional in his letter: "Man you don't know how that made me feel when I got a letter from you shit my fam don't even write me you are a real nigga that ain't to much out there like thank you for being there my boy man you did not have to put that money on my books but good looking out."

It felt good to keep my word, but then I never wrote them again. I wasn't upset with any of them or trying to distance myself. In fact, I kept feeling bad about it. I just became preoccupied with the job hunt, caring for Micah, and figuring out how to put my life back together. Once a year, or so, I spend a little bit of time trying to find them, but if I'm honest, that's more about my intellectual curiosity than a longing to connect with old friends. If I found them, I don't imagine that those transient friendships kindled during the worst of our lives would turn into anything meaningful.

This is not to say that my friendship with Paul was any less transient. It was more so in the sense that I only talked with him during a mental health visit. But Paul appreciated our transactional friendship as much as I did. In contrasting our conversations with those he had with other residents, he noted that it hurt "when you're pouring your heart out to a guy," and he's not listening. I nodded in agreement. "I wish you were my psychiatrist," he said, and I could see the sincerity in his eyes—not that he actually wanted me to be his doctor but that he was thankful for the empathy I showed him. He said his celly "tends to get down" and that he often felt emotionally drained as a result. Our conversations lifted both our spirits.

Respite and a Hustle

There were other more basic reasons to take a mental health visit. Flip used to say that going was like a field trip. Paul said the same. I can't say I gained any enjoyment from the walk to mental health, but I used those trips to speak with deputies and take in other parts of the jail. The paisa I described above and another wood, who were regulars, said that it was good to escape the politics of their respective dayrooms and gain license to vent complaints a bit. The latter benefit may seem trivial, but complaining about the food, the cold, the deputies, or what have you, was considered annoying among the residents and it wasn't always easy to repress all those frustrations. For instance, one day, as I lined up in the hallway for a mental health visit, an older black resident from Z-2 launched into a story about how another black resident was "crying like a baby" and how "nobody wants to see that."

At first, I understood his comments as an example of masculinity getting in the way of a resident's ability to express frustration, but restricting emotional expression is not a gender-specific move. It is always the case that some emotions are more or less appropriately expressed given the time and place. Jail is not special in that regard. I came to a different understanding of that older resident's statements once I experienced a Minnesota winter.

At first, I used to send screenshots to friends and family in California: "Real feel: -32° F." During that first winter, I complained about the single-digit weather and negative wind chills. Then came mid-April and two feet of snow fell. I was flabbergasted. I'd been whining, off and on, as my colleagues blandly fended off my weather-related comments: "You've gotta get used to it . . . It's all about the layers . . . You gotta get out there! Enjoy it . . . I'll take you ice fishing." *Black folk ain't ice fishing.* But sometimes, native Minnesotans just smiled to acknowledge that they heard me but they didn't feel the cold warranted any kind of conversation.

Eventually I got it. In their nice way, they were trying to tell me the same thing that older resident in Z-2 had: "nobody wants to [hear] that." It wasn't that residents weren't allowed to have feelings or to be sad, but the appropriateness of emotional expression is always emplaced. If we are all suffering the same things, who wants to entertain your complaints about the conditions? It's January and you're cold in Minneapolis? Everyone is! You don't like jail? Shit. No one does!

You could do that kind of complaining in the mental health holding cells, though, and someone would listen. Like church, those holding cells were marked as places where it was safe to just whine a bit. Others would even commiserate with you on your complaints. Some conversations attacked the politics or just found us bitching about the courts and the process of going to court while in custody.

During my final visit with mental health staff, I listened to a group of black residents in the adjoining holding cell discuss the lack of "unity" among the black residents and the problems they were having with deputies. They spoke like a nervous cabal with their voices piled atop one another, jockeying to be heard. Finally, one voice rose, saying that "guys [are] facing triple life" and were "afraid" to sign grievances against the deputies but that there needed to be limits to being submissive to deputies "beating" and "bullying guys."

There were a lot of grumbles, and one resident kept repeating, "They just gon' keep fuckin' wit' us."

I had the sense that they had been using more than one trip to mental health to discuss those issues.

Laying aside the benefits of respite from the housing units, I learned that some residents took mental health visits as a *hustle—an exploitation of gaps in rule systems.* In jail, hustles were just another kind of endurance strategy, and the most successful hustlers learned the rules and procedures that governed situations they hoped to exploit. The main hustle related to mental health was to take a visit just to use the phones in the mental health holding cells.

On a day in which I was feeling particularly rundown, the pod summoned my cell through the intercom: "Walker. Do you want to go to mental health?" I declined, but as the hours rolled by, I was offered two more times! The third offer came at 8:45 p.m. *I guess they really wanna see me.* Before then, I didn't know it was possible to have a mental health appointment so late, but my curiosity was piqued.

When I got the sally port, Deputy Brown looked me over and said that I didn't "look like" I needed to go to mental health. He added that I was probably just going to use the phones. I shrugged off what he said, and my appointment was unremarkable, but as we lined up to return to our respective housing units, Deputy Brown told a nearby ADSEG resident: "You just wanna use the phones. I know that's why you come down here. I'm not stupid."

At that moment, I remembered Deputy Brown's earlier comment to me about the phones, but until then it had not occurred to me that some residents visited mental health just to use a phone. It was a simple hustle. Deputies made us wait in a mental health holding cell until we were called to a booth to speak with staff. Those holding cells usually had one to three phones, and in subsequent visits, I paid closer attention to phone use. Sure enough, some residents ambled to spots on the benches while others shot straight for a phone and chatted delightfully.

It was all a chase. We chased more sleep, a better quality of sleep, more vivid dreams, and less vivid nightmares. We chased an empathic ear, someone who would just listen. We chased respite from the hardships imposed by social life in the housing units and, I learned, some of us chased an opportunity to call a friend or loved one. My sleep never improved though.

Sisqo

I still think about Sisqo from time to time. I don't recall who gave him that nickname—maybe D-Double—but he looked a lot like the singer Sisqo from Dru Hill but about 45-years-old, six inches taller, with some dad weight and a bumbling personality. He was a walking tragic comedy in that his funniest moments tended to be his saddest. We used to give him whatever food items we didn't want, and he would scurry off to his cell with the spoils in a Styrofoam container or two.

This one time, a bag of chips was accidentally crushed on the ground, and Sisqo's first thought was to ask if he could have them. LK said he saw Sisqo digging used food containers out of the trash, and eventually he brought those containers to mealtimes, expecting the extras. He once had two containers of extras and a big cup of beans, but he tripped going up the steel steps to the top tier. Beans went flying, and his fall was so loud and looked so painful that the dayroom paused to see what had happened. He turned around and sat on the stairs with a shocked look and beans spilled on his arm. His bottom lip was busted and bleeding, and his top teeth were chipped.

We were genuinely concerned for him. A couple of us ran to help him up, and D-Double ensured that Sisqo got some replacement beans. I took them up to him. Later during dayroom time, I asked him how he was doing, and I was surprised that he was genuinely hurt that the deputies hadn't checked on him. His head was hung between his legs, and then he slyly looked up and said, "Well you know what would make it better?"

"I know! Chips!"

He said it simultaneously with a laugh, but I wasn't going for his chip hustling that time. I've still never met anyone who loves chips more than Sisqo.

I remember the night he left. It was the evening after another Sunday clothing exchange. Earlier in the day, Sisqo was caught trying to sneak an extra pair of boxers. He was open about having hemorrhoids, and he frequently complained to deputies that he needed to wear at least two pairs of boxers. Having caught Sisqo with an extra pair, a deputy asked him his cell number and which bunk was his. Then two deputies tossed the hell out of his cell. They were indiscriminate about it, too. TJ's stuff was equally thrown everywhere, their bedrolls were untucked and partially hanging off their bunks, and the deputies took the newspaper and chip bags that TJ and Sisqo had been using to cover the lights.

I guess all of that was on his mind as he stared out his cell door window into the dayroom at nothing in particular. From next door, I heard the pod buzz Sisqo's cell: "Are you staring at me or the TV?"

The television wasn't on, and when in the bright lights of a cell, it was really difficult to see inside the darkened pod. Sisqo might not have known whether he was staring at a deputy. "Just meditating," he said.

"Well, don't look at me. Look elsewhere."

A little while later, the runner came by his cell to formally give Sisqo his punishment for the extra pair of boxers: a week of no rec time. That wouldn't matter for two reasons. Sometimes a week went by and we didn't get rec time, and just hours after that, Sisqo rolled out.

About a year after I came home, I saw Sisqo in a church just a few pews from where I was. There was a woman testifying about how happy she was to have him in her life, and I was excited to see him. I stared until we made eye contact, and when we did, I waved like a child seeing Mickey Mouse. We didn't talk, though. In fact, he ignored my wave and ducked out before I could catch up with him. Guess I was the past.

9

Complexities of Care

There were two black tables in Sunland's Z-4 with a high school status hierarchical feel to who sat where. One table was for the *cool guys*. From the top tier, that included D-Double and Ken, Herc and LK, and Toll and Lee, though Lee floated a bit between the tables. Each of those guys had a running count of at least two years of consecutive jail time. They understood jail culture. They knew a lot of the same people, and though they had not done all their time in Z-4, they had a collective history as a group within our group. There were only two blacks on the bottom tier, Curtis and Kinsley, and they sat together without the status distinctions I'm about to describe. The other table was known as the "weirdo" table. "Weirdo" is one of those California slang terms that can take on few meanings, but in general, it refers to people or actions that are unconventional in ways that lower one's social status. In this case, just being at the weirdo table marked you. Residents at the weirdo table were mostly new and relatively inexperienced. That group included me, Scott, and Flip before he left; Dago and Brian; and TJ and "the Minister," who replaced Sisqo. Of those, only me, Scott, and Sisqo were in for charges other than domestic violence.

I started out at the weirdo table, which I learned when a conversation at the cool table led Herc to pretend to pack up his food tray and protest in jest, "I'm going over to the weirdo table."

He was talking about where I was sitting, so I spoke up in a kneejerk way: "Naw. You can't come over here." I chuckled, but I really did feel offended at the implication.

A week or so after that exchange, Toll invited me to sit at the cool table. "No more weirdos for you, eh, Mike," Herc said with a laugh. I happily took my seat without looking back—so to speak.

I'd been at the weirdo table for about a month—give or take, and the change to the cool table indicated that I'd developed a relationship with the cool guys. I didn't notice it at first, but after I changed tables, I came to see how status, seating arrangements, charges, and care mapped onto each other. Somehow, I'd missed that the cool table residents tended to condescend to

the weirdo table residents in ways that didn't happen in the opposite direction—that a resident's position in the black status hierarchy afforded him
greater or lesser liberties to be dismissive and jokingly disparaging to others.

No matter your table, though, with time, you would have your moment in the limelight of a scathing "bagging" session where (mostly cool)
guys ritualistically made you the butt of jokes. The session might start with
an observation about your oranges. My hairline was a frequent target. D-
Double stuttered. Sisqo's gut was tight, and he was always begging for chips.
TJ had a ponytail. These were perennially low-hanging fruit, but it was
during conversations about women that distinctions between the tables became clear.

At the cool table, discussions of women revolved around "game"—*the
ability to walk, talk, dress, and relate in ways that gain the romantic interests
of others.* Such discussions sprung from the smallest observation. Someone
would comment on an actress on a show we were watching, or there would be
a discussion about characters in a "hood book." Toll sometimes rapped lyrics
about sexual prowess, and Herc quipped that Toll "couldn't get no bitches."

"Yeah, aight, nigga," Toll said.

Dago, who sat at the weirdo table, was a self-proclaimed pimp who spent
a lot of dayroom time on the phone, and just as much time telling us that he
could give us pointers if anyone was interested. He said he needed to make
calls to ensure that the women he ran were doing what they were supposed to
do and that his house—his physical "four-bedroom house," as he frequently
told us—was in order. He once showed us a picture of his "bottom bitch"; she
was a spiritless white woman. He grinned and nodded while we looked at the
picture, being more excited than that picture warranted, and he insisted that
he could give us tips on how to get a woman like that.

Toll jumped in to offer his two cents on the matter: "You gotta break a
bitch. She'll sell her soul to *you* if you talk to her right. You gotta crack her."
To "crack a bitch" is California slang for saying something clever to catch a
woman's attention so that she's agreeable to talking more.

Then came the familiar discussion about who had the most "bad bitches"
before being locked up. Toll and D-Double were long-time opponents on the
issue, but in this conversation, Herc looked slyly at Dago and said, with a
challenge, that there was a resident in a neighboring dayroom who claimed
to be pimp. Dago didn't get to respond before LK jumped in: "Eh, but did he
have bitches?"

Dago said something about being a better salesman than everyone else. Whether "selling pussy" or "selling drugs, niggas can't fuck with me."

Toll said he used to be like a character in one of the "hood books" that we had all read. He said he used to "get 30-year-old bitches."

I voiced incredulousness about a teenager attracting grown women with professional careers, but I was immediately argued down, and there ensued a series of comments in which Toll, D-Double, and Herc gave anecdotes about guys they knew with that level of game. Others nodded, and the exchange became about how little game I have and how I probably have to "pay for it."

Looking at me but pointing at Dago, Herc said, "You be settin' up appointments with this nigga's bitches, Mike?"

I threw my hands up as if to say, "C'mon." There was an eruption of laughter because I'd long been pegged as having no game, in part, because I sometimes spoke against using the word "bitch" as if it meant "Black woman." But by the time of that conversation, I'd given up talking as if I had the moral high ground. During an early discussion about women, I told Toll that someone would be calling his daughter a bitch in the same way he calls every woman a bitch.

"Oh well. It's gotta happen," Toll said.

Herc laughed, and I said, "Bitch doesn't mean woman."

"Nigga. Yes, it does. It means FEMALE dog," Herc said.

I told him that surely men refer to his mama that way.

Laughing, Herc said, "I wanna be able to get my turn to say it since everyone else is."

After that, I mostly kept my silence about how men talked about women. I didn't want to be ostracized, and I didn't want to present myself as if I were better than anyone.

Anyhow, as our collective laughter died down, Ken chuckled through a final comment: "Somebody needs to pray for these guys."

Nearly every conversation about game followed the same path and had the same pulse of casual misogyny and blithe denigration of women. We never established a consensus on attracting women, keeping women, or who had broader appeal to women, but none of that was the goal. Those were community-building events—a way of ritualistically endorsing and validating one another as group members. Even if, as the butt of jokes and with differences in opinion, the laughs and one-upmanship in those exchanges lingered long enough to momentarily lift spirits and consolidate a feeling of we-ness.[1]

They reminded me of a scene in the movie *Jungle Fever*. It had been discovered that one of the men had cheated on his wife with a white woman, and a group of Black women gathered in support at the home of the woman who had been cheated on. There was a discussion about the pitfalls of race and colorism, and the challenges to finding and sustaining romantic relationships with Black men. It's a thoughtful scene that connects the women as much as it reveals how their experiences diverge and why. Like our many conversations about women, nothing was solved during their discussion. Neither did the women come to an agreement about what to do next about the problems discussed. What they gained nevertheless was a strengthening of bonds between them.

That bonding is a way of expressing and receiving *care*. Our conversations about women weren't always as sophisticated as what the actresses in Spike Lee's *Junger Fever* gave us, and they weren't always about game, but the resulting care was very real, and it was different from typical conceptions of the criminal object as a conniving, emotionally atrophied,[2] homophobic, and violent[3] man. In fact, you can be all those things, and more, and still being caring. You can still *tend to the emotional, material, and symbolic well-being of others* because people are more than one thing in the world; each of us has multiple ways of *being*, as the sociologist Reuben Miller once reminded me.

What I learned was that caring was one of the most common ways of being in jail. The laughter we shared—the camaraderie—it bonded us. We built friendships that way. We kept each other's secrets and validated and looked out for one another. It felt good even as so many of our mutual endorsements were threaded through patriarchy, misogyny, and in some instances, naked advocacy of rape[4]—especially those commiserating sessions about women that originated from the weirdo table.

We all knew TJ was in for beating his wife. He was fuzzy on whether she was three weeks or three months pregnant at the time. The latter seems more likely, unless they were closely tracking her menstrual cycle and then got a pregnancy test. His main concern was whether the beating would lead to a miscarriage and how that might add to his legal jeopardy. "She said I beat her with a trophy and a broomstick," he said. He frequently opened a talk about his circumstances in that blunt way. I came to see that salvo as his way of care-seeking. "Everybody in my family know [sic] she lies." I didn't much like TJ, so I could barely hide my disgust when I plainly asked him if he had hit her. "Yeah. I admit I hit her—slapped her around, but I didn't know she was pregnant at the time."

"Women be lying," Scott said, right on time.

TJ and Scott had a near ritualistic call-and-response performance that they often did. TJ started it off with a complaint about his wife; Scott offered explanations to assuage how TJ felt. Repeat.

"It's his Indian blood," Scott said while making a chess move against me. "It's too much . . . He probably was drunk. Indians can't hold their liquor."[5] He never said which one, but TJ claimed to be a member of an Indian nation. In Scott's mind, Indian genetics explained what happened between TJ and his wife, and TJ never disconfirmed the explanation Scott offered.

So common was this call-and-response among weirdo-table residents that I understood it as the *Delilah trope*.[6] In biblical lore, Delilah was one of Samson's favorite lovers; however, she conspired with the Philistines to learn the secret to Samson's strength. Twice he lied about the source of his strength, but after a little prodding, Sampson finally told her that it was his hair. He took a nap. She cut his hair and summoned the Philistines to take him away. There are a number of lessons to be learned in the story, but in practice, the Delilah trope centers women as a social problem and the locus of any man's potential downfall. Women are not to be trusted, so goes the thinking, and as a corollary, a man cannot be totally to blame for whatever ignoble actions a woman drives him to take.[7]

Hence, after the "Indian blood" explanation, there came a cascade of endorsements about how women push men to do things they wouldn't ordinarily do—how the Minister's Delilah resulted in him being jailed and how "the mouth" on Brian's Delilah caused problems in his life. This was the typical arc of conversations about women at the weirdo table: a care-seeking call, supportive validations, and a series of endorsements through similar narratives.

Sometimes cool-table residents just shook their heads in disagreement, and sometimes they weren't in the conversations at all. Just as often, a care-seeking call went unendorsed when no one responded. I ignored Byron, my last celly, when he used the Delilah trope to explain his circumstances. It was his second offense with the same woman. The first was a misdemeanor: summary probation and 52 weeks of domestic violence classes. The second was a felony, with bail set at $50,000. He volunteered all that information, including that he was on "week 36."

He was a constant mix of mad, sad, and disappointed in our cell. "I ain't messin' with her anymore," he said without my asking him a question. "I shoulda known cuz her baby daddy used to beat on her, so that shoulda told me something." I stared at my books on the table. He turned and saw I wasn't engaging. He climbed to the top bunk and went to sleep.

I didn't feel the need say a thing to him, but every now and then, someone expressed clear disapproval of the justifications some residents used for intimate partner violence—often on the grounds of game. After a brief exchange about men feeling forced to "put hands on women," Herc said if a man "gotta beat a bitch . . . he don't need to be with her."

A different time we were watching television in the dayroom. Most of the programs we watched were on AMC, USA, and TNT—channels packed with shows covering themes related to crime: *Law and Order, Monk,* and so on. In fact, I was introduced to *Breaking Bad* while in jail. Whatever we were watching that day included a rape enactment. I made some comment about the thinking of a man who forces himself into a woman while she kicks at him—how an unaroused woman is a turnoff.

Women "get wet during rape," D-Double responded. He added that "if you really think about it," rape "is an ultimate fantasy" for women.[8]

There was a shock of silence. I looked around to see that I wasn't the only one puzzled by the comment. D-Double shrugged, and Herc spoke up: "Nigga. That's that weirdo shit."

Aside from the occasional criticism, part of what was happening at the two black tables was two very different kinds of care. The demarcation wasn't perfect, but cool-table residents didn't need the same kind of care weirdo-table residents did. The former had long been in jail for years. We used "game" as a group dynamic to establish a status hierarchy[9] and to bond ourselves to the group through the symbolic validation of one another.

The Delilah trope did a different kind of work. The newer guys were at the weirdo table. They hadn't yet established a monthly or biweekly schedule of court appearances to monotonize jail living even further. Their arrests were still fresh and in need of sense-making. The Delilah trope did that for them. It offered an explanation for how they came to be in jail and, through validation, they could feel better about themselves. It was men commiserating about having done and being charged with doing terrible things to the women in their lives, and it was a way of processing their feelings and being told that it was OK. Given my experiences with the mental health staff, it's doubtful weirdo-table residents would have received that kind of care from anyone other than us.

However, the Delilah trope wasn't and isn't exclusive to penal residents. It's a broad cultural frame that skillfully uses misogyny to prescribe how men should interact with women. While awaiting my turn to see the nurse, I caught the end of a conversation between a deputy and a resident who explained that his wife "started all this mess" that landed him in jail. It should be noted that I don't know the veracity of any of these claims. It may well have been that a turbulent relationship and a web of lies resulted mood disorders, illegal activity, and eventually jail time for some residents. What concerns me here is how the Delilah trope was rolled out to galvanize emotional support.

The deputy listened and nodded with interest. He told the resident that he understood, and then he told a story about the changes he had made to keep women from stymying his personal progress as a man. "I don't have a girl-friend—nothing," the 30-something-year-old deputy said proudly. "I own two houses I don't even live in. I live with my parents." He continued on to explain how he had once been near financial ruin because he was trying to keep up with the interests of women. He apparently made a miraculous turn-around once he gave up on pleasing women, and he had shared that gospel with his brother, who "saved up $35,000 in two years"—apparently because he wasn't with a woman. The resident smiled wide in response, and the exchange carried on a bit more, as the two laughed and nodded in support of each other like old friends in a bar, trading war stories about how they had survived women—well, one of them at least. The deputy told the resident to "hang in there."

The Delilah trope showed up in church, too—quite often, in fact. One of the Bible study volunteers once opened a discussion by lamenting that he had kids with a "crazy woman." Residents nodded and grumbled their agreement. He explained that, as a result of his time with her, he got into drugs and petty crimes and eventually prison time. He explained that "even" his wife's lawyer agreed that his wife "should be locked up." Laughs traced along our prayer circle, and then came a few Delilah stories from residents. When the last one was told, there was a moment of collective resolution that we needed to get better at spotting and avoiding Delilahs.

Intimacy

The differences between the tables broke down completely when our discussions were about our families. Then it was hard—improper even—to compartmentalize men as essentially the worst behavior they had displayed. Each of us was more than the charges we faced. We comforted each other during frequent and inevitable moments of vulnerability and somber talks about missing daughters, mothers, girlfriends, and wives.

TJ spoke with his wife nearly every day, and he frequently updated our interested ears about her health and that of their unborn child. In his final update before leaving, both were doing well. His wife had showed up in court to support him, and he was looking forward to being reunited after completing his sentence. I was cautiously hopeful for his family. We offered words of encouragement, and he looked off in a moment of romantic nostalgia before saying that he needed his braids redone. He smiled: "She used to do my braids a little crooked and shit and fuck my shit up a bit just so another bitch won't want me." He was miles away from us in that moment—someplace warm and loving. LK added that he missed the way his wife smelled. Scott talked about his girlfriend's cooking. Those of us who had romantic partnerships took the moment to reminisce on what we missed the most.

The Minister bemoaned the distance that jail put between him and his girlfriend. He noted that his charges were from an event that occurred seven years prior and that he had long since come to understand "a woman is the closest thing to a man's heart." He said he was sure that god had a plan about it him being in jail.

Many of LK's bouts of hard-timing-it had to do with how much he missed his wife and daughters. "I gotta get outta here," he sometimes announced. He would be weepy-eyed in talking about how "useless" jail time is—that he wished he could be home to support his daughters, and I used to worry about what would happen to him if his wife met another man or stopped supporting him. We would encourage him to be strong and remind him that his wife was still there, so he needed to find ways to endure.

My triggers for hard-timing-it were similar to LK's. I wrote Micah, trying to be a father from a damned jail cell. I kept starting a letter, balling up the paper, and starting over because I didn't feel I had the right to give my eight-year-old advice. I wasn't always comfortable with how my mother handled situations with my son, but I wasn't there. Pressure, like an elephant standing on my chest, the burning and stinging in my tear ducts before my emotional levees broke, the uncontrollable gaping of my mouth and sucking in and out of my bottom lip between soundless cries and attempts to catch my breath while burying my face into my bed mat: Not every period of hard-timing-it was days long. Some were seconds of intense collapse. And sometimes, I let Scott be there for me. He'd tell me that my son loved me, and I hoped that he was right.

Often enough, there was an outpouring of support for a resident crying in church about how much he missed his family. You would see a guy in the dayroom living his life without any outward signs of inner turmoil. His endurance strategies were keeping him upright, but then you would see him in church sobbing about his mother with strangers caring for him. It was a reminder: Beyond the charges and sentences, many of us were brothers, fathers, closest cousins, best friends, and there was a kind of phantom pain to being severed from those roles. But you couldn't always see the wounds from a distance. Sometimes you had to be up close.

I credit Toll for teaching me that lesson—that intimacy was needed in its own right and to know what was truly going on with us. We had been engrossed in a conversation that started off about what we would do when free, but it veered into a philosophical discussion about life and parenthood. The pod flashed the dayroom lights, and seeing that, Toll said he was going to hang out with us in our cell until the next dayroom time. I felt some way about him telling and not asking if that was cool with us, but I didn't say anything.

His plan was to "jump cells," which is to hide out in someone else's cell during the periods between dayroom time. Jumping cells was a risky business. First, dayroom time was never guaranteed. We might end up on lockdown, and then it would only be a matter of time before we were caught. Second, jumping cells placed some level of responsibility on your celly to cover for you. You might bunch up the blanket on the bed mat and sheet as if your celly is asleep, or string a sheet up from the vent to the top bunk frame to give the illusion that your celly was on the toilet. Most of the time, we could rely upon the runner to half-ass the security checks and not notice anything strange in the cell. Most of the time.

I once returned from a mental health visit to see two southsiders handcuffed in the program room while deputies threw their clothes into the dayroom and then kicked them here and there for good measure. Deputies tossed toilet paper rolls from the cell that unraveled as they descended from the top to the bottom tier. I later learned that deputies had caught them jumping cells.

So, when Toll first entered our cell, Scott and I were so nervous that the conversation we had been having stalled. Actually, the first thing I noticed was how small our cell was with a third person in there. It didn't help that Toll was tall and solidly built, but eventually, Scott and I calmed down enough to hold a conversation. Toll revealed that he was constantly stressed about his brother, his parents, and his three-year-old daughter. He said he would find himself laughing and joking in the dayroom to keep from crying. Jail made it a major effort, he explained, just to *be*.

I felt a rush of shame at hearing him say that. I'm going to blame this on the imperious nature of research, but I'd made the shockingly absurd assumption that if residents laughed, that meant jail wasn't so bad for them. No less egregious, I'd felt righteous indignation when Deputy Brown made the same assumption of me. Yet somehow, I'd created a sense that I was different from others—that my training made me more introspective and therefore more discerning of experiences than *those* guys could be. And that disrespectful thinking gave me a false sense of superiority—an authority to explain the experiences that residents couldn't possibly understand. And here's the kicker: I'd had innumerable exchanges in which it was it clear that I was in no position to understand something that others had missed—that I didn't have any special insights—yet I was surprised to hear Toll talk about how sad and troubled he was while being sad and troubled myself. I felt stripped naked in that moment. I could see myself clearly, and I didn't like what I saw.

"Walking!" a deputy exclaimed upon entering our dayroom for a security check, and as he approached our cell, Toll dashed under the bottom bunk.

After the deputy passed, Toll emerged with a complaint: "Y'all need to sweep under there." Then our conversation continued, and Toll said he was just trying to maintain hope that things would get better and that he would soon go to trial. Scott shifted the conversation back to our families. He had a daughter that he worried about all the time, too. She was only a few months old (he never said how many), and he was afraid that she would forget him. Toll and I struggled to say anything definitive about whether Scott's concerns were likely. We offered reassurances just the same. I revealed that I'd told Micah that I was off at some months-long academic workshop and that I was scared he would find out that I was in jail before I was ready to explain myself. Toll said he could tell I'm a "good dad," and it was bittersweet. Scott said something about being near tears on a regular basis, and Toll responded that being sad all the time would only "make things unbearable." A second security check interrupted us, and again, Toll emerged from under the bottom bunk with a complaint that we needed to do a better job at getting the dust bunnies when sweeping.

Having Toll in our cell that day changed the way I saw everyone, and it triggered a reevaluation of my previous preliminary conclusions about social life in jail. It was a reminder that I didn't know what someone was dealing with and that I would do well to withhold my judgments.[10] Our time together was intimate and caring, and it ended with a comment and a look on Toll's face that is burned in my memory. The pod popped the top tier doors for dayroom time, and as Toll stood in the doorway putting on his slippers, he looked back and said, "Y'all niggas boring." I still laugh at how disappointed he looked when he said that. It was a very strange thing to say given the discussion we had had. Sure. At the start he had made a couple of complaints about us not having any dominos, dice, or cards made when he jumped cells. We hadn't planned on entertaining him that day, but the tonal switch in that statement is akin to the emotional switch residents made when leaving church in the program room to reenter the dayroom.

Despite that dramatic switch, the dayroom wasn't off limits for showing intimacy. I lived in South Korea for three-and-a-half years and graduated from Seoul American High School. It was common for Korean teenaged boys to sit on each other's laps and walk hand-in-hand as an indication of affection. That kind of affection is, perhaps, less common in US culture, but there are plenty of other ways men share affectionate touches. We need only give a brief thought to boys and men in sports and fraternities, and it is with this frame of reference in mind that I first took notice of how southsiders in Z-4 shared affectionate touches.

It was mainly a subgroup of close southsiders. They frequently sat hip-to-hip in the dayroom with their legs intertwined and their arms draped over each other. It reminded me of a group of kindergarteners hugging and loving on one another, but that doesn't mean everyone understood physical affection in jail the same way. During one such occasion, LK approached me, and in directing my attention to the southsiders, he said: "Mexicans man. That's how they do." Beast and Tiny were sitting on a table near the phones with their legs interlocked. "It's worse in YA. They be jackin' each other off."

My mind went to Flip's stories about "Messicans" in juvenile detention centers using sexual assault as a status marker. I'd ignored him at the time, but I found myself wondering, for the first time, whether GENPOP residents were having sex—consensual or otherwise. I'd once seen Beast pinching Tiny's butt as they headed upstairs at the end of dayroom time, and I'd also seen Beast approach a chest-naked southsider, standing at his cell door looking into the dayroom. Beast licked his pointer fingers and gestured as if he were stimulating the southsider's nipples through the glass. The southsider feigned a shiver. It was, of course, possible that some affection between residents was more intimate than others.

During a separate southsider huddle-and-cuddle session in the dayroom, Herc said, "They do that gay shit." Then he volunteered a story about the previous black rep in Z-3 who, apparently, was rolled out because "he had an Asian celly he used to bash."[11] It wasn't clear to me whether Herc was talking about rape or consensual sex; either way, that was the only story about sex between residents that I ever heard.

Whatever was the nature of intimacy between those few southsiders, they were virtually alone in their public displays. I never saw woods engage in any public affection, and some black residents more than others were against "sex play" or *playful erotic touching and gestures*. Carter from Providence 16D raised his voice against sex play around him on several occasions. In Sunland's Z-4 dayroom, it was TJ who was most vocally against sex play: "Eh! I ain't wit' none of that sex play!" he would say if there was playfighting around him or homoerotic jokes or comments directed toward him.

At the opposite end of the spectrum on attitudes about intimacy was D-Double. He was more openly affectionate than any other black resident I met: a hand on Ken's knee; running his fingers through Lee's hair to straighten it; a hand on my shoulder. After a phone call, D-Double approached Scott from behind and took it upon himself to pick Scott's hair out. "There," he said while looking at his work, "You look 100% better." That moment raised eyebrows but nothing more.

D-Double's affection stood out against others because no one else was as affectionate, and there seemed to be a consensus that he was gay. He sagged his orange bottoms and his boxers enough so that the top of buttocks showed—never without admonishment: "Nigga! Pull your pants up!" and "Nigga, you gay" were typical refrains. Ken once wrote "D-Double is a homosexual" on the dayroom calendar for anyone to see. These weren't harmless objective observations but insults within accusations.

D-Double's usual response was some half-hearted claim to how many women he had been with, yet he frequently made homoerotic comments and gestures. During a bagging session, LK called D-Double "a boy." D-Double moved closer to LK, pulled his waistband away from his body as if to encourage LK to take a look and said: "I don't have a boy's dick size."

"Gay ass shit!" LK exclaimed while moving away.

More than anything, he seemed lonely to me, and I count these moments of intimacy as the predictable outcome of social life because despite being jailed, residents are people with the same need for intimacy that free society persons have. In any case, if others were bothered by his care-seeking and intimate behaviors, it was of little practical consequence. No one took action to have him removed from our unit. No one campaigned to have him removed as rep. He remained our legitimate rep until I left.

Jail life was as complex and resistant of compartmentalization as life is in any other social arena. The same man facing violent charges sought your support and offered you a caring ear. He was the same man who would dole out violent discipline if it were determined that you deserved it, and he shared his food, knowledge, and books with you—whatever he had. The care came with the violence and misogyny and everything else because the matters of life are messy like that.

In some ways, sharing between residents was the most significant form of care. It cost money to share with others, and very often, the sharing was among residents who were just a step above being strangers to one another. Beast fed quite a few southsiders in Z-4, and I'd seen him punch in his phone card code on many occasions for others. In small open units, southsiders periodically held spreads for indigent southsiders who could not contribute to the feast. The black rep in the Cardinal Detention Center offered me some chips that I declined in our very first conversation following the orientation. And in general, there was a moderate expectation that your celly would bring food back to the cell for you if you were hard-timing-it, and if you had a positive relationship with your celly, he would be the one sharing food stores to help you survive the night's hunger.

Sharing wasn't exclusive to reps and cellies, though. I'd never known Curtis to ask anyone for food, but Flip sometimes gave Curtis a soup or two. Toll, however, was Curtis's big homie[12] and his main benefactor. Still, after I chatted with Curtis from outside his bottom-tier cell door, I ended up promising to give him a few soups and some chips. It was hard to see someone hungry in jail when I knew that a bag of chips could be the difference between getting some sleep and having a hunger headache. That day, however, deputies put us on lockdown, so there wouldn't be dayroom time to give him the food. His hunger weighed on me, and I can't say I gave this much thought before I tried it, but I hit my cell intercom button and asked the pod whether I could deliver food to Curtis. To my great surprise, the pod popped my cell door. *A cool dep'.* I beelined to Curtis's cell, set the soups and chips outside his cell door, and on my way back, I passed Toll who was delivering food to Herc—a cool deputy, indeed! We greeted each other, but we didn't ruin the momentary privilege we had been given by trying to chat.

Because Lee and Herc were in chronically indigent families, D-Double and Ken sometimes made sure the mealtime extras went to one or both of them. It was hard to ask for food. Lee said he didn't want to owe anyone, and he worried that if someone gave him something, he would have to do something for it later, so he chose hunger to the precarity of that situation.

Sisqo was the least inhibited person I met in jail. Very early into his time in Sunland, he submitted and received a $30 order from the commissary. Then, he ate it all in a single night. My guess was that he thought he would be free the next day. He wasn't. Or, maybe he thought he would have more money for future orders. He didn't. Instead, he turned himself into a sitcom character whose main role in every dayroom skit was to hustle for chips. "My life would be better if I had some chips," Sisqo used to say. He always appeared tragically hungry. We couldn't always tell when he was hustling, so sometimes we leaned into care and gave him the extras or a food item or two from our individual stashes.

But of all the episodes of food sharing that I witnessed and participated in, none impressed me more than the way we handled the news that Ken had signed his "deal" for 14 years of prison time. Toll collected apples from each of us so he could make "pruno"—an alcoholic drink made from fermented fruit. D-Double, being Ken's celly, took it upon himself to make a "cake" of sorts. The day came to give Ken a respectable send off, and D-Double brought out that cake in a Styrofoam container. He opened the container to oohs and aahs! It was a five-pound sugar fiend's dream: an inventory of every high fructose corn syrup item available for purchase from the commissary. There were honeybuns, little donuts, M&M's, and other insulin spiking catalysts with chocolate spread heavily drizzled over it all. D-Double gave a brief speech about wishing Ken the best, and we dug in. I had my customary two bites before germaphobia got the better of me.

Food wasn't the only resource that residents shared. It was common to share soap and lotion and other basic hygiene products with those less fortunate. In nearly every housing unit, there was a talented artist who would decorate a birthday, Mother's Day, and Valentine's Day card for you. Kinsley drew two tattoos for me. He was about 6'1", caramel-skinned, and he wore his hair short all around—the way Black men did during the 1980s. Though he was a big guy, he presented as nonthreatening and he was accommodating when it came to his art. He never asked for anything, but I gave him some chips and a soup for his work. He made an exceptional Mother's Day card for

LK, and he served as our dayroom's black barber and hair braider. All these caring activities, he did without asking for a thing in return.

In one way, the politics was a system of sharing and caring for one another. After all, by the politics, residents were guaranteed access to facilities. Still, as I explained earlier, a resident sometimes shared across racial boundaries—even if we had to be sneaky about it. Nearly everyone used Beast's stash of *Smooth Girl Magazines*. I often lent out books—well, they were "weirdo books" according to Herc, but I lent them out without concern for race.

For a while, there was interest in my copy of Erving Goffman's *Asylums*. I think the title misled expectations. I gave it out like a mischievous kid handing a deceptively sour piece of candy to a friend. Residents returned the book with disappointment and curiosity as to why I'd be interested in something like that. TJ never finished it or told me what, if anything, he thought of the book. D-Double looked at the books on my table: *Asylums*, *Forced Passages*, *Seeking the Sakhu*, the second edition of *Feminist Theory*, and the third edition of *Gender Inequality*. I suppose *Asylums* had the most agreeable look among them.

"This book is about being in here?" D-Double asked while holding *Asylums*.

I said he should just read it and tell me what he thought.

He flipped through a few pages, put it back on the table, and said that he didn't want to be aware of "everything going on in here every day; I don't need that level of consciousness."

Sometime later, Beast asked to read it in exchange for a *Smooth Girl Magazine*. I declined the magazine and offered him *Asylums* anyhow. A week or so later, he returned it to me, saying: "It was weird." That gave me a chuckle for days, and I never asked whether he completed the book, but I did think it was noteworthy that even in jail, where there was virtually nothing else to do and residents read everything within reach multiple times, I couldn't persuade some to read a classic sociological text.

A Lesson

At lunch I put in my bid to use the phone during dayroom time. I wanted to give a friend an update on how I was doing. She wasn't home, but her partner answered. I said I'd call another time, and though we didn't know each other, he kept me on the phone longer than I wanted to be. It was awkward—and costly, throwing away precious phone time on him. He said something that led me to reply that I wasn't ever going to jail again.

"It could happen again," he replied.

I doubled down on my initial response, and so did he.

Months later, I was home and trying to put my life back together. I relayed that conversation to a future colleague, who expressed sympathy that someone had said that to me but, in the same breath, suggested that perhaps I was supposed to have had that uncomfortable exchange—that there may have been a lesson in it for me.

I have since given quite a few research presentations after which I was approached by people eager to give my life meaning. If I wasn't so disappointed, I might be intrigued by the sliminess with which I've been told that I'm "lucky" to have gone to jail "to collect data." More than a few persons have bemoaned not having "the access" that I had while in jail—that I'm "fortunate"—yes, it was my fortune—to have gone to jail. "Yeah, but you used it to build a career, so it all worked out for you." "You've got this [sic] amazing data, though!" "Well, look at you now. You've got an amazing story."

I used to be shocked by these kinds of statements, but then I decided that there were just more rude and ridiculous people walking the Earth than I'd once thought. Now, however, I see these exchanges as meaning-making situations, but for others. It's their way of comforting themselves about me and setting right the basic causal nature of life. I went through something so that I could have something else. More importantly, they weren't as "fortunate" as I was to go through that same something, and that's why they don't have whatever it is they want. It all makes sense.

10

It Is What It Is

What should you wear to surrender yourself for a county jail sentence? And "surrender" is definitely the appropriate term. If that's what you're doing, it means you have agreed with your public defender or defense attorney on "a good deal." Lots of residents talked about that—"a good deal." By the time the date of my surrender came, the goodness of the deal was irrelevant. I was tired, and if you have never needed to appear in court for a civil or criminal matter, it's an incredibly jeopardizing experience that sucks up the energy from all corners of your life. Even if you expect a favorable outcome, just thinking about a pending court appearance can be exhausting. You find yourself fighting to keep from ruminating on what could happen. Imagine that: Your thought is that you need to *not* think about the case. After you have gone to a bunch of hearings, lost countless hours of sleep, survived migraines (if you're like me), and been through bouts of emotional eating, surrendering to a plea deal can be a sweet relief—well, maybe not sweet. I knew not to wear a suit or something nice. My appearance in court was a process formality—no point in primping for a judge. I wore a T-shirt, sweat pants, socks, and a pair of Adidas slides. You might as well be comfortable.

My mother, brother, and I snickered in the courtroom gallery. All morning we had wisecracked through intermittent moments of resignation like a movie scene in which there's not enough oxygen for everyone, so you tell a few jokes to ease the anxiety of imminent death. The court session began, and there weren't many people there: my immediate family and a handful of others—the judge, his clerk, a deputy, the counselors, and a couple of in-custody residents. As the process got underway, there was a moment of clarity for me when I noticed the clerk sipping something from a straw in her tumbler, and I watched the deputy and counselors move about the courtroom with ease. The rest of us—those of us in the gallery and the residents shackled in their seats—were sitting still in our chairs like we were chained to them. The comfort with which the court personnel moved about emphasized how dominated and uncertain I felt in that moment.

Whatever were the specifics of the first case, it was handled with the cool, distant objectivity of a professional. The judge started to monotone through the second case in the same way, but then he noticed that the resident had been doing state prison time before being brought to Providence. He told the resident that he had a choice as to where to finish his sentence. "You'd rather go back [to prison], right?" The resident nodded eagerly. "That's usually how it works."[1]

The exchange reminded me of a conversation I'd had in a court holding cell weeks earlier. A resident told me: "In prison, you're home. You're just home. They try to make it comfortable for you. Jail is punishment. Prison is like working for the government. You'll be taken care of. You just do your job, and you'll be OK. Jail is like working at McDonald's. You could be fired. The pay sucks. The whole thing sucks." He freestyled that brilliant analysis, and it remains my go-to description of the difference between jail and prison.

My case was next. I stood at the sound of my name, looked back at my family, and I stepped forward. I don't recall whether I was asked to give an affirmative response to anything. A deafening shock crept into my ears as the judge said some words at me. It's one thing to plan a surrender. It's another to be there on schedule. And it's quite another for it to actually happen. I understood that I was to do 180 days in jail. I got that, and I remember that my public defender had told me I'd "only" have to do 120 of those days and that, most likely, I'd "be out in three days because of gov-boots." So, I understood my sentence, and I also understood that I wasn't returning to my seat in the gallery. I'm not sure how I thought things would go, but the judge was still talking when the deputy ghosted to my side and had a hand around one of my wrists for the handcuffs. He turned me around, and I put on my smile mask for my weepy-eyed mother. Then they took me away.

Jail. There's no catharsis, no lasting revelation of god, no gaining of a deeper self-meaning. There most certainly isn't any righteousness-making or correction. There's no organized series of steps to constitute some sort of moral process. There is only sequence: this happened, then that happened, and the order is inconsequential. That never stopped residents from narrating themselves as the protagonists in a grand adventure in which jail is a mystical stronghold where painful lessons must be learned before freedom can be obtained. We have a basic socioemotional need for events to make sense—especially windfalls and suffering. We go through some awful experience or are given an unplanned victory, and we feel impelled to fit what happened into a digestible story. That's thing about jail time, though: there is no neat story arc from arrest to incarceration to release. But if it's comforting to believe there's a plot, it's this: It is what it is.

You have likely heard or said that before: "It is what it is." There are at least two appropriate uses. It could be that you don't care about what could happen if you do or don't do a thing, or it could be that your current circumstances or impending consequences are out of your control. The main difference between the two usages is in the degree of self-efficacy—more in the former than in the latter. As an example of the first, I spent the better part of a day carefully carving out domino-sized rectangles from the cardboard back to a notepad. I'd made significant progress in drawing the dots on each domino when Scott reminded me that the Sunday clothing exchange was the next day. I paused for a second. He was warning me. Having contraband in the form of dominos might give cover to an asshole dep to toss our food, books, and toilet paper around the cell. I shrugged my thought: *It is what it is.* Seeing my attitude, Scott said I might regret working so hard for something that I'd only have for a few hours and that he just wanted to remind me of that fact. Now, I might have stopped making the dominos and avoided the possibility of a deputy ransacking our cell, but making the dominos was a productive project, and I figured I'd just deal with whatever came later.

I also had occasion to use the other meaning of *it is what it is.* I'd gotten into a brief altercation in the dayroom with Lee. During breakfast, there were extra food items, and when I reached for a hardboiled egg, he slapped the back of my hand. (I never learned why. Maybe he thought it would be funny.) The smack sound was loud, and in a split second, I heard Toll or Herc say, "Ooh!" and in that moment, I intuited that the smack required a response or perhaps I'd be perceived as someone who could be picked on. I wasn't upset, so I turned reluctantly toward Lee to give him one of those sudden, strong pushes in the chest that can feel like a punch. Lee tumbled like clothes in a dryer into a cell door on the bottom tier with a loud and echoing crash. I moved toward him, but I wasn't angry. I didn't even want to fight, and neither did he. I let him stand, and we squared up for a couple of seconds without doing anything. We were saved from the inertia of the moment by D-Double yelling to take the conflict to the cells. That's where fights in closed dayrooms were sanctioned—the cells. No one wanted dayroom time ruined. The pod popped the cell doors, and I waited in my cell for Lee to come. I was hoping he wouldn't, but he did.

He stood in the doorway and lectured me about what I'd done. "Do you understand what you did? Do you? Do you understand what you did?"

I didn't. He left without explaining what I'd done—and without a fight, thank goodness. For the next couple of days, though, I didn't let Lee stand behind me, and I paid close attention to how others behaved around me. He had been in Sunland longer than I had, and I figured he had friends among the other black residents; maybe they were protective of him. He was a little guy. Eventually, I asked D-Double whether I'd have to watch my back for the rest of my sentence. He said he didn't know, and I decided right then: *It is what it is.* I couldn't live every day in fear of a fight. If it was coming, it was out of my control.

In Golden County jails, *it is what it is* was another endurance strategy—a way of saying, "There's no point in whining about this negative issue," so repress it. Maybe she didn't put money on your books like she promised you; maybe you decided against your rep's instructions to come out for dayroom time; or perhaps the public defender didn't show. There was nothing that you could do about any of those matters. And because there was little value in complaining about what might happen, *it is what it is* summed up your level of self-efficacy.

This is not fatalism, however. Residents understood well that if they were better resourced, perhaps things would be very different for them. *It is what it is* can mean you don't get the favorable outcomes no matter how hard you try and having exhausted whatever you could do to keep bad things from happening, the cancer returns. The hot water is shut off. The eviction moves forward. The arrest happens. The gov-boot doesn't happen. The sun is going to rise tomorrow, and you will still be short a couple of hundred dollars of paying your car note, so you go to the movies. May as well have some momentary enjoyment. *It is what it is.*

But whereas residents used *it is what it is* to resign themselves to some circumstances—or at least to avoid openly discussing how they felt—they were just as likely to use *it is as it should be* to endure. No one ever comes out and says it just like that, but *it is as it should be* is the principle that connects platitudes like "god's got a plan," "everything happens for a reason," "it wasn't meant to be," "it's karma," "things have a way of working out," and perhaps most common and powerful of them all: "I'm glad I went through [X] because now I've learned/gained [Y]." *It is as it should be* nearly raises these broad cultural memes to the level of a religion. In short, the idea is that nothing happens without meaning for each of us, so the stank of jail, the cold, Deputy Dog, the Palace de Excreta, cool deps—you have all those experiences for a purpose, even if you don't realize it until after you're onto a new set of experiences.

Life is conceived as a highly individual process with everything that happens being part of that process for you. Believing that to be true constitutes strong emotional armor because it points to there being something better in the end, so you needn't be in despair now. Your life is purposeful.[2] The catch is that however strongly you believe that to be true, the process may be hidden from you until *after* you have completed it. Then you look back and note: My first love failed, and in finding my second love, I realize that my first love was just a process I had to go through to be ready for this new love. That is a very tidy way of injecting meaning and endurance into all sorts of life experiences.

Whichever perspective residents chose for whatever situations in which they found themselves, *it is what it is* and *it is as it should be* constitute philosophies of life for enduring troubling circumstances. And like every other endurance strategy, emotional entropy guaranteed their failure at some point. That may be one reason why residents employed both strategies—sometimes in the same moment. They aren't mutually exclusive philosophies.

I frequently heard a mixing of the two strategies while in church. During one meeting, a southsider started talking about how his girlfriend had stopped supporting him, and it had taken some time for him to realize that she was gone. He had tears in his voice at first, so it seemed to me that he was still dealing with the abandonment, but then he pivoted, "It is what it is, ya know?" A few of us nodded in response. "I guess it wasn't meant to be," he added, giving purpose to his abandonment. One of the volunteers said something about everything being part of god's plan, and there were gestures of agreement around the room. We all took part, more or less, in vacillating between *it is what it is* and *it is as it should be*.

One of the main benefits of going to church was to give life meaning. This is where *it is as it should be* was most often called upon to do the work of making our suffering purposeful. Residents could marshal a biblical character's story as an analog of the trials and tribulations they were experiencing. We weren't just in jail. We were in the belly of a great fish like Jonah. We weren't just being abandoned. We were being tested like Job. Sometimes the discussion revolved around the idea that god was trying to get our attention with all our suffering—that jail was "an opportunity for growth," as a volunteer once claimed to much agreement. It was, therefore, up to us to learn whatever was being taught so we could move on to the next stage in our respective life processes.

But like so many characters in religious stories the world over, residents couldn't always see whatever it was that they were supposed to learn, and there was a quiet desperation in many of us. Some expressed it openly, but I heard that desperation in voices. I discerned it in word choice. I saw it scrawled amid gang writing on the metal frame in a Providence open day-room: "Lord please cure my [sic]" and "Jesus save me from this Hell take me home I know I sinned for give [sic] my sin and show me mercy in the name of the Holy Spirit and Jesus Christ Amen." And in the Providence trustee pod: "Thank Jesus" and "I Love you J." I'm assuming "J" was short for "Jesus" in that last one—perhaps the writer was cut short before finishing. Those prayers remind me of sweaty hours in Church of God in Christ revivals where faith mixed with desperation for a breakthrough as the church musicians and praise team sent energy waves through the sanctuary. We would leave church exhausted and with a new perspective on our same circumstances. That's the central of the work of *it is as it should be*: perspective to endure a little longer.

In Z-Pod, no resident was as consistent with *it is as it should be* as the Minister. It didn't even have to be his news. Bad or good, he would say, "god is working." He had been homeless before his arrest, and he was full of Black church sound bites: "Let go and let god"; "PUSH—pray until something happens"; "Let god work." In one instance, no one was talking to him but he butted in to say, "Everything happens for a reason." *Everything?* My mind went to the Rwandan genocide and my childhood neighbor in "the green house" who my grandmother forbade me to play with because his parents were crack addicts. Did "everything" include that visceral moment at the green house wherein we opened his trash to throw away our Pop Ice packets and we saw a burnt and broken crack pipe.

"So!" he said in response to how I must have been looking at him. "That don't mean nothing!" Maybe *I* was supposed to learn to trust my grand-mother in that moment, but what about him? At 10 years old, what was the reason that everything was happening to him?

The Minister aside, *it is as it should be* had broad appeal. In one instance, I must have been openly wearing my burdens because Scott told me to stop stressing and that I should just "make love to that woman" and "everything'll work out for the best." I'm still not sure why he thought I was stressing over a woman, that making love to that imaginary woman—while I was in jail, no less—was a solution, or why the concerns that I hadn't shared with him would "work out for the best." But I understood the essence of his point: Life's processes were for my betterment. He gave me a final *it is as it should be* moment just before leaving.

When a judge issued Scott a "failure to appear" because deputies didn't call him for court, he was understandably despondent. But he went the next day, and about two weeks later, he was released. In the minutes between when he learned he was to be released and when the pod popped the cell door, he could barely stand his joy. He breathed new meaning into having been left behind for court weeks earlier: "Man! I was stressin'—like I didn't know what was happening, but everything happens for a reason. Do you want my razor?" I declined the razor. It was something to see him recast his previous woes as mystical events with meaning because he signed a deal for summary probation and hours of community service in lieu of jail time.

Similarly, on the latest stint that brought us together, Flip explained: "My wife said I need to do about four months to clean my life up."

"You agree?"

"Shit. It got me to stop drankin' last time."

"So how did you end up in here this time?"

"Shit," he snorted with a smile. "Drankin'! Ha! Ha!"

It Is What It Is

Some of the most poignant moments I experienced in jail had to do with *it is what it is*. During a conversation, a bunch of us tried to convince Sisqo that two years in prison was better than the decades he was facing. The circumstances around his case were not at all in his favor. The discussion segued into what we might do after jail. It was a familiar discussion. Lee said he would report to his probation officer, head to a homeless shelter, and "get some homeless pussy." I asked him if he had a family, and he said he could tell his mother wouldn't support him. He added, "I don't wanna live with my mom."

Scott said he was going to be a truck driver and make "$3,000 a month." Before jail, I'd never made more than $25,000 a year, so $36,000 sounded like pretty good money to me. Herc and Toll talked about possibly joining a branch of the Armed Forces. Sisqo, however, said he planned to keep stealing.

A few of us laughed. "Yeah. Nigga. First finish this case. Stupid mufucka," Herc said while shaking his head. "Nigga need to get a job."

"I *been* working. I just started stealing," Sisqo said.

"You haven't learned anything," Chino said. Chino had done state time, and between regaling us with examples of how much better state time is than jail time, he often spoke of his daughters and the need to get home.

D-Double said he didn't "believe in that," and it wasn't clear what he meant at first. He explained that you're supposed to get smarter at doing dirt—not quit. "If you get caught for the same crime twice, you're just stupid," he said.

"Well, I must be dumb as a mufucka," Chino laughed.

We all got a laugh at that one, but not Sisqo. He changed the tone of the discussion altogether when he said that if given "a lot of years, I'm just gonna hang myself with a sheet from the top tier." The statement was floating there between us with no one knowing immediately what to do about it.

I told him not to do that while I was there—that I wouldn't be able to handle it.

"Naw. Don't do that shit," D-Double said.

Sisqo shrugged.

He wasn't the only one with an *it is what it is* attitude toward suicide. At 19, Curtis was facing life in prison. "How do you deal with that?" I asked.

"Shit. Nigga. I'm just gon' kill myself; it's as simple as that." Curtis didn't flinch or seem afraid. I stared at him through his cell door window. "I just don't think about it, really," he continued.

"Until you go to court?" I asked.

"Not even then."

The finality in his voice was unnerving. He would kill himself if given a life sentence, and it was what it was. It reminded me of the finality in D-Double's voice when he explained that he could "focus on the bad" and that "missing family and children is bad," but "Whatever. If I gotta go to prison, I gotta go. I ain't gonna cry like some would."

In response, Toll spoke up about hope. He said without hope, he "really would be lost—gotta have hope."

His appeal to hope stood out to me because just a few days prior, he was told that a rival gang member in another dayroom was talking about killing him. There was a good chance they would see one another during a court day. At the threat of losing his life, Toll didn't speak of hope. He decided that there was little he could do about it: "Oh well, nigga. I ain't gon' live forever."

On this note, Ken embodied *it is what it is*. I'd never seen him do a day of hard time—something I can't say for anyone else. In fact, he was often pleasant in his attitude toward others. When he signed his "deal" for 14 years in prison, he was unbothered—almost chipper. I don't think he was cheerful about going to prison, but he wasn't down about it either. I asked him what he thought of his sentence, and he said that ever since he was little, he "knew" he would go to prison. As for this sentence, he smiled: "I'm guilty, so . . . " He shrugged, and that was that. He had long decided that *it is what it is.*

But let me tell you of a marathon of exchanges I'd had with Flip. By the time, what I'm about to recount happened, I was sick and goddamned tired of Flip's presence, and I could no longer hide it from him. We had been on bad terms for a while and being at odds with your celly is like beef between a married couple, only there's no going to another room or to work to avoid each other. I'd stopped talking to him altogether, and I wonder how Flip would describe me, but he was reputed to be a "bad celly."

During the week that I stopped talking to him, jail was more annoying than it would ever be for me. I guess Flip decided that he didn't need me to talk. Each and every day for a week he held complete conversations with himself in the cell. He voiced different characters in make believe scenes, and when he tired of that—or when his mind interrupted his mouth with a new plan—he started reciting lines from the Steven Segal movie, *Marked for Death.* During better times in our cell, I recited lines with him. We took turns being "Screwface" and some of the Jamaican minions that Steven Segal's character whooped on. But I wasn't having any of that.

Everything about him annoyed me. The tap-shh sound of his slippers in the cell was extra loud. I hated how he paced constantly. I hated seeing his brain grasp for the slightest project. He picked at the lint covering the vents for a while; then he started to clean the walls, sucking his teeth when he saw the filthy rag he was using added as much muck as he was trying to remove. *How many times you gonna do that same shit before you learn?* I hated how he "cleaned." We used to argue all the time about it before I resigned that I'd just have to clean whatever he thought he was cleaning. *It is what it is.* I went behind him with a soapy rag because Flip didn't bother with soap. He just smeared sink water on the toilet-sink. I'd complain, and he would respond, "Nigga! There's nothing there! It's *stainless* steel!" That used to break up the argument, and I'd laugh at his ridiculous logic while cleaning the mess, but I was sick of him.

I no longer got a chuckle at the songs he sang off key and with the wrong lyrics. I didn't want to join in with my 99 Cents Only store version of Sam Cooke's "A Change Is Gonna Come" like I used to. And maybe Flip was doing "Screwface" and Sam Cooke as olive branches, but I had long been done with him. So, he cawed and squawked out "A Change Is Gonna Come" like he had a personal complaint against Sam. Poor Sam wasn't the only victim, though. Flip desecrated 50 Cent's "Hustla's Ambition" all the time. The beat was stuck in his head, but he didn't know any of the lyrics, so he made them up. So many times, I tried to teach him the hook—he should at least know the hook—but he said he *preferred* to use his own words, and well, what can anyone do with that?

Eventually, he would tire of singing and conversing with himself enough to lay down, but there was a whole ordeal to him falling asleep. He had a "need," he once told me, to hum or talk to "clear" his mind for sleep. He would lay in bed saying whatever phrase flashed on the screen in his mind, emptying his every thought into the cell's air. To hell with my sleep. He needed to babble. Sometimes, he focused enough to treat me to him struggling to read a magazine or book aloud. He didn't have his reading glasses, and it was hard for him to see. I stared at the underside of the top bunk barely able to contain my anger.

Worse, I had been accepting whatever gastrointestinal issues Flip had because, I told myself, *We're in this cell together.* But things had changed, and Flip seemed to have more gas than others and more potent doses, too. Increasingly, he ignored toilet etiquette. He waited until there was some fecal sillage from his gas before flushing. Still, I refused to talk to him. He smacked loudly while eating, and I said nothing. I kept my silence as he hummed and talked to his food like a little kid while eating on his bunk. Even when he stood over the toilet, shifted his weight to either leg, bit the skin off apples and spit them into his hand to then drop them into the toilet, I refused to say a damned thing. If the toilet clogged, oh well, I thought.

I survived a week of that. Then came the day that Flip returned from a mental health visit to immediately start his daily annoyances. It was early in the afternoon, and I decided that if he kept that up after lights out, I'd say something. After dinner, he sang to himself and fashioned a knife from a plastic spoon. I wondered whether that was for me. Maybe. For sure, though, he wanted me to see that he had made it. *Is this a threat?* Around 11:30 p.m., he was snoring. Yes! He snores, too. Alas, his sleep was short lived. We hadn't covered the lights, and they were burning through his eyelids, no doubt.

At 1:15 a.m., he started shuffling around the cell before climbing back onto his bunk and moaning to himself. He tried a few "Screwface" lines, but he wasn't getting back to sleep. Meanwhile, I'd been up, writing a letter, which I stopped to record what he was doing. He launched into a full-voiced conversation with himself, and I tried to wait him out, but I couldn't. "Say man. Can we have one night where you don't talk to yourself?" I asked.

"Look here, bruh. You and me ain't been talking—"

"I know," I interrupted him. "And yet you keep talking to yourself day and night. Goddamn! It's late."

"You do things that are pretty rude, too." The implied equivalence annoyed me. I was indignant, in fact, as I stood from my bunk to face him on the top bunk. The fight might have looked imminent, but I still had some posturing to do. "You can just hit the button," he said nervously.

I remembered the spoon-knife he had made, but I pushed ahead: "I'm about to push the button on yo' eye!"

He shrugged: "Hey. That's jail."

The comment sent thoughts spiraling as I moved to sit on my bunk. "That's jail" summed up so much. Havocc had to hurry to let a nurse take a culture of his urethra in the presence of a brusque deputy, sometimes no one visited you, sometimes you were thrown in the Palace de Excreta, sometimes your slippers fell apart, sometimes you hard-timed-it, and sometimes your celly socked you because you were annoying. It was what it was because that's jail—all of it.

"Just shut the fuck up," I more begged than commanded. After all, I didn't want to fight. I wanted peace. "It's late! It's time to go to sleep or at least be quiet! Damn. It's fuckin' 1:30 in the mornin'." I sat on my bunk, and after a few huffs to himself, Flip shut up.

A few hours later, it was time for breakfast. Flip didn't get up. I asked Toll and Herc if they heard Flip and I arguing in the middle of the night. They hadn't, so I gave them the highlights. Ken, Lee, and D-Double had quite the laugh, and each told a personal story about Flip. D-Double and Flip had been cellies, but they didn't get along, so D-Double had Flip transferred to the cell he was in when I met him. "The nigga is weird," D-Double said.

"He be up talking to himself," I said.

Ken laughed: "That's hard time."

"Is he schizo?" Lee asked.

"No, but he takes medication, and I know he has problems; he's on disability."

Our conversation ended there, but I'd never before made that observation about Flip aloud: that he was on disability. If I'm honest, I never took it seriously. I ate my breakfast in silence, thinking about the two times before in which Flip apologized to me for his mood swings. I'd told him that it was sometimes better for me to ignore him when he was flipping out, to which he empathized with me and was genuinely apologetic. In that moment at break-fast, I felt awful. I wasn't nearly as empathic as I could have been.

A few hours later came the morning pill call. Flip didn't hear it. If he didn't get up, his back and shoulder would ache all day, and he would groan in pain. Plus, deputies would ignore his pleas to get medication off schedule. I'd seen it happen to him before. He would end up waiting until the night pill call—10 hours or so later. His pain was on my mind, so I woke him, and while we never returned to the playful banter that defined the beginning of our cell-lationship, we didn't have beef for the rest of the time he was there. I acknowl-edged (for myself) that he was dealing with more than his annoying habits. I wasn't in constant pain, I wasn't taking his medication, and I didn't need to be uncaring.

A week later, Flip was released on schedule. I marked the time: 8:40 p.m. "Maxwell," a deputy's voice came through the intercom, startling us.

"Yeah," Flip responded.

"Roll it up. You're getting released."

If he had smiled any wider, the corners of his mouth would have touched in the back of his head. He did a child-like dance step, and honestly, I was happy for him. I gave him some chips "for the road."

"Learn from This"

When I was in the Providence trustee pod, I oriented the head of my blue "boat" sleeping apparatus such that when I looked up, I was staring under the table and my feet were at the cell door. Looking up, directly in my line of sight, someone had scratched, "Learn from this." There were other things there, too—various gang signatures and what not, but I sometimes think about the guy who wrote "Learn from this." I wonder about the conditions he was experiencing at the time. I'm sure the outline of his life when he wrote that was similar to mine when I was reading it, but I wonder about the details that made his experience unique. What did he think he was supposed to learn?

Some of my closest friends were raised in Chicago, Minnesota, the Bronx, St. Louis, Detroit, Virginia, Nashville, and various parts of northern and southern California. Among the commonalities that truly link us are the en-durance strategies we grew up using—a kind of jailing but for poor people in free society.[3] We ate condiment sandwiches—I preferred A-1 Sauce to syrup. We considered eggs, bread, and American cheese the makings of a mini-feast. Many of us ran little hustles to get things we wanted and needed. I pumped gas for spare change. We intimately understand what it means to "put something on" a bill because the ends weren't going to meet no matter what, so you may as well spend some of money on having fun. We hadn't merited those conditions[4] any more than the kid in the green house merited crack-addicted parents. But when your life experiences are dotted by uncertainty, hunger, thwarted dreams, and the knowledge that things could have been better if only you had been born with better resources, jailing becomes a way of life and *it is what it is* and *it is as it should be* are indispensable strategies to endure a little longer.

But the questions remain: Was there a lesson in all our tribulations? Is that what jail is—one big lesson?

I wonder because I didn't learn a damned thing—not if the lessons are moral or spiritual or otherwise lofty. I did learn some practical realities, if those count. I learned that someone could be in jail for nine years while fighting a case, and if you can be there for nine, you can be there for much longer. On that point, I learned that the presumption of innocence is often little more than a cool ideal. It's not a practical reality. I learned that the best-case scenario for mental health treatment in jail is a kind ear and some medication. The Palace de Excreta was awful, but I'm guessing it's not the worst-case scenario. I learned that race relations are built into the managerial functions of jail. I learned that bad sleep isn't your kid keeping you up at night—it's the county forcing you to sleep on a metal slab with a thin, bacteria-infested sponge mattress in the cold, under lights that never cut off. For that matter, it turns out, I learned that not seeing the sun for days and weeks at a time can play havoc with basic bodily functions. I came to find out that nightmares converge in cloistered living, and so does the smell in everyone's skin and their body waste. I still find it interesting that deputies solutioned an answer to problems which they largely contributed. Who knew that Doritos, grape jelly, mayonnaise, pepperoni, and cheese squeeze on flayed Top Ramen noodles constituted a good start toward a "pizza"? In the movies, jail is loud. But I learned it was the quiet that was so often unsettling. I'd been to court as a free person, but I have newfound empathy for those appearing while in custody. I've heard the phrase "hard time" more times than I can count, but I had no understanding of it until I was hard-timing-it. I suppose I can say I learned that some deputies found a sort of primitive limbic gratification in mistreating us while others were kind enough to ignore us with music. You gotta take the good with the bad. I could go on—maybe name some of the indelible memories I have from jail: the sound of a man masturbating above me, being berated by the dentist, Nurse Bee and Dr. Cross, various exchanges with deputies, conversations with residents about their families, and the one-armed man. And all that stuff was happening more or less at the same time—despite my having broken things up into chapters. Let's be clear: even if you have never been to jail and know nothing about it, you know you don't want to go, so "Don't go to jail" can't be the lesson. But was there a morality to it all because it's wild to me that jails are run the way they are.

Jail time counts among the most meaningless kinds of time you can you do. I had more empty experiences in jail than I can put in one book, and after all of it, all I can say is *it is what it is.* This doesn't mean I don't empathize with those who lean toward *it is as it should be.* A foundational idea in sociological and social psychological research is that we are all trying to avoid discomforting feelings.[5] It can be upsetting to think of trauma and tragedy as totally purposeless—awful things happen that are just random and without process, and that we don't always have the agency that we think we have to shape our lives. This is not the same as saying social structure is so rigid that it cannot change. I am saying that the existence of a structure is not evidence of purpose. That's what I got out of jail. Perhaps you will "learn from this."

Notes

Introduction

1. The Bureau of Justice Statistics defines jail as "a confinement facility operating under the authority of a sheriff, police chief, or county or city administrator. Facilities include jails, detention centers, county or city correctional centers, special jail facilities (such as a medical or treatment centers and pre-release centers), and temporary holding or lockup facilities that are part of the jail's combined function" (Zheng and Minton 2021, 3).
2. All names of persons and places are pseudonyms.
3. I am reminded of a question that Lorna Rhodes (2004, 4) used to frame her ethnography of a maximum-security prison: "What assumptions about dangerousness, self-control, and individual choice are contained in, and signaled by, measures of extreme confinement?" It may seem natural to assume that places of punishment are justified by who is put in them, but it is just as valid—if not more revealing—to ask about the motives of an organization that conceives of such places to put people in.
4. Goffman (1961, 4–5). Goffman's (1961) study of an asylum as a kind of total institution remains a masterful examination of organizational living.
5. Carson (2020).
6. Zheng and Minton (2021).
7. For a discussion on the popularity of prison films, see Rafter (2000, 123–128).
8. Turney and Conner (2019) published a recent review of the literature on jails. For a discussion on the impact of penal time on families, see Miller (2021), Western (2018), and McKay et al. (2016). Additionally, Sufrin (2017) is, quite frankly, a heartbreaking study of mothering in jail. For an examination of changes in visitation methods for jail residents, see Tartaro and Levy (2017). May et al. (2013) published a revealing study about the perceived punitiveness of jail versus prison that mirrors May and Wood's (2010) finding that people with experiential knowledge of both jail and prison perceive jail to be the more punishing environment. Still, none of this work has led to sustained research efforts into American jails.
9. Goldfarb's (1975) book, *Jails*, has a subtitle that summarizes the undercurrent in Irwin (1985) and Spradley (1970): "The Ultimate Ghetto of the Criminal Justice System." All three are connected by the idea that jails are how local governments get rid of disreputable people. Goldfarb, however, spends considerably more time describing how reckless and criminally negligent penal administrators could be. Additionally, Octavio Ballesteros (1979) published a study of jails that is rarely cited. He worked as an educator in "Southwest Jail," and though he barely veiled his antipathies toward penal residents, he nevertheless produced an interesting account of his time as an educator

in jail, where he set for himself the task of rehabilitating the residents. Indeed, he put together a very practical list of rehabilitative programs should a penal administrator have interest in bettering the lives of the residents and reducing recidivism.

10. Carson and Cowhig (2020); Slate, Buffington-Vollum, and Johnson (2013). For a discussion of suicide in jails that considers specific cases, see Roth (2018).

11. Carson and Cowhig (2020).

12. Zeng (2019); Beck, Karberg, and Harrison (2002); Gilliard and Beck (1996); Schlesinger (1983).

13. When discussing "The Kalief Browder Story" in my courses, my students are always shocked by how long he was kept at Rikers Correctional Facility without any progress on his case.

14. This is an ongoing issue in sociology. As specializations separate researchers into camps, there is less integrative work across subspecialties. Scholars interested in prisons and jails should also be interested in more general theoretical developments in studies of organizations and institutions, but the two groups remain largely separate. Of course, not every scholar sticks to their subspecialties like that. My general approach to social science is best expressed in Turner's (1991, 1990) discussion of building cumulative knowledge. In both articles, Turner lays out a set of principles by which he abides. All are useful and, in particular, he believes we should abstract above the context for theoretical power, not be wedded to any theorist as much as we are the ideas in a theoretical program, avoid ideological argumentation, and search for points of convergence across theories and studies.

15. Russell-Brown (2009, 14).

16. Muhammad (2010), Russell-Brown (2009), Mendelberg (2001).

17. A central finding in Pager (2007) was that hiring managers were more likely to call back White applicants with criminal records than they were Black applicants with the same resumes but no criminal record. The study is a fascinating, if not poignant, analysis of how race and blameworthiness intersect in the minds of some hiring managers to deepen racial inequality. For a similar and no less important study, see Royster (2003).

18. Goffman (1961).

19. I have in mind Tuan's (1977, 8) conception of "experience" as "a cover-all term for the various modes though which a person knows and constructs a reality." This includes sensation, perception, and conception which are funneled through emotion and thought.

20. According to Mills ([1959] 2000), sociological research should connect history with biography in society to make sense of what's going on in a given situation.

21. I was inspired by Abbott's (2007, 74) description of "lyrical sociology" and the value of writing in an emotionally engaged way that doesn't pretend as though the researcher is somehow outside of emotional experience being described.

22. Scheff (2003, 254) discussed shame as a master emotion that signals a threat to social bonds as well as indication that one has failed to meet a standard. I didn't want to ask what "truck" meant because I didn't want to appear culturally incompetent and risk being ostracized in some way.

23. For an interesting read on how an ethnographer felt about his research and the participants, see Malinowski ([1967] 1989).

24. It's not easy to balance these three voices in an academic text. Gardner ([1983] 1991, 30–32) has an illuminating discussion about narrative inviting the reader into a dream world, how immersion in the dream can be quite satisfying, and the dissatisfying experience e of being "woken" from that vivid dream. As an academic book, interrupting the dream state of deep description is sometimes necessary to provide analysis.

25. Goffman (1989, 125–126).

26. Abbott (2007).

27. Abbott (2007, 69) described "momentaneity" as a style of sociological writing in which—among other matters—the scholar captures the state of being in a time and freely gives a natural reaction to it.

28. The origin of this observation—for me at least—is found in Abbott (2004, 99).

29. Becker (2003) has a useful discussion on this matter. The central point is that nomenclature matters. Researchers should not ignore word connotations.

30. Alper and Durose (2018).

Chapter 1

1. Foucault ([1978] 1995, 194) summarizes this point, too—namely that penal organizations produce "criminals" as a kind of object—a category of social living. Reuben Miller has a working paper, entitled "Making Up the Ex-Offender" that makes the argument that as a social institution, punishment "makes" the ex-offender as a social category, and that institution includes the rules, practices, and policies that govern how we should understand and behave toward the ex-offender.

2. This definition is borrowed from Fredrickson and Roberts (1997, 174) who introduced us to "sexual objectification theory." For an updated discussion of how Frederickson and Robert's (1997) "objectification theory" has developed, see Moradi and Huang (2008). My discussion of objectification also borrows from Garfinkel's (1956, 420) discussion of a "total identity"—a scope condition that is often ignored when Garfinkel's discussion of status degradation is cited.

3. The American Bar Association (2011) published standards for the treatment of prisoners, and what's notable is how often so much of what's in there was ignored by Golden County custodial deputies as a matter of practice.

4. Tran (2017).

5. Carter et al. (2017).

6. Sassoon (2020), Kornfield (2020).

7. Zender (2018).

8. There is no shortage of historical or contemporary examples. Attempted genocides always include the denigration and objectification of personhood at the population level. Three books on this subject come to mind immediately. Richard L. Miller's

(1966) study of the politics around drug use includes a theory of population-level subjugation and destruction. *Medical Apartheid*, by Harriet Washington, traces how medical scientists and primary and secondary care personnel experimented on black bodies and the history racial inequality in access to medical care in America. *Judging State-Sponsored Violence*, by Bronwyn Leebaw, examines human atrocities while pointing to how justice was conceived in the aftermath.

9. This is precisely the point in Donald Black's (1976, 37–55) discussion of the relationship between morphology and law. As relational distance increases, so does the degree of punitive versus reconciliatory efforts.

10. Goffman (1961, 20).

11. The American Bar Association's (2011, 88) "Standards for Criminal Justice: Treatment of Prisoners" includes the following relevant statements regarding presumed guilt and a jail uniform: "For a person on trial in criminal court, being observed in jail clothing may create an impression of dangerousness or guilt. In order to protect the presumption of innocence, such a prisoner is entitled to wear civilian clothes on request when appearing before a jury. Typically, the prisoners' lawyer or family brings the clothes to the courthouse; subdivision (b) requires correctional authorities to implement procedures that allow the prisoner an opportunity to put the clothes on prior to being seen in court—and to leave them with the lawyer or family member upon leaving court, so that they are available the next time, as well." If this provision applies only to those who go to trial, it is woefully unhelpful because over 90 percent of criminal cases don't go to trial. During my time in Golden County jails, I saw only one resident dressed in street clothes, and I never heard of anyone being offered an opportunity to wear anything other than their county oranges for trial, pre-trial hearings, or arraignment.

12. I have purposely left off some numbers for the sake of anonymity.

13. For useful discussions on "place" and "identity," see Gieryn (2002, 2000); Proshansky, Fabian, and Kaminoff (1983); and Twigger-Ross and Uzzell (1996).

14. I was inspired by Roth's ([1963] 1976) study of uncertainty and time in a hospital ward for persons with tuberculosis. It's a fascinating study that examines how patients made sense of and managed time and progress when they could not know when or whether they would be released from the hospital. Christakis (2001, 31–33) has a similar analysis of the distress patients feel when they don't yet have a prognosis.

15. Racial categories are not proper nouns, but I want to avoid confusion in subsequent chapters where there is overlap between labels for racial categories and labels for racial classifications in jail.

16. My definition is borrowed from Vaughan ([1996] 2016, 64). But for an exhaustive study of conceptions of culture in social science, see Kroeber and Kluckhohn (2018).

17. See Brennan (1999, 1987), Wells and Demory (2004), Austin and Hardyman (2004), and Clements (1996) for overviews of penal classification. For a California-specific examination of penal classification, see the "Expert Panel Study of the Inmate Classification Score System" published in 2011 for the California Department of Corrections and Rehabilitation. See AELE (2010) for a discussion of the laws and practices around using race in penal classification.

18. Part of the issue is that social behaviors must be labeled as prosocial or antisocial and risk assessments tend to include measures of "self-control" (for a review see Andrews, Bonta, and Wormith 2006). I am reminded of Becker's (1963) book *Outsiders* and a less well-known but no less sophisticated and important book by Jane Mercer (1973) called *Labeling the Mentally Retarded*. Labeling social behavior is not an objective practice, and this is especially obvious when the label will be used to determine levels of punishment and care. For recent review of risk assessment in criminal justice processing, see Berk (2021).

19. Many thanks to Professor Robert Weide for sharing his knowledge on this matter.

Chapter 2

1. I graduated from Seoul American High School, where I played varsity basketball. During my time there, our team made the Far East Tournament, and we traveled to Kadena to play against teams from Department of Defense high schools in nearby Asian countries. We stayed in a Marine barracks, and one of the many memories I have from my time there is of the short and abrasive wool blankets we were given. My friends and I wondered whether the blankets hurt to toughen Marines, to keep them ready to wake at a moment's notice, or whether the Department of Defense couldn't afford better blankets. No one seriously thought the third option was likely.

2. I never learned a trusted origin story of this term; however, penal lore holds that the term began as a put down aimed at rural whites in the South before becoming linked with white power comrades.

3. On this issue, Sen and Wasow (2016) should be part of the canon for social scientific methods and those who want to study race relations. See also Zuberi (2001).

4. Organizations have always played a central role in how race is constructed and lived. For a theoretical development of the relationship between race and organizations, see Ray (2019).

5. For an outstanding history and analysis of the U.S. census and political fights over race, see Anderson ([1988] 2015).

6. See Roediger (2005) for a historical analysis that traces the construction of whiteness in the United States. For a study that intersects racial classification, law, and political and economic interests in California, see Almaguer (1994). In recent decades, some race scholars have come to see Omi and Winant's *Racial Formation in the United States* as a kind of soft version of race theory. Nevertheless, the arguments hold up well if one wants to understand how racial categories are constructed and destroyed and why. For a sophisticated philosophical argument on the issue of race and racial classification, see Mills (1999). Finally, Ibram Kendi's *Stamped from the Beginning* is an exhaustive study of the history of race making and race relations.

7. State of California Department of Justice, Criminal Justice Statistics (2008).

8. These terms come from Goffman's (1959, 112–139) dramaturgical approach to the study of how we ready and present ourselves to the social world.

9. Meyer and Rowan (1977, 342). For an application of the concept, see Hallett (2010).

10. See Brittany Friedman's forthcoming book, *Born in Blood: Death Work, White Power, and the Rise of the Black Guerilla Family*, for an indispensable historical tracing of the development of these logics. She shows how contemporary systems of racial classification are built upon early penological efforts to suppress the Black freedom movement. See also AELE (2010).

11. Trulson and Marquart (2002) analyzed 39,000 acts of violence among penal residents in the Texas prison system. They found that 55 percent of the violent incidents were intraracial and 45 percent were interracial. In the 10 years after Texas desegregated its housing units, there were 35,579 acts of violence but only 1,691 were racially motivated, and of those, only 333 occurred in desegregated, two-man cell units. Thus, one of the most racially segregated prison systems in the United States (Trulson et al. 2008) desegregated its housing units without there being mass interracial violence.

12. Walker (2016).

13. Another example of this is the failed "building tender" program in Texas prisons (Crouch and Marquart 1989).

14. University of Minnesota (2018).

15. One way to think of reps is to see them as "brokers" (Stovel and Shaw 2012, 141) whose role it is connect actors who would otherwise be disconnected.

16. A search for "race riots" and related mass incidents of violence in Golden County jails yields no results in many decades. Of course, it may be that there were large violent events that deputies were able to keep out of the news.

17. Seim (2020, 53–56) provides a useful analog in his study of ambulatory work. Ambulance teams regarded some calls as "legit" and others as "bullshit." However harrowing were legitimate calls, crews were excited to respond because legit calls justified the crew's resources and gave them an opportunity to use their training. Bullshit calls, however, were seen as trivial and unworthy of resources because they provided no opportunity to use paramedic training. In jail, a lot of caretaking work is analogous to the bullshit calls in Seim's ethnography.

18. For a similar and thorough discussion of different kinds of organizational mortifications, see Goffman (1961, 22–48).

19. Reps were sometimes referred to as "trustees" presumably because of the work they did; but strictly speaking, reps were not "trustees," an official classification for sentenced residents who held official jobs in jail.

Chapter 3

1. As Simmel (1950, 160) noted: When two competing parties end their competition and unite, so ends the exploitive power of the *tertius*.

2. Omi and Winant (1994, 55–56) define "racial projects" as the ideological connections between race as a structural phenomenon that organizes how people and resources

are distributed across racial categories and race as a system of meanings and social statuses.

3. This is Gieryn's (2000) whole point: Social behavior happens somewhere, and that somewhere matters—indeed "place" shapes how social interactions unfold and the rules therein.

4. *Frontline PBS* (2019).

5. Tilly (1998).

6. Giddens (1984, 62) refers to this as "ontological insecurity."

7. The politics is at least partially based on intergang relations. In southern California, the politics refers to codes for how gang members ought to conduct themselves in relation to members of their own gangs, their allies, and their enemies.

8. "Social status" is "inequality based on differences in honor, esteem, and respect" (Ridgeway 2014, 2).

9. For recent work on this, see Contreras (2018, 2017).

10. Charles (2006, 39–63) provides a useful review of the many explanations of patterns of residential segregation. Racism goes a long way toward explaining those patterns.

11. A single book comes immediately to mind, though I could certainly think of others: *Steppin' on the Blues* by Jacqui Malone. I read it during my undergraduate career around the time I'd discovered *The African Origin of Civilization* by Cheikh Anta Diop. The latter stretched Black history beyond a month and far beyond chattel slavery. Malone's book, as much a celebration of Blackness as it is a well-studied historical analysis of African American dance, music, and style, gave me an appreciation for being Black that I'd not encountered before then. More to the point, both books demonstrate the complex of legal, social, and pseudo-scientific efforts taken to control what Black people do and how peoples of the African diaspora understand themselves.

12. Rawls and Duck (2020, 182) briefly discuss aversions some Jamaicans have to being associated with African Americans. It's common, in fact, for Africans and Caribbean or West Indians to hold antipathies about African Americans (see also Waters 1999). In Nigeria, the term "akata" is used pejoratively to refer to African Americans. As is too often the case, African Americans equally hold may hold antipathies toward African diasporic ethnicities.

13. The change in emotional energy was an excellent example of Collins's (2008) theory of micro-interactional violence in practice. Ken excelled at managing what Collins called "confrontational tension/fear" (cf/t)—an emotion that worked like a barrier keeping individuals from doing violence. The more skilled a person is at turning cf/t against an opponent, the easier it is for that person to do violence.

14. Gieryn (2000). See also Giddens (1984, 117–143).

15. I never saw or knew of a rep going to church, and I wonder whether they, too, would ignore the politics for the sake of church.

16. His story was as likely to be untrue as it was true. It's less exciting to say you have been DPed by other black residents for some violation or another than it is to say you rushed someone with whom you had an old beef.

17. I do wonder how that fight would be coded by penal staff. It wasn't racially motivated, but it was interracial.
18. Durkheim (1995 [1912]).

Chapter 4

1. Liebling, Price, and Shefer (2011) have a useful officer-focused study of correctional work.
2. One of the best analyses on culture wars and the role of ethnographers in recreating tropes about Black communities is in Chapter 1 of Robin Kelley's *Yo' Mama's Dysfunktional!*
3. Russell-Brown (2009).
4. Both Irwin (1985) and Goldfarb (1976) make a similar analogy. In both books, the argument is that jails are filled with our nation's disreputable peoples—that the ghetto is being reproduced behind bars. Wacquant (2010) took this point further in his explanation for the growth of incarceration rates for Black America. He argued that incarceration rates increased first as an attack on the poor and then by targeting Black people, resulting in the prison being "ghettoized" and the ghetto being "prisonized" (Wacquant 2010:82).
5. I imagined then and now that even if music was sometimes a nuisance for some, we would rather have it than not. It connected us to a world beyond our four walls. McCall (1994, 189–190).

Chapter 5

1. For research on race, class, blameworthiness, and criminal case processing, see Johnson and King (2017), Lara-Millan and Van Cleve (2017), Kutateladeze et al. (2014), Wooldredge et al. (2015), and Miller (2021).
2. See Ridgeway (2006) for a discussion of status and the significance of status beliefs. We use hair color and texture, lip shape, height, eye color, degree of attractiveness, and so on, not as mere markers of gender, ethnicity, race, and the like, but as "status characteristics": shorthand for one's competence and yes, blameworthiness. See Ridgeway (2014) for the role of status in producing and reproducing inequality.
3. For an exhaustive discussion of stratification and inequality in the United States, see Massey (2007).
4. See Thomas (1988, 192–218) for a formal discussion of jailhouse lawyering.
5. Van Cleve (2016, 29–31) describes the experience of families waiting in court, having taken time off from work, and in some cases having driven long distances to be made to wait hours for what will be a brief moment in court with a loved one. My mind goes to those realities in remembering how Scott was given a "failure to appear" while in custody and knowing that his mother and girlfriend were in court angry, in part,

because Scott wasn't permitted to show in court but also because it was a massive waste of their time, energy, and money.

6. I have in mind here an extension of Collins' (2004, 38–42) discussion of "emotional energy" and synchronized "mutual stimulation."

7. See Collins (2008, 345–348) for a discussion of bluster as a pre-fight ritual.

8. Tupac Shakur is one of the more quotable artists to have ever rapped. See Shakur (1996) for the "bomb first" reference.

9. For problems related to legalese as a barrier to information, see Butt (2001), Gordon and Breaux (2014), and Hartley (2000).

10. See Feeley ([1979] 1992, 199–243) for an exploration of pre-trial processes as punishment in and of themselves.

11. Devers (2011).

12. My mind goes to Kalief Browder and how his case was handled by the judge Patricia DiMango, who kept sending him back to jail with unnecessary continuances despite his mental health deteriorating and the violence he was suffering there. See Carter et al. (2017).

Chapter 6

1. What I mean to highlight here is that a great deal of what it means to be jailed is not overcome and there is scarcely a time when one's emotional guards can be let down. For a deep discussion of coping and adaptation in prison, see Toch ([1992] 2002). Irwin's (1985, especially Chapter 3) "rabble thesis" is a way of arguing that penal residents become adapted to jail life. Clemmer's (1940) conception of "prisonization" is the heavily used term to indicate adaptation to penal life. More recently, Crewe (2009, 149–244) provides an excellent review and analysis of "adaptation" in prisons.

2. Way (2007).

3. *MacGyver* was a 1980s television program in which the lead character, MacGyver, constantly found himself trapped in ridiculous situations with almost no tools or resources around. In every episode, he would take something like a match, a shoelace, and an empty soda bottle and he would jumpstart a car or wire a bomb or something totally unsuspected like that. The show was edutainment at its finest because at its heart, it was about demonstrating the usefulness of science to get things done.

4. Goffman (1971, 56–58).

5. Here we have one of Sykes's (2007 [1958], 64–78) classic arguments about the "pains of imprisonment" associated with a group of common deprivations that penal residents experience. Loss of heterosexual relations is one.

6. My use of this term comes from Goffman (1961).

7. I have since conducted a series of courtroom observations with a student. On one occasion, we used an unfamiliar entrance to the building where the courtrooms were. We were nearer the jail than usual, and I knew that because I smelled the entrance to the jail before we ever saw signs directing us there.

8. My understanding of "frustration" is owed to Turner (2011b, 18–19). He theorizes emotional arousal under one of two conditions: "meeting or failing to meet expectations" and "receiving positive or negative sanctions." In this case of batched living, our normal expectations about personal space and personal time to handle personal matters are violated, and those violations build up frustration. Jail sets up structural conditions whereby failure to meet expectations and negative sanctions are guaranteed. Consequently, frustrations and irritations run high among residents. For a discussion of major theoretical traditions in terms of emotions, see Turner and Stets ([2005] 2009). For useful compendium of sociological research on emotions, see Stets and Turner (2007).

9. Sufrin (2017) offers, as much as anything else, an exploration of the indignities of women's healthcare in jail.

10. Though my experience was surely less extreme, I am reminded of Sufrin's (2017, 147–152) recounting of having delivered a baby while the mother was in chains—how normal and extremely abnormal and unforgettable that experience was.

11. I observed a video conferencing set up in Omaha's Douglas County Jail during a carceral tour. There is a website that has a clearinghouse of recently published material regarding video conferencing and remote viewing (www.prisonpolicy.org/visitation). Increasingly, jails are adopting a video conferencing style of visitation in which, instead of meeting with a visitor in a designated room, residents pick up a phone and stare into a monitor to make "eye contact" with their visitors. In practical terms, the resident never leaves the housing unit.

12. This reality made some parts of this organic ethnography particularly difficult. I wanted answers to lots of questions about matters that appeared to be the natural way of things, but I didn't want to raise suspicions or develop a reputation for asking questions about basic matters that everyone seemed to understand. I might have been ostracized.

Chapter 7

1. Zerubavel (1981, 1976), Lauer (1981), Levine (1997), Lewis and Weigert (1981).

2. Some insightful discussions about inequality and time include Auyero (2012), Comfort (2008, 35–44), Lauer (1981, 86–102), and Schwartz (1974).

3. An essential fact of life in penal organizations is that you are far more likely to be supported by a woman in free society than you are by any man. For a deep dive into the complexities, problems, experiences, and consequences to women and families in their efforts to support incarcerated men, see Comfort (2008).

4. For an interesting normative argument about time and place, see Lynch ([1972] 1993).

5. Bluedorn (2002), Davis ([1963] 1991, 74–76), Roth ([1963] 1976).

6. For discussions on "event time" versus "clock time," see Hall ([1983] 1989) and Levine (1997). See Roth ([1963] 1976) for a study in using events to mark progression through a career.

7. Spradley's (1970, 193–224) study inspired me to think more deeply about the kinds of time in jail and how they mattered.
8. Lauer (1981, 70–73).
9. Nathan McCall (1994, 180–183) has a useful description of the experience of "hard time."
10. Turner (2011b, 7) theorizes negative emotions like shame as discomforting and painful, so we repress them, but those emotions transmute into what he calls "diffuse anger," and it is that undirected and often misdirected anger that increases the likelihood of violent situations. See also (Turner 2002).
11. I'm reminded of the rapper J. Cole's (2011) story about how he found out about winning a music recording deal. He was pulled over and sent to jail for a night knowing he was about to sign that deal and eventually make millions. He said: "That was the easiest night in jail a nigga could ever do, son."
12. Comfort (2008, 65–92) makes this point. Ultimately, it is families who bear the financial hardship of caring for penal residents, and it can be extraordinarily taxing. For a recent analysis on this, see Miller (2021, 237–260).
13. Miller (2021, 129–160) has an exceptional analysis of what he calls the "economy of favors" upon which incarcerated and formerly incarcerated persons subsist.

Chapter 8

1. This likely applies to all cloistered living.
2. There is remarkable stability in the content and therefore the categories of dreams humans have. For a recent review, see Yu (2016). For an empirical study, see Nielsen et al. (2003). Documentation of themes in dreams goes back before Freud's (2010) *The Interpretation of Dreams*. Most of the analytical work on dreams relevant to the current discussion has been done by anthropologists (Caughey 1984, 77–117; Domhoff 1996; Spaulding 1981; Griffith, Miyagi, and Tago 1958) and psychologists publishing in what seems to be the only social scientific journal on the topic: *Dreaming*. My argument that dream content is, in part, a function of one's social conditions has been made in different ways, if not with less formality. Fine and Leighton (1993) were distinctly sociological in their approach to the subject, abstracting above the particulars of dreams to develop a framework for analyzing dreams as collective phenomena. Halton (1992) made an appeal to study dreams on methodological grounds but also because he viewed the study of dreams as a potentially fruitful link between biology and sociology. Hartmann (1996) presented a very interesting perspective on dreams as vehicles for processing dominant emotions. The larger takeaway from these efforts is that there is productive work to be done in something like the *sociology of dreams*, if you will.
3. See Yu (2013) and Yu and Fu (2011) for studies of erotic content in dreams.

4. Sykes ([1958] 2007, 70–72) describes "the deprivation of heterosexual relationships" as one of several "pains of imprisonment" or difficulties germane to incarceration that make the experience as punishing as it is. See also McCall (1994, 191–201).
5. Chung et al. (2018); Tononi and Cirelli (2014).
6. For an interesting review of research intersecting loneliness and mood disorders, see Hawkley and Cacioppo (2010).
7. Lorde ([1984] 2007, 112).
8. Carlen (2002, 3–20).
9. Bedrosian, Fonken, and Nelson (2016).
10. Albrecht (2012); Bedrosian, Fonken, and Nelson (2016); Buysse (2013); Baglioni et al. (2011); Konjarksi et al. (2018); McClung (2013); see also Morin and Benca (2012).
11. There were interruptions all throughout the night. New residents entering, others being released. Those scheduled for court appearances were summoned as early as 2:30 a.m. Prison transfers occurred around midnight, and deputies performed regular security checks—sometimes with a modicum of respect for the sleep we were trying to get and sometimes not.
12. Albrecht (2012); Bedrosian, Fonken, and Nelson (2016).
13. Buysse (2014).
14. Reddy and Chakrabarty (2011).
15. According to the American Heart Association, about seven hours of quality, uninterrupted sleep is the most beneficial kind (Yin et al. 2016).
16. For a review of the relationship between sleep and the "emotional brain," see Goldstein and Walker (2014) and Kahn, Sheppes, and Sadeh (2013). For research directly speaking to emotion processing and sleep, see Killgore et al. (2017) and van der Helm, Gujar, and Walker (2010).
17. Buysse (2014), Parthasarathy et al. (2015), St-Onge et al. (2016), and Yin et al. (2017).
18. See Lawler, Thye, and Yoon (2000) for a discussion of the role of emotion in social exchange.

Chapter 9

1. The sense of "we-ness" is a central motive that drives social interaction. We seek it out and experience negative affect when we feel separated from the group. See Fiske ([2004] 2010)—especially Chapter 12—for a psychological social psychological discussion of the "core motives" of social interaction. See Turner (2011b, 2002), who calls the need to be included in a group a "transactional need."
2. For a general discussion of emotions in penological research, see Crewe (2014), Crewe et al. (2014), and Laws and Crewe (2015).
3. There is a set of criminological researchers whose project involves investigating the misconduct of penal residents with the chief concern being rates of interpersonal violence. For a review, see Steiner, Butler, and Ellison (2014).
4. For a meta-analysis of "rape myths acceptance," see Suarez and Gadalla (2010).

5. For a recent research related to alcohol abuse and Native Americans, see Spillane et al. (2020).

6. Berns's (2001) concept of "patriarchal resistance" is similar in connotation. See also Coates and Wade (2007).

7. See Berns (2001) and Thapar-Björkert and Morgan (2010).

8. For a discussion on "rape myths," see Burt (1980), and Lonsway and Fitzgerald (1994).

9. Fine (2012, 30–31) discusses the strong research program of the role of groups in establishing status hierarchies.

10. This is another way the paired field notes paid dividends because the reality was that I wasn't going to withhold my judgments completely, but in expressing them in my personal field notes, I *got it out my system* so to speak, so that I could deal more fairly with what was sociologically interesting and relevant.

11. "Bash" may or may not connote sexual assault, as consensual sex is associated with slang terms like "hit," "smash," "beat," and so forth.

12. The "big homie" refers to the senior gang member who inducted and supports a new member.

Chapter 10

1. May and Wood (2010); May et al. (2013).

2. Mattis (2002) provides a useful analysis on the relationship between struggle, "religious/spirituality," and meaning-making. The women in the study used a sense of divine purpose to ease and make sense of their struggles. Holt et al. (2009) reported similar findings: namely that research participants made sense of their cancer diagnosis as part of a divine plan—as part of a divine purpose. See also Mkuu et al. (2021) and Pendergrass (2017) for similar arguments about meaning-making, religion, and uncertainty or difficulties.

3. Duck (2015, 71) makes this point by noting that "stray bullets are ever-present" threats. There is a relentlessness to living precarious lives, and one tries to endure as long as possible. Ladner (1995 [1971], 47–66) makes a similar point in noting that Black parents "are unable to offer" an expected standard of "protection and comfort to their children because of their own vulnerability to the discriminative practices of the larger society," and that, as a consequence, Black parents devise a different mode of parenting that is "predicated upon the principle that children in the Black community must be taught to survive in a hostile society." Racial discrimination is relentless and dynamic. It is therefore wise for parents to give their children strategies to endure until methods of overcoming come to fruition.

4. Sharkey (2013).

5. Turner (2002).

Bibiliography

AELE Law Enforcement Legal Center. 2010. "Racial Classifications and Inmate Housing Assignments." *AELE Monthly Law Journal* (1): 301–309.

American Bar Association. 2011. *ABA Standards for Criminal Justice: Treatment of Prisoners*. Washington, D.C. Retrieved March 27, 2021 (https://www.americanbar.org/content/dam/aba/publications/criminal_justice_standards/treatment_of_prisoners.pdf).

Abbott, Andrew. 2004. *Methods of Discovery: Heuristics for the Social Sciences*. New York: W. W. Norton & Company, Inc.

Abbott, Andrew. 2007. "Against Narrative: A Preface to Lyrical Sociology." *Sociological Theory* 25 (1): 67–99.

Albrecht, Urs. 2012. "Timing to Perfection: The Biology of Central and Peripheral Circadian Clocks." *Neuron* 74: 246–260.

Alexander, Michelle. 2010. *The New Jim Crow: Mass Incarceration in the Age of Colorblindness*. New York: New Press.

Almaguer, Tomas. 1994. *Racial Fault Lines: The Historical Origins of White Supremacy in California*. Berkeley, CA: University of California Press.

Alper, Mariel, and Matthew R. Durose. 2018. "2018 Update on Prisoner Recidivism: A 9-Year Follow-Up Period (2005–2014). NCJ 25–975. Retrieved March 27, 2021 (https://www.bjs.gov/content/pub/pdf/18upr9yfup0514.pdf).

Anderson, Margo J. [1988] 2015. *The American Census: A Social History*. New Haven, CT: Yale University Press.

Andrews, D. A., James Bonta, and J. Stephen Wormith. 2006. "The Recent Past and Near Future of Risk and/or Need Assessment." *Crime & Delinquency* 52 (1): 7–27.

Austin, James, and Patricia L. Hardyman. 2004. "Objective Prison Classification: A Guide for Correctional Agencies." *National Institute of Corrections*, Retrieved March 27, 2021 (https://s3.amazonaws.com/static.nicic.gov/Library/019319.pdf).

Auyero, Javier. 2012. *Patients of the State: The Politics of Waiting in Argentina*. Durham, NC: Duke University Press.

Baglioni, Chiara, Gemma Battagliese, Bernd Feige, Kai Spiegelhalder, Christoph Nissen, Ulrich Voderholzer, Caterina Lombardo, and Dieter Riemann. 2011. "Insomnia as a Predictor of Depression: A Meta-Analytic Evaluation of Longitudinal Epidemiological Studies." *Journal of Affective Disorders* 135: 10–19.

Ballesteros, Octavio Antonio. 1979. *Behind Jail Bars*. New York: Philosophical Library, Inc.

Beck, Allen J., Jennifer C. Karberg, and Paige M. Harrison. 2002. "Prison and Jail Inmates at Midyear 2001." NCJ 191702. Retrieved March 27, 2021 (https://www.bjs.gov/content/pub/pdf/pjim01.pdf).

Becker, Howard S. 1963. *Outsiders: Studies in the Sociology of Deviance*. New York: The Free Press.

Becker, Howard S. 2003. "The Politics of Presentation: Goffman and Total Institutions." *Symbolic Interaction* 26 (4): 659–669.

Bedrosian, Tracy A., Laura K. Fonken, and Randy J. Nelson. 2016. "Endocrine Effects of Circadian Disruption." *Annual Review of Physiology* 78: 109–131.

Berk, Richard A. 2021. "Artificial Intelligence, Predictive Policing, and Risk Assessment for Law Enforcement." *Annual Review of Criminology* 4: 209–237.

Berns, Nancy. 2001. "Degendering the Problem and Gendering the Blame: Political Discourse on Women and Violence." *Gender & Society* 15 (2): 262–281.

Black, Donald. 1976. *The Behavior of Law*. New York: Academic Press, Inc.

Bluedorn, Allen C. 2002. *The Human Organization of Time: Temporal Realities and Experience*. Stanford, CA: Stanford Business Books.

Burt, Martha R. 1980. "Cultural Myths and Supports for Rape." *Journal of Personality and Social Psychology* 38 (2): 217–230.

Butt, Peter. 2001. "Legalese versus Plain Language." *Amicus Curiae* 35: 28–32.

Brennan, Tim. 1987. "Classification for Control in Jails and Prisons." *Crime and Justice* 9: 323–366.

Brennan, Tim. 1999. "Implementing Organizational Change in Criminal Justice: Some Lessons from Jail Classification Systems." *Northpointe Institute for Public Management*. Retrieved March 27, 2021 (http://www.northpointeinc.com/downloads/classification/1999CMQ_-_Implementation.pdf).

Brennan, Tim, Dave Wells, and Lt. Randy Demory. 2004. "Classification Implementation Manual for Smaller Jails." *Northpointe Institute for Public Management*. Retrieved March 27, 2021 (http://www.northpointeinc.com/files/publications/Smalls_Jails_Manual_Complete.pdf).

Buysse, Daniel J. 2013. "Insomnia." *Journal of the American Medical Association* 309 (7): 706–716.

Buysse, Daniel J. 2014. "Sleep Health: Can We Define It? Does It Matter?" *Sleep* 37 (1): 9–17.

Carlen, Pat, ed. 2002. *Women and Punishment: The Struggle for Justice*. New York: Routledge.

Carson, E. Ann. 2020. "Prisoners in 2019." NCJ 255115. Retrieved March 27, 2021 (https://www.bjs.gov/content/pub/pdf/p19.pdf).

Carson, E. Ann, and Mary P. Cowhig. 2020. "Mortality in Local Jails, 2000–2016: Statistical Tables." NCJ 251921. Retrieved March 27, 2021 (https://www.bjs.gov/content/pub/pdf/mlj0016st.pdf).

Carson, E. Ann and Mary P. Cowhig. 2020. "Mortality in State and Federal Prisons, 2001–2016, Statistical Tables." Washington, D.C.: Bureau of Justice Statistics. Retrieved May 2, 2021. (https://bjs.ojp.gov/content/pub/pdf/msfp0116st.pdf).

Carter, Shawn, Jenner Furst, Nick Sandow, Julia Willoughby-Nason, Michael Gasparro, and Chachi Senior. 2017. *The Kalief Browder Story*. Netflix.

Caughey, John L. 1984. *Imaginary Social Worlds*. Lincoln, NE: University of Nebraska Press.

Charles, Camille Zubrinsky. 2006. *Won't You Be My Neighbor?: Race, Class, and Residence in Los Angeles*. New York: Russell Sage Foundation.

Christakis, Nicholas A. 2001. *Death Foretold: Prophecy and Prognosis in Medical Care*. Chicago, IL: University of Chicago Press.

Chung, Kai-Fai, Chit-Tat Lee, Wing-Fai Yeung, Man-Sum Chan, Emily Wing-Yue Chung, and Wai-Ling Lin. 2018. "Sleep Hygiene Education as a Treatment Insomnia: A Systematic Review and Meta-Analysis." *Family Practice* 35 (4): 365–375.

Clements, Carl B. 1996. "Offender Classification: Two Decades of Progress." *Criminal Justice and Behavior* 23 (1): 121–143.

Clemmer, Donald. 1940. *The Prisoner Community*. New York: Rinehart.

Coates, Linda, and Allan Wade. 2007. "Language and Violence: Analysis of Four Discursive Operations." *Journal of Family Violence* 22: 511–522.

Cole, Jermaine. 2011. "Interlude." New York: RocNation.

Collins, Randall. 2004. *Interaction Ritual Chains*. Princeton, NJ: Princeton University Press.

Collins, Randall. 2008. *Violence: A Micro-Sociological Theory*. Princeton, NJ: Princeton University Press.

Comfort, Megan. 2008. *Doing Time Together: Love and Family in the Shadow of the Prison*. Chicago, IL: University of Chicago Press.

Contreras, Randol. 2017. "There's No Sunshine: Spatial Anguish, Deflections, and Intersectionality in Compton and South Central." *Society and Space* 35 (4): 656–673.

Contreras, Randol. 2018. "From Nowhere: Space, Race, and Time in How Young Minority Men Understand Encounters with Gangs." *Qualitative Sociology* 41: 263–280.

Crewe, Ben. 2009. *The Prisoner Society: Power, Adaptation and Social Life in an English Prison*. Oxford: Oxford University Press.

Crewe, Ben. 2014. "Not Looking Hard Enough: Masculinity, Emotion, and Prison Research." *Qualitative Inquiry* 20 (4): 392–403.

Crewe, Ben, Jason Warr, Peter Bennett, and Alan Smith. 2014. "The Emotional Geography of Prison Life." *Theoretical Criminology* 18 (1): 56–74.

Crouch, Ben M., and James W. Marquart. 1989. *An Appeal to Justice*. Austin, TX: University of Texas Press.

Davis, Fred. [1963] 1991. *Passage through Crisis: Polio Victims and Their Families*. New Brunswick, NJ: Transaction Publishers.

Devers, Lindsey. 2011. "Plea and Charge Bargaining: Research Summary." Bureau of Justice Assistance. Retrieved March 27, 2021 (https://bja.ojp.gov/sites/g/files/xyckuh 186/files/media/document/PleaBargainingResearchSummary.pdf).

Diop, Cheikh Anta.1974. *The African Origin of Civilization: Myth or Reality*. Chicago, IL: Lawrence Hill Books.

Domhoff, G. William. 1996. *Finding Meaning in Dreams: A Quantitative Approach*. New York: Plenum.

Duck, Waverly. 2015. *No Way Out: Precarious Living in the Shadow of Poverty and Drug Dealing*. Chicago, IL: University of Chicago Press.

Durkheim, Emile. [1912] 1995. *The Elementary Forms of Religious Life*. Translated by K. E. Fields. New York: The Free Press.

Feeley, Malcolm M. [1979] 1992. *The Process Is the Punishment: Handling Cases in a Lower Criminal Court*. New York: Russell Sage Foundation.

Fine, Gary Alan, and Laura Fischer Leighton. 1993. "Nocturnal Omissions: Steps toward a Sociology of Dreams." *Symbolic Interaction* 16 (2): 95–104.

Fine, Gary Alan. 2012. *Tiny Publics: A Theory of Group Action and Culture*. New York: Russell Sage Foundation.

Fiske, Susan T. [2004] 2010. *Social Beings: Core Motives in Social Psychology*. Hoboken, NJ: John Wiley & Sons, Inc.

Foucault, Michel. [1978]1995. *Discipline and Punish: The Birth of the Prison*. New York, NY: Vintage Books.

Fredrickson, Barbara, and Tomi-Ann Roberts. 1997. "Objectification 'Theory': Toward Understanding Women's Lived Experiences and Mental Health Risks." *Psychology of Women Quarterly* 21: 173–206.

Freud, Sigmund. [1955] 2010. *The Interpretation of Dreams: The Complete and Definitive Text.* Translated by J. Strachey. New York, NY: Basic Books.

Friedman, Brittany. Forthcoming. *Born in Blood: Death Work, White Power, and the Rise of the Black Guerilla Family.*

Frontline PBS. [1985] 2019. "A Class Divided." YouTube. Retrieved March 27, 2021 (https://www.youtube.com/watch?v=1mcCLm_LwpE).

Gardner, John. [1983] 1991. *The Art of Fiction: Notes on Craft for Young Writers.* New York: Vintage Books.

Garfinkel, Harold. 1956. "Conditions of Successful Degradation Ceremonies." *American Journal of Sociology* 61 (5): 420–424.

Giddens, Anthony. 1984. *The Constitution of Society: Outline of a Theory of Structuration.* Berkeley, CA: University of California Press.

Gieryn, Thomas F. 2000. "A Space for Place in Sociology." *Annual Review of Sociology* 26: 463–496.

Gieryn, Thomas F. 2002. "What Buildings Do." *Theory and Society* 31: 35–74.

Gilliard, Darrell K., and Allen J. Beck. 1996. "Prison and Jail Inmates, 1995." NCJ 161132. Retrieved March 27, 2021 (https://www.bjs.gov/content/pub/pdf/PJI95.PDF).

Goffman, Erving. 1959. *The Presentation of Self in Everyday Life.* New York: Anchor Books.

Goffman, Erving. 1961. *Asylums: Essays on the Social Situation of Mental Patients and Other Inmates.* New York: Anchor.

Goffman, Erving. 1971. *Relations in Public: Microstudies of the Public Order.* New York, NY: Basic Books.

Goffman, Erving. 1989. "On Fieldwork." *Journal of Contemporary Ethnography* 18 (2): 123–132.

Goldfarb, Ronald. 1976. *Jails: The Ultimate Ghetto.* Garden City, NY. Anchor.

Goldstein, Andrea, and Matthew P. Walker. 2014. "The Role of Sleep in Emotional Brain Function." *Annual Review of Clinical Psychology* 10: 679–708.

Gordon, David G., and Travis D. Breaux. 2014. "The Role of Legal Expertise in Interpretation Legal Requirements and Definitions." *IEEE International Requirements Engineering Conference,* 273–282.

Griffith, Richard M., Otoya Miyagi, and Akira Tago. 1958. "The Universality of Typical Dreams: Japanese vs. Americans." *American Anthropologist* 60 (6): 1173–1179.

Hall, Edward T. [1983] 1989. *The Dance of Life: The Other Dimension of Time.* New York: Anchor Books.

Hallett, Tim. 2010. "The Myth Incarnate: Recoupling Processes, Turmoil, and Inhabited Institutions in an Urban Elementary School." *American Sociological Review* 75 (1): 52–74.

Halton, Eugene. 1992. "The Reality of Dreaming." *Theory, Culture & Society* 9: 119–139.

Hartley, James. 2000. "Legal Ease and 'Legalese.'" *Psychology, Crime & Law* 6 (1): 1–20.

Hartmann, Ernest. 1996. "Outline for a Theory on the Nature and Functions of Dreaming." *Dreaming* 6 (2): 147–170.

Hawkley, Louise C., and John T. Cacioppo. 2010. "Loneliness Matters: A Theoretical and Empirical Review of Consequences and Mechanisms." *Annals of Behavioral Medicine* 40 (2): 218–227.

Holt, Cheryl L., Theresa Ann Wynn, Mark S. Litaker, Penny Southward, Sanford E. Jeames, Emily K. Schulz. 2009. "A Comparison of a Spirituality Based and Non-Spiritually Based Educational Intervention for Informed Decision Making for Prostate Cancer Screening Among Church-Attending African American Men." *Urologic Nursing* 29 (4): 249–58.

Irwin, John. 1985. *The Jail: Managing the Underclass in American Society*. Berkeley, CA: University of California Press.

Johnson, Brian D. and Ryan D. King. 2017. "Facial Profiling: Race, Physical Appearance, and Punishment." *Criminology* 55 (3): 520–47.

Kahn, Michal, Gal Sheppes, and Avi Sadeh. 2013. "Sleep and Emotions: Bidirectional Links and Underlying Mechanisms." *International Journal of Psychophysiology* 89: 218–228.

Kelley, Robin D. G. 1998. *Yo' Mama's Disfunktional!: Fighting the Culture Wars in Urban America*. Boston, MA: Beacon Press.

Kendi, Ibram X. 2016. *Stamped from the Beginning: The Definitive History of Racist Ideas in America*. New York: Nation Books.

Killgore, William D. S., Thomas J. Balkin, Angela M. Yarnell, and Vincent F. Capaldi, II. 2017. "Sleep Deprivation Impairs Recognition and Specific Emotions." *Neurobiology of Sleep and Circadian Rhythms* 3: 10–16.

Konjarski, Monika, Greg Murray, V. Vien Lee, and Melinda L. Jackson. 2018. "Reciprocal Relationships between Daily Sleep and Mood: A Systematic Review of Naturalistic Prospective Studies." *Sleep Medicine Reviews* 42: 47–58.

Kornfield, Meryl. 2020. "A Veteran Died in a Florida Jail. Two Years Later, Video Shows He Was Tased, Left Convulsing in a Cell." *Washington Post*, November 13 (https://www.washingtonpost.com/nation/2020/11/13/veteran-police-death/).

Kroeber, A. L., and Clyde Kluckhohn. 2018. *Culture: A Critical Review of Concepts and Definitions*. London, UK: Forgotten Books.

Kutateladze, Besiki L., Nancy R. Andiloro, Brian D. Johnson, and Cassia C. Spohn. 2014. "Cumulative Disadvantage: Examining Racial and Ethnic Disparity in Prosecution and Sentencing." *Criminology* 52 (3): 514–551.

Ladner, Joyce A. [1971] 1995. *Tomorrow's Tomorrow*. Lincoln, NE: University of Nebraska Press.

Lara-Millan, Armando, and Nicole Gonzalez Van Cleve. 2017. "Interorganizational Utility of Welfare Stigma in the Criminal Justice System." *Criminology* 55 (1): 59–84.

Lauer, Robert H. 1981. *Temporal Man: The Meaning and Uses of Social Time*. New York: Praeger Publishers.

Laws, Ben, and Ben Crewe. 2015. "Emotion Regulation among Male Prisoners." *Theoretical Criminology* 20 (4): 1–19.

Lawler, Edward J., Shane R. Thye, and Jeongkoo Yoon. 2000. "Emotion and Group Cohesion in Productive Exchange." *American Journal of Sociology* 106 (3): 616–657.

Leebaw, Bronwyn. 2011. *Judging State-Sponsored Violence, Imagining Political Change*. Cambridge, MA: Cambridge University Press.

Levine, Robert. 1997. *A Geography of Time: The Temporal Misadventures of a Social Psychologist*. New York: Basic Books.

Lewis, J. David., and Andrew J. Weigert. 1981. "The Structure and Meaning of Social Time." *Social Forces* 60 (2): 432–462.

Liebling, Alison, David Price, and Guy Shefer. 2011. *The Prison Officer*. New York: Willan Publishing.

Lonsway, Kimberly A., and Louise F. Fitzgerald. 1994. "Rape Myths: In Review." *Psychology of Women Quarterly* 18 (2): 133–164.

Lopez-Aguado, Patrick. 2018. *Stick Together and Come Back Home: Racial Sorting and the Spillover of Carceral Identity*. Berkeley, CA: University of California Press.

Lynch, Kevin. [1972] 1993. *What Time Is This Place?* Cambridge, MA: The MIT Press.

Lorde, Audre. [1984] 2007. *Sister Outsider: Essays and Speeches*. New York: Ten Speed Press.

Malinowski, Bronislaw. [1967] 1989. *A Diary in the Strict Sense of the Term*. Stanford, CA: Stanford University Press.

Malone, Jacqui. 1996. *Steppin' on the Blues: The Visible Rhythms of African American Dance*. Urbana, IL: University of Illinois Press.

Massey, Douglas S. 2007. *Categorically Unequal: The American Stratification System*. New York: Russell Sage Foundation.

Mattis, Jacqueline S. 2002. "Religion and Spirituality in the Meaning-Making and Coping Experiences of African American Women: A Qualitative Analysis." *Psychology of Women Quarterly* 26: 309–321.

May, David C., and Peter B. Wood. 2010. *Ranking Correctional Punishments: Views from Offenders, Practitioners, and the Public*. Durham, NC: Carolina Academic Press.

May, David C., Brandon K. Applegate, Rick Ruddell, and Peter B. Wood. 2013. "Going to Jail Sucks (and It Really Doesn't Matter Who You Ask)." *American Journal of Criminal Justice* 39 (2): 250–266.

McCall, Nathan. 1994. *Makes Me Wanna Holler: A Young Black Man in America*. New York: Vintage Books.

McClung, Colleen A. 2013. "How Might Circadian Rhythms Control Mood? Let Me Count the Ways . . . " *Biological Psychiatry* 74: 242–249.

McKay, Tasseli, Megan Comfort, Christine Lindquist, and Anupa Bir. 2016. "If Family Matters: Supporting Family Relationships During Incarceration and Reentry." *Criminology & Public Policy* 15 (2): 529–42.

Mendelberg, Tali. 2001. *The Race Card: Campaign Strategy, Implicit Messages, and the Norm of Equality*. Princeton, NJ: Princeton University Press.

Mercer, Jane R. 1973. *Labeling the Mentally Retarded*. Berkeley, CA: University of California Press.

Meyer, W. John, and Brian Rowan. 1977. "Institutionalized Organizations: Formal Structure as Myth and Ceremony." *American Journal of Sociology* 83 (2): 340–363.

Miller, Reuben Jonathan. 2021. *Halfway Home: Race, Punishment, and the Afterlife of Mass Incarceration*. New York: Little, Brown and Company.

Miller, Reuben Jonathan. "Making up the Ex-Offender." Unpublished manuscript, last modified 2020. Microsoft Word file.

Miller, Richard L. 1996. *Drug Warriors and Their Prey: From Police Power to Police State*. Westport, CT: Praeger Publishers.

Mills, C. Wright. [1959] 2000. *The Sociological Imagination*. New York: Oxford University Press.

Mills, Charles W. 1999. *The Racial Contract*. Ithaca, NY: Cornell University Press.

Mkuu, Rahma S., Idethia S. Harvey, Edna Brown, Erica C. Spears, Miryan G. Jira, Kenné L. Johnson, Tyra Montour, and Janae Alexander. 2021. "'I Struggle with Breast Cancer and I Struggle with God': Insights from African American Breast Cancer Survivors." *Journal of Racial and Ethnic Health Disparities* 1–10. 47. Published electronically February 10, 2021. doi: 10.1007/s40615-021-00986-w.

Moradi, Bonnie, and Yu-Ping Huang. 2008. "Objectification Theory and Psychology of Women: A Decade of Advance and Future Directions." *Psychology of Women Quarterly* 32: 377–398.

Morin, Charles M., and Ruth Benca. 2012. "Chronic Insomnia." *Lancet* 379: 1129–1141.

Muhammad, Khalil Gibran. 2010. *The Condemnation of Blackness: Race, Crime, and the Making of Modern Urban America*. Cambridge, MA: Harvard University Press.

Nielsen, Tore A., Antonio L. Zadra, Valérie Simard, Sébastien Saucier, Philippe Stenstrom, Carlyle Smith, and Don Kuiken. 2003. "The Typical Dreams of Canadian University Students." *Dreaming* 13 (4): 211–235.

Omi, Michael, and Howard Winant. 1994. *Racial Formation in the United States from the 1960s to the 1990s*. New York: Routledge.

Pager, Devah. 2007. *Marked: Race, Crime, and Finding Work in an Era of Mass Incarceration*. Chicago, IL: The University of Chicago Press.

Parthasarathy, Sairam, Monica M. Vasquez, Marilyn Halonen, Richard Bootzin, Stuart F. Quan, Fernando D. Martinez, and Stefano Guerra. 2015. "Persistent Insomnia Is Associated with Mortality Risk." *The American Journal of Medicine* 128: 268–275.

Pendergrass, Sabrina. 2017. "No Longer 'Bound for the Promised Land': African Americans' Religious Experiences in the Reversal of the Great Migration." *Race and Social Problems* 9: 19–28.

Proshansky, Harold M., Abbee K. Fabian, and Robert Kaminoff. 1983. "Place-Identity: Physical World Socialization of the Self." *Journal of Environmental Psychology* 3: 57–83.

Rafter, Nicole. 2000. *Shots in the Mirror: Crime Films and Society*. New York: Oxford University Press.

Rawls, Anne Warfield, and Waverly Duck. 2020. *Tacit Racism*. Chicago, IL: University of Chicago Press.

Ray, Victor. 2019. "A Theory of Racialized Organizations." *American Sociological Review* 84 (1): 26–53.

Reddy, M. S., and Arindam Chakrabaarty. 2011. "'Comorbid' Insomnia." *Indian Journal of Psychological Medicine* 33 (1): 1–4.

Rhodes, Lorna A. 2004. *Total Confinement: Madness and Reason in the Maximum Security Prison*. Berkeley, CA: University of California Press.

Ridgeway, Cecilia L. 2006. "Status Construction Theory." In *Contemporary Social Psychological Theories*, edited by P. J. Burke, 301–323. Stanford, CA: Stanford Social Sciences.

Ridgeway, Cecilia L. 2014. "Why Status Matters for Inequality." *American Sociological Review* 79 (1): 1–16.

Roediger, David R. 2005. *Working toward Whiteness: How America's Immigrants Became White*. New York: Basic Books.

Roth, Alisa. 2018. *Insane: America's Criminal Treatment of Mental Illness*. New York: Basic Books.

Roth, Julius. [1963] 1976. *Timetables: Structuring the Passage of Time in Hospital Treatment and Other Careers*. Indianapolis, IN: The Bobbs-Merrill Company, Inc.

Royster, Deirdre. 2003. *Race and the Invisible Hand: How White Networks Exclude Black Men from Blue-Collar Jobs*. Berkeley, CA: University of California Press.

Russell-Brown, Katheryn. 2009. *The Color of Crime*. New York: New York University Press.

Sassoon, Alessandro Marazzi. [2019] 2020. "A Death in Custody: Army Veteran's Treatment in Brevard Jail Violated Sheriff's Office Policies." *Florida Today* February

17   (https://www.floridatoday.com/in-depth/news/crime/2019/11/06/death-custody-army-vets-jail-treatment-violated-policy/1991676001/).

Scheff, Thomas J. 2003. "Shame in Self and Society." *Symbolic Interaction* 26 (2): 239–262.

Schlesinger, Steven R. 1983. "Jail Inmates 1982." Washington, D.C.: Bureau of Justice Statistics. Retrieved March 27, 2021 (https://www.bjs.gov/content/pub/pdf/ji82.pdf).

Schwartz, Barry. 1974. "Waiting, Exchange, and Power: The Distribution of Time in Social Systems." *American Journal of Sociology* 79 (4): 841–870.

Seim, Josh. 2020. *Bandage, Sort, and Hustle: Ambulance Crews on the Front Lines of Urban Suffering.* Berkeley, CA: University of California Press.

Sen, Maya, and Omar Wasow. 2016. "Race as a Bundle of Sticks: Designs that Estimate Effects of Seemingly Immutable Characteristics." *Annual Review of Political Science* 19: 499–522.

Shakur, Tupac. 1996. *Bomb First (My Second Reply).* Los Angeles, CA: Death Row Records.

Sharkey, Patrick. 2013. *Stuck in Place: Urban Neighborhoods and the End of Progress Toward Racial Equality.* Chicago, IL: University of Chicago Press.

Simmel, Georg. 1950. *The Sociology of Georg Simmel.* Translated by K. H. Wolff. New York: The Free Press.

Slate, Risdon N., Jacqueline K. Buffington-Vollum, and W. Wesley Johnson. 2013. *The Criminalization of Mental Illness.* Durham, NC: Carolina Academic Press.

Spradley, James P. 1970. *You Owe Yourself a Drunk: An Ethnography of Urban Nomads.* Boston, MA: Little, Brown and Company.

Spaulding, John. 1981. "The Dream in Other Cultures: Anthropological Studies of Dreams and Dreaming." *Dreamworks* 1 (4): 330–342.

Spillane, Nichea S., Katelyn T. Kirk-Provencher, Melissa R. Schick, Tessa Nalven, Silvi C. Goldstein, and Christopher W. Kahler. 2020. "Identifying Competing Life Reinforcers for Substance Use in First Nation Adolescents." *Substance Use & Misuse* 55 (6): 886–895.

St-Onge, Marie-Pierre, Michael A. Grandner, Devin Brown, Molly B. Conroy, Girardin Jean-Louis, Michael Coons, and Deepak L. Bhatt. 2016. "Sleep Duration and Quality: Impact on Lifestyle Behaviors and Cardiometabolic Health." *Circulation* 134 (18): 367–386.

Steiner, Benjamin, H. Daniel Butler, and Jared M. Ellison. 2014. "Causes and Correlates of Prison Inmate Misconduct: A Systematic Review of the Evidence." *Journal of Criminal Justice* 42: 462–470.

Stets, Jan E., and Jonathan H. Turner., eds. 2007. *Handbook of the Sociology of Emotions.* New York: Springer.

Stovel, Katherine, and Lynette Shaw. 2012. "Brokerage." *Annual Review of Sociology* 38: 139–158.

Suarez, Eliana, and Tahany M. Gadalla. 2010. "Stop Blaming the Victim: A Meta-Analysis on Rape Myths." *Journal of Interpersonal Violence* 25 (11): 2010–2035.

Sufrin, Carolyn. 2017. *Jailcare: Finding the Safety Net for Women behind Bars.* Berkeley, CA: University of California Press.

Sykes, Gresham M. [1958] 2007. *The Society of Captives: A Study of a Maximum Security Prison.* Princeton, NJ: Princeton University Press.

Tartaro, Christine, and Marissa P. Levy. 2017. "Visitation Modality Preferences for Adults Visiting Jails." *The Prison Journal* 97 (5): 562–584.

Thapar-Björkert, Suruchi, and Karen J. Morgan. 2010. "'But Sometimes I Think . . . They Put Themselves in the Situation': Exploring Blame and Responsibility in Interpersonal Violence." *Violence against Women* 16 (1): 32–59.

Thomas, Jim. 1988. *The Paradox of the Jailhouse Lawyer*. Totowa, NJ: Rowman & Littlefield Publishers.

Tilly, Charles. 1998. *Durable Inequality*. Berkeley, CA: University of California Press.

Toch, Hans. [1992] 2002. *Living in Prison: The Ecology Survival*. Hyattsville, MD: American Psychological Association.

Tononi, Guilio, and Chiara Cirelli. 2014. "Sleep and the Price of Plasticity: From Synaptic and Cellular Homeostasis to Memory Consolidation and Integration." *Neuron* 81 (1): 12–34.

Tran, Linh. 2017. "Inmate Died after Going 7 Days without Water, Prosecutors Say." *CNN* May 1 (https://www.cnn.com/2017/04/30/us/terrill-thomas-milwaukee-county-jail-death/index.html).

Trulson, Chad, and James W. Marquart. 2002. "The Caged Melting Pot: Toward an Understanding of the Consequences of Desegregation Prisons." *Law & Society Review* 36 (4): 743–782.

Trulson, Chad, James W. Marquart, Craig Hemmens, and Leo Carroll. 2008. "Racial Desegration in Prisons." *Prison Journal* 88 (2): 270–299.

Tuan, Yi-Fu. 1977. *Space and Place: The Perspective of Experience*. Minneapolis, MN: University of Minnesota Press.

Turner, Jonathan H. 1990. "The Misuse and Use of Metatheory." *Sociological Forum* 5 (1): 37–53.

Turner, Jonathan H. 1991. "Developing Cumulative and Practical Knowledge through Metatheorizing." *Sociological Perspectives* 34 (3): 249–268.

Turner, Jonathan H. 2002. *Face to Face: Toward a Sociological Theory of Interpersonal Behavior*. Stanford, CA: Stanford University Press.

Turner, Jonathan H. 2011a. *The Problem of Emotions in Societies*. New York: Routledge.

Turner, Jonathan H. 2011b. "Extending the Symbolic Interactionist Theory of Interaction Processes: A Conceptual Outline." *Symbolic Interaction* 34 (3): 330–339.

Turner, Jonathan H., and Jan E. Stets. 2005. *The Sociology of Emotions*. Cambridge, MA: Cambridge University Press.

Turney, Kristin, and Emma Conner. 2019. "Jail Incarceration: A Common and Consequential Form of Criminal Justice Contact." *Annual Review of Criminology* 2: 265–290.

Twigger-Ross, Clare, and David L. Uzzell. 1996. "Place and Identity Processes." *Journal of Environmental Psychology* 16: 205–220.

University of Minnesota. 2018. "The 2018 Stein Lecture: John G. Roberts, Jr., Chief Justice of the United States." YouTube. Retrieved March 27, 2021 (https://www.youtube.com/watch?v=9i3RwW0y_kE).

Van Cleve, Nicole Gonzalez. 2016. *Crook County: Racism and Injustice in America's Largest Criminal Court*. Stanford, CA: Stanford University Press.

Van der Helm, Els, Ninad Gujar, and Matthew P. Walker. 2010. "Sleep Deprivation Impairs the Accurate Recognition of Human Emotions." *Sleep* 33 (3): 335–342.

Vaughan, Diane. [1996] 2016. *The Challenger Launch Decision: Risky Technology, Culture, and Deviance at NASA*. Chicago, IL: University of Chicago Press.

Wacquant, Loïc. 2010. "Class, Race & Hyperincarceration in Revanchist America." *Dædalus* 139 (3): 74–90.

Walker, Michael L. 2016. "Race Making in a Penal Institution." *American Journal of Sociology* 121 (4): 1051–1078.

Washington, Harriet. 2006. *Medical Apartheid: The Dark History of Medical Experimentation on Black Americans from Colonial Times to the Present*. New York: Harlem Moon.

Waters, Mary C. 1999. *Black Identities: West Indian Immigrant Dreams and American Realities*. Cambridge, MA: Harvard University Press.

Way, DeAndre. 2007. *Yahhh!* Atlanta, GA: Collipark Music.

Western, Bruce. 2018. *Homeward: Life in the Year after Prison*. New York: Russell Sage Foundation.

Wooldredge, John, James Frank, Natalie Goulette, and Lawrence Travis, III. 2015. "Is the Impact of Cumulative Disadvantage on Sentencing Greater for Black Defendants?" *Criminology & Public Policy* 14 (2): 187–223.

Yin, Jiawei, Xiaoling Jin, Zhilei Shan, Shuzhen Li, Hao Huang, Peiyun Li, Xiaobo Peng, Zhao Peng, Kaifeng Yu, Wei Bao, Wei Yang, Xiaoyi Chen, and Liegang Liu. 2017. "Relationship of Sleep Duration with All-Cause Mortality and Cardiovascular Events: A Systematic Review and Dose-Response Meta-Analysis of Prospective Cohort Studies." *Journal of American Heart Association* 6 (9): 1–82.

Yu, Calvin Kai-Ching. 2013. "Lust, Pornography, and Erotic Dreams." *Dreams* 23 (3): 175–193.

Yu, Calvin Kai-Ching. 2016. "We Dream Typical Themes Every Single Night." *Dreaming* 26 (4): 319–329.

Yu, Calvin Kai-Ching, and Wai Fu. 2011. "Sex Dreams, Wet Dreams, and Nocturnal Emissions." *Dreaming* 21 (3): 197–212.

Zender, Bree. 2018. "Revisiting the Life and Death of Andrew Holland." *KCBX* February 22 (https://www.kcbx.org/post/revisiting-life-and-death-andrew-holland#stream/0).

Zeng, Zhen. 2017. "Jail Inmates in 2017." Washington, D.C.: Bureau of Justice Statistics. Retrieved March 27, 2021 (https://bjs.ojp.gov/content/pub/pdf/ji17.pdf).

Zeng, Zhen, and Todd D. Minton. 2021. "Jail Inmates in 2019." NCJ 255608. Retrieved March 27, 2021 (https://www.bjs.gov/content/pub/pdf/ji19.pdf).

Zerubavel, Eviatar. 1976. "Timetables and Scheduling: On the Social Organization of Time." *Sociological Inquiry* 46 (2): 87–94.

Zerubavel, Eviatar. 1981. *Hidden Rhythms: Schedules and Calendars in Social Life*. Berkeley, CA: University of California Press.

Zuberi, Tukufu. 2001. *Thicker than Blood: How Racial Statistics Lie*. Minneapolis, MN: University of Minnesota Press.

Index

For the benefit of digital users, indexed terms that span two pages (e.g., 52–53) may, on occasion, appear on only one of those pages.

Figures and tables are indicated by *f* and *t* following the page number